Organised Crime

Organised Crime

Alan Wright

WILLAN
PUBLISHING

Published by

Willan Publishing
Culmcott House
Mill Street, Uffculme
Cullompton, Devon
EX15 3AT, UK
Tel: +44(0)1884 840337
Fax: +44(0)1884 840251
website: www.willanpublishing.co.uk
e-mail: info@willanpublishing.co.uk

Published simultaneously in the USA and Canada by

Willan Publishing
c/o ISBS, 920 NE 58th Ave, Suite 300
Portland, Oregon 97213-3786, USA
Tel: +001(0)503 287 3093
Fax: +001(0)503 280 8832
e-mail: info@isbs.com
website: www.isbs.com

First published 2006

Paperback
ISBN-10: 1-84392-140-5
ISBN-13: 978-1-84392-140-0
Hardback
ISBN-10: 1-84392-141-3
ISBN-13: 978-1-84392-141-7

British Library Cataloguing-in-Publication Data

A catalogue record for this book is available from the British Library

Typeset by GCS, Leighton Buzzard, Beds
Project management by Deer Park Productions, Tavistock, Devon
Printed and bound by T.J. International, Padstow, Cornwall

Contents

For Patricia, with love

Preface

The primary aim of this book is to provide an accessible introduction to the study of organised crime: for undergraduate and postgraduate students who need an overview of the subject for their studies; for professional investigators with a need for knowledge of historical context and contemporary theory but with little time for research; and for the general reader who wants to know more about organised crime, beyond the news headlines.

A number of people have both fuelled my interest over the years and provided practical help to enable me to complete the book. First, my thanks go to Frank Gregory of the Department of Politics, Southampton University, who encouraged me to engage in the subject during the late 1980s and thereafter. I worked closely with Frank and with Alan Waymont on my first piece of academic research: a study of drugs squads and intelligence in England and Wales in the wake of the setting up of the new Regional Crime Squad Drugs Wings (Wright and Waymont 1989; Wright *et al.* 1993). Later, the 'Chilworth Conferences' that Frank organised under the aegis of the Department of Politics of Southampton University during the 1990s led to many interesting discussions with other academics and practitioners. In particular, Gerald Brookes, Mike Levi, Paddy Rawlinson and Phil Williams were the origin of a number of ideas and trains of thought on the subject, which extended my knowledge and sharpened my interest.

Secondly, my thanks go to Professor Geza Katona, Dr Miklos Benke and other colleagues in the Hungarian Police Research Association for their help with a study of organised crime in Hungary (Wright 1997).

This research forms part of Chapter 7 in relation to organised crime in Eastern and Central Europe. Thirdly, my thanks go to Assistant Commissioner Tarique Ghaffur and colleagues in the Specialist Crime Directorate at New Scotland Yard for inviting me to help define a performance framework for Operation Maxim in 2003–4. This, with regular and frequent contact with police officers and academic colleagues over recent years, has sustained my interest and extended my knowledge of the subject of organised crime.

A number of other people also deserve thanks for their help in encouraging the completion of this text. Professor Steve Savage and Dr Paul Norman of the Institute of Criminal Justice Studies (ICJS), University of Portsmouth, kindly agreed that I could make use of some of the material that I produced for the Institute's distance-learning units on the subject. My thanks go to Professor Tim Hope, Dr Rob Mawby, Professor Anne Worrall and other colleagues at the Department of Criminology at Keele University for granting me a visiting research fellowship in 2004 to help me complete this and other work. My thanks also go to Chris Lewis and Tom Williamson of ICJS, University of Portsmouth and to Rob Mawby of Keele University for their kindness and generosity in reading the manuscript and for making a number of suggestions for improvement. Finally, my thanks go to my wife Patricia, to whom I dedicate this book. Without her loving support (and some valuable practical help with the proof-reading), I could not have completed it.

Alan Wright
Keele University
October 2005

Introduction

This is a book about organised crime: about those who commit it and the effect that it has on individuals, businesses and states. To a lesser extent, it is also about the ways in which states and the international community have sought to contain it. Many books are already available on organised crime, in both the popular and academic literature. With regard to the popular literature, browsing the bookshops and scanning internet sources reveals an increasing number of books that fall within the genre of 'true crime'. These books provide the general reader with dramatic accounts of organised crime gangs and their exploits. As such, they are the kind of thing that might break the tedium of waiting at an airport. However, their appeal is to a mass market rather than to the somewhat more limited number of people who are making a serious study of the subject. Of course, this is not to say that many of the writers who have contributed to this popular literature have not taken the subject seriously. Indeed, accounts of the subject by investigative journalists have often been at the very forefront of probing the clandestine world of organised crime.

In recent years, former gang members have taken advantage of the popularity of the subject to publish accounts of their criminal activities. Readers might justifiably suppose that the authors of such books have written them to explain away their criminality or simply to make money. In many respects, these books sit more comfortably alongside the fictional accounts of gangster life that have had their niche in the popular literature since the 1930s than with more rigorous accounts of the subject. However, it is certainly true that both 'true crime' and fictional accounts provide interesting insights into organised crime and its people. Nevertheless, serious students of the subject need to approach these popular texts with a great deal of caution and to distinguish well-researched reporting and analysis from the less reliable material that is widely available.

Academic writers have published an increasing number of valuable texts on the subject in recent years, in the form both of books and journal articles. These texts often consist of rigorous analysis of specialised aspects of organised crime. Hobbs, for example, provides penetrating accounts of organised crime in London, its social context and the attitudes of detectives who investigate it (1988, 1995). Much of the recent academic writing in the field consists of chapter contributions to edited volumes or articles in journals. For example, Passas (1995) provides a useful edited collection of classic and exploratory studies of aspects of the subject. Edwards and Gill (2003) and Beare (2003) provide edited collections of critical papers on the troublesome concept of transnational organised crime and responses to it. Journals such as *Transnational Organized Crime* and *Trends in Organized Crime* provide useful articles on a range of connected topics. The *British Journal of Criminology* frequently publishes articles on empirical research on the subject that are of interest to academics and to policy makers.

The literature from the United States includes a number of textbooks on the subject, although written mainly with the American market in mind. Here, Albanese and Abadinsky provide wide-ranging studies of organised crime that have gone to several editions (Albanese 1996; Abadinsky 2002). The text by Lyman and Potter, which is now in its third edition, is detailed and useful, although again the authors appear to have aimed it mainly at the American market (1997, 1999, 2004). Nash (1993) and Kelly (2000) represent a comparatively new genre in the literature on organised crime, namely handbooks and encyclopaedias on the subject, which have increased in number in recent years. These contain extensive sources of material, although some prior knowledge is necessary to enable readers to make best use of them. By their very nature, however, such works do not present a holistic overview of the subject.

The predominance of collections and specialist texts means that few books are currently available to introduce the subject to those who are new to it. It is certainly true that overviews of the subject are available. For example, the chapters by Hobbs, Levi and Nelken in the various editions of the *Oxford Handbook of Criminology* provide scholarly material from experts of high international reputation (Hobbs 1994; Levi 2002; Nelken 2002). With these exceptions, few academic texts provide a broadly-based introduction that reviews the components of the debate in a critical yet systematic way.

This book seeks to address this perceived gap in the literature. Overall, it aims to provide an introductory analysis of the subject at a reasonable theoretical level. However, it should be accessible to readers who do not have extensive prior knowledge. Throughout, the text makes use of examples and case studies to highlight the problems that organised crime presents. It includes an extensive review of the literature through which readers can assess and evaluate the subject. The book has four predominant themes:

- the nature and central concepts of organised crime;
- the specific activities with which it is associated;
- its origins and growth nationally, regionally and globally; and
- the efforts by the international community and law enforcement agencies to contain, regulate and control the risks that it poses.

The book examines each of these themes in turn. Chapter 1 deals with the problems of defining organised crime and locating it conceptually and geographically. Chapter 2 deals with gang life and the violence that often accompanies it. Chapters 3 and 4 deal with some of the key activities of organised crime: 'enterprise' crime, drug trafficking and people trafficking. Chapters 5 to 8 cover the origins and growth of organised crime in various parts of the world. Chapter 9 explores the law enforcement measures and the control and regulatory strategies through which states and the international community have sought to tackle organised crime. A more detailed outline of each chapter is as follows.

Chapter 1 examines the problems of defining organised crime and discusses a number of examples drawn from both official and criminological sources. It explores the contestability of meaning that surrounds the subject, suggesting that the very nature of organised crime makes its definition a problem. It examines social perspectives on organised crime, exploring conflicting theories about the rationality of specific criminal groups and the extent to which analysts can legitimately say that such crime groups are 'organised'. The chapter examines critical claims from writers such as Reuter (1983) who argue that gang activity in illegal markets is in fact radically 'disorganised'. The chapter concludes with a review of the loci of organised crime, exploring the distinctions between national, international and transnational levels and between its manifestations in the social, political and economic domains. It also examines the extent of the pluralisation of organised crime in recent years and begins to elaborate on its impact and the importance of locating it within the contemporary discourse about risk.

Chapter 2 examines the rise of gangs, questioning the extent to which criminal groups have distinctive organisational dynamics and pose specific risks to communities. Based upon a review of research into gang life and culture, it first examines the socialisation of gang members and the role played by delinquency in encouraging gang membership. Secondly, the chapter discusses the typology of gangs and organised crime groups. This includes their structure, the way in which they are organised, their cohesion and their relationships with the authorities and with local communities. It also critically assesses the degree of rationality that they demonstrate in goal setting. This chapter also discusses the crucial roles of drug dealing, violence and coercion, including the potential for youth and street gangs to provide a pathway into more sophisticated forms of organised crime.

Economic or 'business' crime is central to the activities of most organised criminal groups. Chapter 3 discusses the historical development of economic crime and recognises that not all organised crime is associated with gangs. It sets out a number of historical and contemporary examples, examining the extent to which they pose specific risks in the political, social and economic domains. To place this in perspective, this chapter examines the so-called 'enterprise' theory of organised crime. It compares the activities of organised crime groups with those of legitimate business. It explores enterprise crime its many forms, including money laundering. This chapter also examines issues in the development of corporate fraud and so-called 'white-collar' crime. It questions whether an analysis of the subject should distinguish this from other forms of organised crime or regard it as part of the same phenomenon.

Because of their central importance to questions of international organised crime, drug and people trafficking deserve a more holistic analysis than the study of a particular region or group can provide. Chapter 4 examines the scope of these problems, discussing the typologies of drug and people traffickers and the supply chain through which they operate. It illustrates the relationship between drug trafficking and organised crime, including a number of examples relating to particular jurisdictions and to the activity of criminal and terrorist groups in the USA, Asia, Europe and South America. In recent years, the smuggling of economic and political migrants has become an important source of revenue for organised criminal groups. Many of the criminal groups discussed in later chapters have this activity at the centre of their operations. In addition to economic and political factors, changing conceptions of nationality and the willingness of criminal groups to develop lucrative new markets have encouraged this form of organised crime. The movement of women and children for sexual and other purposes has become part of the activity of specialist groups, especially those from Eastern and Central Europe. Chapter 4 examines this particular area of activity in more detail.

Chapter 5 begins to examine the subject in a comparative perspective, through an examination of so-called 'traditional' organised crime groups including the Mafia, the Chinese Tongs and Triads and the Japanese Yakuza. First, it examines the rise of organised crime in Europe, in particular, the growth of the Sicilian Mafia and other groups emanating from southern Italy. It discusses the activities of such groups, especially the predominance of illicit protection and its early role in Italy of providing social control in the absence of effective government. It examines the Mafia diaspora, whereby their activities have spread beyond their original roots. Secondly, this chapter examines organised crime of Chinese origin. In particular, it explores the activities of Triad and Tong groups, whose operations have extended to Europe, to the USA and elsewhere. This includes people smuggling by so-called 'snakehead' gangs, and participation in every level of the illicit drug trade from production through to local distribution. Thirdly, the chapter examines the activities of Japanese organised crime, in particular the Yakuza, who have been heavily involved in political corruption and drug trafficking. It also discusses the activities of the Yakuza in developing their financial interests in the USA and elsewhere.

Chapter 6 explores the growth of organised crime within the territory which provides the paradigm example of free-market capitalism: the United States of America. Beginning with early examples of the development of crime groups of Irish, Jewish and Italian-American origin, this chapter reviews the history of organised crime in the USA, comparing different types of organisations and their activities. It discusses the importance of the prohibition era and the ways in which this contributed to the growth of syndicated crime. Building on the discussion in Chapters 1 and 2, this chapter examines the pluralisation of organised crime in the USA since the 1960s, including the growth of youth gangs, motorcycle gangs, prison gangs and the development of other, non-traditional forms of organised crime. In particular, it examines the role of ethnic groups of Hispanic, African-American and Asian origin, referring to what Ianni (1974) has called the 'ethnic succession thesis' (see Chapter 6 for the main discussion of this concept). It sets out a critique of US federal policy on organised crime since 1967, including the impact that this has had on control measures. It indicates the role that the US government has accorded to organised crime in developing its foreign policy. Finally, this chapter examines the importance of the gangster image in American popular culture and its influence beyond the USA. It examines the relationship between gang life, public perceptions and the media, including the propensity of the fashion and entertainment industries to promote gangster chic and the cult of celebrity.

Chapter 7 examines the growth of the new wave of organised crime groups. First, it examines the rise of non-traditional forms of organised crime in Europe, including the growth of corporate fraud and smuggling of contraband. Secondly, it discusses the growth of organised crime in the post-Soviet states since the demise of communism. This includes a review of the impact of the history of the Soviet era and the political changes of the late 1980s on organised crime. It examines Russian organised crime, setting out its main characteristics and activities. It discusses the growth of organised crime in Eastern and Central Europe and the Baltic Sea states. It assesses the efforts to control organised crime in these jurisdictions, including the implications of best and worst case scenarios. Thirdly, this chapter examines organised crime that emanates from the developing world, and that which criminal gangs perpetrate upon developing countries. Following Passas (1998), it discusses the impact of the 'criminogenic asymmetries' that exist between the states of the developed and the developing world. To illustrate some of the difficulties, it sets out a case study of organised crime emanating from Nigeria. Finally, it reviews the internationalisation of organised crime in the collaboration between the Mafia, Asian groups, Colombian drug cartels and others. It discusses the viability of the so-called *pax mafiosa* and 'merger' theses in the work of Sterling (1994) and Robinson (2002).

Chapter 8 examines the character and dynamics of organised crime in one jurisdiction, focusing on the development of criminal gangs in Britain as a case study. In particular, it examines the history of gangs in relation to the development of an 'underworld' of criminal groups in the 1920s and thereafter. It reviews the growth and the present state of such enterprise through an examination of what Morton (2002) has called 'Britain's gangland'. This chapter also discusses the rise and fall of particular criminal groups, including the Richardson and Kray gangs and those who followed them. In doing so, it contrasts the operation of these earlier types of British criminal gang with more recent developments, highlighting their activities in relation to both violent and 'enterprise' crime, especially drug trafficking. Finally, the chapter briefly explores the relationship between organised crime and new communities in Britain.

Chapter 9 discusses the ways in which Britain, Europe, the USA and the international community generally have sought to tackle the problem of organised crime. First, it examines some of the theoretical and practical problems of using control strategies and other forms of regulation in response to organised crime. It discusses the difficulties of measuring organised crime within and across jurisdictions. Secondly, the chapter discusses the role of investigation and the use of criminal intelligence systems to deal with the problem at national and international levels. It examines issues that relate to law enforcement at three levels: in single jurisdictions; in bilateral co-operation between states; and in multilateral co-operation. Thirdly, this chapter examines the work of international bodies such as the United Nations (UN), the G7/8 group of nations and the European Union (EU) in generating high levels of co-operation through international treaties and agreements. Finally, it discusses the measures that the international community has instituted for the purposes of drug control.

In conclusion, this book argues that organised crime is one of the key problems facing public policy in the early twenty-first century. Although risk is the predominant concept under which we currently subsume organised crime, this chapter suggests that it is necessary to look beyond risk to understand the extent to which the very fabric of capitalist society has organised crime embedded within it.

The fact that organised crime is continually changing to provide new threats and challenges unites the themes that this volume discusses. In particular, there has been a change from gang-related 'underworlds' of the pre- and post-Second World War periods to a more fragmented and diverse panorama of criminal groups at the beginning of the twenty-first century. These changes to the nature and meaning of organised crime have not served to reduce the danger that it presents. New risks are continually emerging. Despite the focus on terrorism since the attack on the World Trade Center in New York on 11 September 2001 (and other events since, especially, in Britain, the London bombings of 7 July 2005), the international community rightly continues to regard organised crime as an important challenge. At the international level, it can affect relationships between states. It has the potential to spell ruin for national economies, especially in the developing world. Locally, it can blight the development of thriving communities.

The extent to which some states might now regard terrorism as 'organised crime against humanity' may well indicate that a combined study is required. However, the intensely political nature of terrorism suggests that it should have its own field of specialist study. Therefore, although this volume will refer to the connection between organised crime and terrorism where necessary, its primary focus is upon organised crime as an important topic in its own right.

The dangers that organised crime presents make it imperative to take seriously its history, the theoretical debates that surround the subject and their practical implications. For all of these reasons, organised crime is a subject worthy of serious study in the universities and in the relevant professions. Accordingly, this book encourages deeper examination of the literature through which readers may further explore the political, economic and social contexts of the subject.

Chapter 1

Mapping rough terrain: the contested concept of organised crime

Organised crime is a subject that has attracted official and public attention for many years. Most governments and law enforcement agencies have long regarded it as a significant policy issue, a point illustrated by the exceptional levels of resources that they expend to deal with it. It is also of considerable public interest, receiving extensive coverage in the press. Frequently the subject of television documentary programmes and of film drama, also it has a wide following in popular literature. Because of its extent, it presents exceptional risks and challenges to the social, political and economic well-being of states and to the international community. For these reasons, if for no others, it is worthy of serious study.

In the light of this extensive interest from many sources, there may be a temptation to plunge into a discussion of substantive examples or into a debate about the means through which states and law enforcement agencies seek to deal with it. The controversy that continues to surround the subject, however, provides a good reason for doing neither. Before dealing with substantive examples or examining how states are tackling organised crime, it is necessary to set out a critical framework that will foster some clarity about its controversial nature. Such a framework is required to set organised crime into a theoretical context through which those who are new to the subject can understand it. The aim in this chapter, therefore, is to clarify some of the conceptual problems identified since theorists and policy makers began to examine organised crime more systematically in the 1960s.

This chapter explores these conceptual problems in three stages in order to tease out the character of the subject. First, it examines a number of definitions of organised crime drawn from both official and criminological sources. Developing arguments about the conceptual contestability that surrounds the subject, it suggests that the very nature of organised crime makes defining it a problem. Secondly, it explores the extent to which we can say that some types of crime groups and their activities are truly 'organised'. This has been a source of disagreement between criminologists, policy makers and law enforcement officials since the 1960s, especially in the USA. As the discussion will show, some criminologists maintain that organised crime may not be 'organised' at all, or at least not organised in the sense of more familiar forms of organisation.

Finally, the chapter comments upon the different loci of organised crime and the way in which a plurality of groups have supplemented, and in some cases replaced, its traditional forms in recent years. It examines ways of defining the locus of organised crime in terms of its spatial distribution worldwide, including its appearance at the national and international levels. It discusses the problems associated with the use of the term 'transnational' to label the phenomenon. In contrast to defining organised crime in terms of its location, it also suggests ways to define it in terms of its logical distribution, through the variety of its manifestations in the social, political and economic domains. Finally, the chapter discusses the way in which organised crime has fragmented into many different groups in recent years. This debate will enable further distinction between types of organised crime group in later chapters and assessment of their relevance and impact. Only after clearing this conceptual undergrowth is it possible to develop satisfactory accounts of substantive examples and to set out a critique of the ways in which states have tackled it.

What is organised crime?

Organised crime has proved difficult to define in terms that satisfy all parties. As Schelling rightly claims, it does not simply mean '...crime that is organised' (1984: 180). Crimes such as robbery and burglary may require organising but criminologists would not necessarily regard them as being part of 'organised crime'. What, therefore, should a rigorous analysis include under the rubric of 'organised crime'? Unfortunately, the official documentation and the critical literature set out almost as many definitions as there are people with an interest in the subject. Some definitions are highly emotive, expressing the attitudes of their authors in language that makes clear their deep feelings about the subject. Some definitions have legal or political aims, seeking to bring about improvements in the ways in which states and law enforcement agencies might tackle the problems that it presents. On one hand, policy makers and investigators seek firm ground upon which to base their operations and to contain the risks that it poses. On the other, criminologists seek definitions that will provide a deeper conceptual basis for their analysis. Definitions vary according to their source. It is perhaps too much to expect to reconcile these diverse interests, although identification of a number of recurring themes in the variety of definitions is certainly possible.

As noted in the Introduction, there is a case for analysing organised crime and terrorism as part of the same continuum. Terrorism certainly suffers from the same problems of meaning and definition as organised crime. States cannot entirely agree on what it is, although it clearly has political aims rather than solely financial ones. A degree of overlap where terrorist groups are involved in other criminality to fund their operations tends to bring confusion about the boundary between terrorism and organised crime. Nevertheless, despite the temptation to include both, this text will regard organised crime and terrorism as separate but linked phenomena. It will, however, draw attention to cases where there is overlap between them, as in the examples of narco-terrorism (Chapter 4).

Although organised crime has a long history, the 1960s were the starting point for extensive debates about its meaning and effect. Much of this emanated from the USA. The prevalence of organised crime in the USA at that time produced a considerable amount of anxiety among policy makers in the wake of the assassination in 1963 of President John F. Kennedy. The assassination in 1968 of his brother, Robert F. Kennedy, the US Attorney-General, who had successfully prosecuted a large number of gang members, further heightened the tension (Lyman and Potter 2004: 33–4). The emotion that characterises some definitions during the 1960s reveals the extent to which it aroused strong feelings. For example, the 1965 Oyster Bay Conference of American Law Enforcement Agents defined organised crime as:

> the product of a self-perpetuating criminal conspiracy to wring exorbitant profits from our society by any means – fair or foul, legal and illegal. Despite personnel changes the conspiratorial entity continues. It is a malignant parasite which fattens on

human weakness. It survives on fear and corruption. By one or other means it obtains a high degree of immunity from law. It is totalitarian in its organisation...

(Oyster Bay Conference 1965)

This definition rightly points to the conspiratorial nature of organised crime and to the way in which it uses corruption and violence to extend its power. However, emotive expressions of this kind also carry with them clear dangers. They are unsafe for policy-making and are likely to encourage ineffective and partisan law enforcement. Indeed, by the mid-1960s it was clear that the subject required a more extensive and rigorous enquiry.

The US President's Commission on Law Enforcement and the Administration of Justice (1967) posed the question: precisely what is organised crime? Donald Cressey, a criminologist who advised the Commission, was one of the first commentators to set out a formal structure for organised crime. He argued that earlier attempts to define the concept had not been a 'smashing success'. They disregarded the important idea that criminal groups were organised and therefore part of a social system. He says:

The organized criminal, by definition, occupies a position in a social system, an 'organization' which has been rationally designed to maximize profits by performing illegal services and providing legally forbidden products demanded by the broader society within which he lives.

(Cressey 1969: 72)

Cressey claimed that organised crime in the USA was comprised mainly of a nationwide alliance of twenty-four tightly-knit criminal 'Mafia families'. For Cressey, these families, with their hierarchy of bosses, captains, 'buffers', 'soldiers' and 'buttonmen' comprised a well-defined criminal organisation that was at the heart of organised crime in that jurisdiction.

According to Cressey, it is important to distinguish between formal and informal organisational structures in any analysis of organised crime. The 'Mafia families', he claims, are both formal in nature and rational in the way in which they organise their affairs. In his words:

The structures of formal organisations are rational. They allocate certain tasks to certain members, limit entrance, and influence the rules established for their own maintenance and survival.

(Cressey 1972: 11)

Although Cressey concedes that there is a blurred dividing line between formal and informal organisations, this is often a matter of degree. The important point is to avoid the confusions caused by uncritical use of terms like 'organised crime' and 'professional crime'. For Cressey, the term organised crime properly used in the USA refers to syndicated crime of the type represented by the Cosa Nostra, 'the Mafia', 'the Mob', 'the Family' and similar names. In such organisations, there is a well-defined hierarchy of roles for leaders and members. There are underlying rules and specific goals that determine their behaviour. According to this theory, such groups are instrumental hierarchies or bureaucracies.

Cressey's report to the Commission (1967, an extensive revision of which is set out in Cressey 1969), provided new definitions of organised crime based upon what criminology has come to know as his Cosa Nostra model. As quoted above, Cressey claimed that the structure he identified was a social system, one that was rationally designed to maximise profits and to provide forbidden goods. In his thinking, it is necessary to guard against legal formalism in relation to the subject of organised crime because too much focus on the legal use of the term alone may hinder a clear understanding of organised crime as a serious social, political and economic problem (Cressey 1969: 311). This work, and others of his which expanded on the topic in the early 1970s (Cressey 1971, 1972), were an important influence on US government policies on organised crime for the next thirty years.

Cressey's claims, however, did not convince other criminologists who were studying the subject during this period. Albini's study of organised crime in Detroit suggests a different picture. For Albini, organised crime consists of networks of patrons and clients, rather than of rational hierarchies or secret societies. These networks are characterised by a loose system of power relationships. Accordingingly:

rather than being a criminal secret society, a criminal syndicate consists of a system of loosely structured relationships functioning primarily because each participant is interested in furthering his own welfare.

(Albini 1971: 288)

The pattern of these networks is similar to that of social exchange networks in communities. They represent a dynamic system rather than a single formal structure.

Patron/client networks carry out a variety of both licit and illicit activities to increase and maintain their power and wealth. In such networks, criminal entrepreneurs (who Albini defines as the 'patrons') exchange information with their 'clients' in order to obtain their support. The 'clients' include members of gangs, local and national politicians, officials of the government, and people engaged in legitimate business. The origin of the power of these networks is in their flexibility and in the abilities of their operatives and contacts. However, the roles of client and patron may change. Relationships between them may dissolve or they may reform over time. Albini's findings concur with those of Cressey in that he agrees that Mafia-style criminal groups have family-like structures. However, he strongly resists Cressey's claim that it is correct to describe the relationship between syndicate members in terms of a hierarchy. Syndicates are not bureaucratic in character. Importantly, he recognises that people involved in the network may not directly be part of a core criminal organisation.

The Iannis, who researched organised crime in the USA in the early 1970s, were also sceptical about the idea of defining crime syndicates as formal hierarchies (Ianni and Ianni 1972). Drawing on evidence relating to the Italian-American crime syndicates that were prevalent in New York and other major cities, they argued that traditional kinship groups are the basis of organised crime, rather than structures of the kind that Cressey had identified. 'Kinship', in this sense, includes fictive godparental and affinitive ties, as well as those based upon blood relations. In their critique, the Iannis set out a behavioural explanation for the activities of Italian-Americans in crime syndicates. According to the Ianni's, instead of regarding them as formal organisations, analysts should think of groups such as the Mafia and the Camorra as traditional social systems. Action, not the status of their members, is their defining attribute. They say:

> Secret societies such as the *Mafia*, however, are not really formal organizations ... They are not rationally designed and consciously constructed; they are responsive to culture and are patterned by tradition. They are not hierarchies of organizational positions which can be diagrammed and then changed by recasting the organizational chart; they are patterns of relationship among

individuals which have the force of kinship and so they can only be changed by drastic, often fatal action.

(Ianni and Ianni 1972: 153)

The Iannis carried out extensive fieldwork among one Mafia 'family' and their associates. They focused upon the behavioural aspects of power within the family and identified a number of rules of conduct that guided the behaviour of members and their associates. They found that the activities of this crime group did not indicate the existence of a specific institution or organisation. According to the Iannis, the activities of this group were simply the output of a particular way of life among a number of closely connected Italian-Americans. Criminologists could explain organised crime of this kind by examination of local kinship or ethnic social networks. This determines the organisational structure of the family and assigns individuals to particular roles within the organisation. In such organisations:

1. The family operates as a social unit with social organization and business functions merged.

2. The group assigns all leadership positions based on kinship, down to 'middle management' level.

3. The higher the position in the organization, the closer the kinship relationship.

4. The group assigns leadership positions to a central group of family members, all of whom have close consanguineal or affinal relationships, which fictive godparental relationships reinforce.

5. Members of this leadership group are assigned primarily to either legal or illegal enterprises, but not both.

6. Transfer of monies from illegal to legal and back into illegal activities takes place through individuals rather than companies and is part of the close kin-organization of the family.

(Ianni and Ianni 1972: 154)

For the Iannis, these groups derive their strong family ties from the traditions of southern Italy, where the family, rather than church or state, is the basis of social order and morality. These themes will be re-examined in Chapter 5, during a more detailed discussion of the Mafia and similar groups.

Since the 1970s, the growth of organised crime and its elevation onto the global stage has encouraged international bodies to set out their own definitions. In 1975, the UN sought to produce a universal definition of organised crime to provide a common basis for the formulation of policy and law. A UN conference held in Toronto said that organised crime:

> is understood to be the large scale and complex criminal activity carried on by groups of persons, however loosely or tightly organized, for the enrichment of those participating and at the expense of the community and its members. It is frequently accomplished through ruthless disregard of any law, including offences against the person, and frequently in connexion with political corruption.
>
> (United Nations 1976)

The European Union (EU) also began to take an increasing interest in organised crime because of its increasing effects on member states. In 1998, the EU set out a definition of organised crime in order to consolidate policy on the subject and to make it a criminal offence to participate in a criminal organisation in the member states of the EU. According to Article 1 of a Joint Action of the Justice and Home Affairs (JHA) Council of the EU:

> A criminal organisation shall mean a lasting, structured association of two or more persons, acting in concert with a view to committing crimes or other offences which are punishable by deprivation of liberty or a detention order of a maximum of at least four years or a more serious penalty, whether such crimes or offences are an end in themselves or a means of obtaining material benefits and, if necessary, of improperly influencing the operation of public authorities.
>
> (European Union 1998)

In 2001, a joint report of the European Commission and Europol set out a list of characteristics comprising a working definition of organised crime in the context of the 1998 definition set out above. Of the eleven characteristics that the report cited, at least six must be present and the four in italics must be among the six:

1. *Collaboration of more than two people;*
2. Each with own appointed tasks;
3. *For a prolonged or indefinite period of time;*
4. Using some form of discipline or control;
5. *Suspected of the commission of serious criminal offences;*
6. Operating at an international level;
7. Using violence or other means suitable for intimidation;
8. Using commercial or businesslike structures;
9. Engaged in money laundering;
10. Exerting influence on politics, the media, public administration, judicial authorities or the economy;
11. *Determined by the pursuit of profit and/or power.*
    (European Commission 2001, quoted in Elvins 2003: 34)

Article 2 of the crucial United Nations Convention against Transnational Organized Crime (2000a) offers a similar definition, again emphasising the relevance of 'structured groups':

For the purposes of this Convention:

(a) 'Organized criminal' group shall mean a structured group of three or more persons, existing for a period of time and acting in concert with the aim of committing one or more serious crimes or offences established in accordance with this Convention, in order to obtain, directly or indirectly, a financial or other material benefit;

(b) 'Serious crime' shall mean conduct constituting an offence punishable by a maximum deprivation of liberty of at least four years or more serious penalty;

(c) 'Structured group' shall mean a group that is not randomly formed for the immediate commission of an offence and that does not need to have formally defined roles for its members, continuity of its membership or a developed structure.

(United Nations 2000a)

Variants of the EU and UN definitions have been included in the definitions of organised crime adopted by law enforcement agencies. For example, according to the National Criminal Intelligence Service (NCIS) definition of organised crime:

> An organised criminal works with others for a profit motive to commit an offence which impacts on the UK and for which a person aged 21 or over on first conviction could expect to be imprisoned for three years or more.
>
> (National Criminal Intelligence Service n.d.)

The definition of organised crime by the US Federal Bureau of Investigation (FBI) contains much the same information. However, it puts more emphasis on the organisational structure of major criminal groups. Structure has long been an important concept in official assessments of organised crime in the USA. According to Grant D. Ashley, Assistant Director of the Criminal Investigation Division, in a statement to the US Congress on Eurasian organised crime in October 2003, the FBI:

> view organized crime as a continuing criminal conspiracy having a firm organizational structure, a conspiracy fed by fear and corruption.
>
> (US Federal Bureau of Investigation 2003)

Why are definitions of this kind important to official bodies such as the UN and the EU? In the above definitions, the specification of offences for which a perpetrator may be detained for three or four years appears to be designed to bring them into line with laws on conspiracy, which have much the same requirements in many states. It also rules out the inclusion of minor offences, even if the authorities regard them as 'organised'. There is also a need for the international community to agree on the character of the subject, to enable members to co-operate effectively. This requires the UN and other international bodies to specify the parameters of the subject in legal or quasi-legal statements set out in the form of treaties, legislation and procedure. It is clearly in the interests of legislators, policy makers and law enforcement agents to regard organised crime as a well-defined concept with identifiable structures. It is something about which they can make rational decisions.

There is also an undoubted need to ensure that criminal justice and law enforcement agencies target their resources effectively. In the UK, the government expects law enforcement agencies to set clear objectives to deal with well-defined problems. The adoption of the principles of so-called New Public Management by recent governments in the UK requires that agencies should be ready to justify their performance against such criteria. It is not surprising, therefore, that law enforcement agencies need strictly to define organised crime in order to justify and to evaluate their actions.

Definitions such as those cited above may be appropriate in the legal and political contexts that generate them. However, they do little to explain the deeper nature of organised crime. In contrast, criminologists have sought to provide comprehensive definitions setting out its meaning. For example, Maltz (1976) identifies nine categories of activity that serve to define organised crime groups. The defining categories include the use of corruption and violence to achieve their goals. They also include a degree of sophistication, continuity and discipline in their operations. Organised crime groups have structure and engage in multiple enterprises, some of which are legitimate. They make use of rituals for bonding members together. According to Maltz, not all groups exhibit the same characteristics or structure. However, violence and corruption, and the pursuit of multiple enterprises and continuity, serve to form the essence of organised criminal activity.

Abadinsky (1994) sets out a similar list of characteristics, high-lighting the importance of power, profit and perpetuity. According to Abadinsky, organised crime (OC) is:

1. *Nonideological:* The primary motivating force for OC is profit. Sometimes the group adopts a worldview and political agenda, but these are supportive of, and secondary to, the goal of making money.

2. *Hierarchical:* The group has a pyramid organization with few elites and many operatives. In between the high and low levels, the organization is supported by mid-level gangsters who handle supply and security.

3. *Having limited or exclusive membership:* The group must maintain secrecy, and loyalty of members must be ensured.

4. *Perpetuating itself:* The group has a recruitment process and policy; new recruits are being attracted as operatives.

5. *Willing to use illegal violence and bribery:* Outside of legal authority, violence is a meaningful resource. Corruption and deceit are the essence of OC.

6. *Having a specialized division of labour:* OC groups can be thought of as task forces with members combining different talents and experiences to reach an organizational goal.

7. *Monopolistic:* Market control is essential to OC because the primary goal is maximizing profits.

8. Having explicit rules and regulations: Members of OC groups have codes of honour.

(Abadinsky 1994: 6)

As will be evident, however, this catalogue of requirements does not meet universal approval. Indeed, comparison of Abadinsky's catalogue with that of other criminologists only serves to demonstrate the extent of the contested nature of the concept. In particular, it fails to highlight the social impacts.

Fijnaut *et al.* (1998) carried out research into the nature of organised crime in the context of the 1994 *Enquiry into Police Investigative Practices* by the Netherlands Ministry of Justice (The Van Traa Commission). Their definition of organised crime recognises the need to bring together its legal and social elements. Organised crime, they emphasise, has widespread social, political and economic effects. It uses violence and corruption to achieve its ends:

> There is talk of organised crime when groups primarily focused on illegal profits systematically commit crimes that adversely affect society and are capable of successfully shielding their activities, in particular by being willing to use physical violence or eliminate individuals by way of corruption.
>
> (Fijnaut *et al.* 1998: 26–7)

Common to criminological definitions of this kind is the 'group' nature of organised crime. Such definitions imply that criminal groups, to some extent at least, are capable of managing their activities. Like Maltz (1976), they emphasise that violence and corruption are enabling activities that help to ensure the success of organised crime.

Other criminologists have argued that definitions such as those set out above do not reflect the reality. For example, Van Duyne (1996) rightly points to the mistake that commentators make in using the term 'organised crime' as though it denotes a clear and well-defined phenomenon. Nothing, he suggests, is further from the truth:

> it is difficult to relate the concepts and theories of 'organized crime' to the existing empirical evidence. This shows a less well-organized, very diversified landscape of organi*zing* criminals… the economic activities of these organizing criminals can better be described from the viewpoint of 'crime enterprises' than from a conceptually unclear framework such as 'organised crime'.
>
> (Van Duyne 1996: 53)

We discuss this thesis in more detail below. Later chapters will revisit these themes and their implications in the discussion of substantive examples.

Although it is possible to pick out some common factors in the definitions set out above, there is only limited agreement between policy makers, law enforcement officers and criminologists about the real nature of organised crime. It is clear that the very nature of the concept makes defining organised crime a problem. There are practical, empirical problems in attempting to provide a definition as well as semantic ones. Many of the definitions emphasise the 'group nature' of organised crime, the 'organisation' of its members, its use of violence and corruption to achieve goals, and its extra-jurisdictional character. However, it is clandestine and polymorphous. It may appear in many forms at different times and in different places.

Because of these anomalies, it is necessary to recognise that the differences between the definitions set out above represent the different frames of reference of those that created them. All may be valid within their own contexts: legal, political and scientific. What is required from academics, from politicians and from practitioners is the recognition that organised crime is an essentially contested concept, over which they may not reach final agreement. It is important to remember, however, that 'organised crime' does not differ from other aspects of crime more generally in relation to its contestability. Crimes such as burglaries and murder are difficult to compare between states because of differences in definition and meaning. Such problems constantly beset the scientific aspirations of criminology, although, as Chapter 9 will show, the EU has made considerable efforts in recent years to resolve these issues to enable EU states to make credible measurements of organised crime. Nevertheless, many of the difficulties of the contestedness of concepts remain. For the seminal discussion of essentially contested concepts in the political and social sciences, see Gallie (1964: 157–91).

The variety of definitions, some of which are set out above, shows that there is an evident danger in asking the question 'What is organised crime?' and expecting a simple answer. However, the question is one that this book will continue to address. As the evidence of the following chapters shows, perhaps the best that criminologists can do is to tease out its complexities through conceptual analysis and through comparative assessment of the activities of the crime groups themselves. In the rest of this chapter, however, before moving on to discuss the realities of the subject in more detail, it is necessary further to elaborate the extent to which organised crime can properly be said to be 'organised'; to discuss its loci and to identify the plurality of ways in which it makes itself manifest across the world.

The 'disorganised crime' thesis

Despite the variety of definitions set out above, one can argue with some justification that a valid analysis of the subject would show the extent to which it is rooted in social organisation. However, the focus of interest should cover both the external and internal dimensions. Analysis should focus on the social context within which organised crime groups operate and on their internal social relationships. This does not mean, however, that crime groups follow the patterns of organisation that one might expect to find in legitimate business, in public sector enterprise or in a military hierarchy. Indeed, one of the most important trends to emerge in criminological thinking about organised crime in recent years is the suggestion that it is not, in a formal sense, 'organised' at all.

A number of empirical studies of organised crime in American cities have made this claim in recent decades. They point to factors in the crime networks they studied to support their assertion. They cite a lack of centralised control, an absence of formal lines of communication, and fragmented organisational structures as evidence that what law enforcement agencies might regard as 'organised crime' is distinctively disorganised. Certainly, crime in the cities studied by these criminologists was not highly systematised. For example, a study by Chambliss (1978) found that Seattle's crime network consisted of groups of businessmen, of politicians and of law enforcement officers. These people had linkages to a national network through the notorious Meyer Lansky, who was a powerful but organisationally ambiguous figure in US organised crime (see Chapter 6). Although there were a number of overlapping crime networks in that city, according to Chambliss there was no evidence that Lansky or anyone else exercised centralised control over them. Block (1983) carried out a study of other forms of organised crime in the USA between 1930 and 1950 and reported similar findings. According to Block (1983), organised crime had become more centralised and hierarchical during that period. However, there was little evidence of a national Cosa Nostra of the kind suggested by Cressey (1969).

Reuter (1983) carried out a study of illegal markets in New York that has been influential in promoting the 'disorganised crime' thesis. The markets he examined included illicit bookmaking, loan-sharking, and dealing in drugs such as heroin. He conceded that some of the criminality he studied involved the well-known criminal hierarchies in the city. However, he argued that their criminal activity was not subject to central management by these hierarchies nor by other controlling groups. Neither was the activity limited to a finite number of objectives. In short, the networks of criminals involved in the crimes he examined did not exhibit organisational cohesion. According to Reuter (1983), the true picture of organised crime in New York was much more diverse and fragmented than that generally espoused by law enforcement. He argued that the relationship between organised crime and illegal markets had too long been the source of myths, especially the myth that the Mafia provided the controlling influence. Although groups such as the Mafia were certainly powerful, they were part of a heterogeneous underworld, a network characterised by complex webs of relationships.

Reuter argued that if the activities he examined were to deserve the label of 'organised crime', they would have to follow the pattern that characterised industrial organisation. The paradigm of industrial organisation to which he subscribed is that set out in Scherer (1970). According to this model, an organisation sets up cartels through which it may maximise effective control of its markets. To do so, it routinely uses structured methods to suppress competition from other groups. Reuter (1983) maintained that the criminal activity that he examined did not fit this model. It was certainly violent on occasions and aimed at making money for participants at its various levels. However, it did not achieve this by setting up a highly structured system. Because of the lack of structure and fragmentation of objectives, Reuter concluded that it was (in his terms), 'disorganised'.

As will be evident in discussing gang life in more detail in Chapter 2, most criminal groups exhibit both instrumental and expressive characteristics. Here it is necessary to be careful to assess the effect of the research methodology itself. For example, it should not be surprising where an interview cohort is that of gang members who are serving prison sentences that they try to give a *post hoc* rational explanation that adds structure to their actions. On the other hand, it may be all too easy to dismiss the rather loose structures and expressive activities of some gangs as 'disorganised'. Because many of these so-called 'organisations' are fragmented and unstable, it is necessary to look at the specific patterns of their association and to avoid drawing unwarranted universal conclusions from the evidence.

This is certainly the case with the Mafia. As will be clear in Chapter 5, the term itself does not stand for a single, hierarchical criminal organisation. The Iannis (1972) are not the only sociologists to point out the problems associated with ascribing an overarching organisational rationality to criminal groups. Some went further. Haller (1990) carried out research on major gangs in the USA that suggested that neither bureaucracy nor kinship groups are the primary structure of much organised crime. It is more like a partnership or series of joint business ventures with a number of partners that change frequently. Even in the heyday of gangsters in the 1930s, Jewish and Irish-based gangs were as much in evidence as were those of Italian-American descent. These findings run contrary to the model generally accepted by the US government and by law enforcement officials.

On one hand, it has certainly become clear since the 1980s that, if such a thing ever existed, analysts should not over-formalise the concept of 'organised' crime. On the other hand, despite the denials by Albini (1971), Chambliss (1978), Block (1983), Reuter (1983) and others of Cressey's claims, there is no doubt that they all observed a degree of managerial activity within the groups they studied. All observed networks that had a degree of persistence, although these may have fallen short of the kinds of relationships that these writers might associate with formal-rational types of organisation. However, the fact that criminal groups did not achieve their aims through the operation of large controlling cartels does not confirm that they were 'disorganised'. The danger of taking an entirely sceptical stance on this question is that the concept of organisation employed by the sceptic might be inappropriate to the subject. Theoretical understanding of the nature of organisations has certainly moved on since the early 1980s. In short, an excessively sceptical approach may tend to rely upon theories of organisation which are inappropriate or which have been superseded.

Scott (1992) claims that theorists may best understand organisations in terms of their role as social systems. He identifies three main theoretical approaches:

- where theory regards organisations as rational systems;
- where theory regards organisations as natural systems; and
- where theory regards organisations as open systems.

Groups that organisational theory regards as having their basis in rational systems have highly formalised structures. Organisational theory defines these structures in terms of bureaucracy and hierarchy, with formal systems of rules that set out the authority and competence of members at all levels. Organisations of this kind seek to achieve highly specific goals. They constantly seek to optimise their performance (Scott 1992: 29–48). This approach was influential during the twentieth century and is still a model against which many analysts judge the nature and effectiveness of the manufacturing and service industries. This model forms the cornerstone of Reuter's thesis. However, it is not the only theoretical perspective through which an analyst can understand the concept of organisation in late modernity.

Natural systems' organisations are those characterised by complexity in their goals, even to the extent that participants may regard the organisation as an end in itself, not merely a means to some other end. Organisations of this kind are characterised by the informality of their structures. Social relationships between their members are also informal, with hierarchies that are very limited in their scope. There is often a degree of loose coupling between parts of the organisation and between the organisation and the environment in which it operates. Natural systems' organisations take great account of the social attitudes expressed by employees and stakeholders. The promotion of group values to maintain solidarity is high on the agenda. Because they are people-centred, organisations of this kind do not rely entirely upon profit maximisation (Scott 1992: 51–75). Although their perversity and violence in respect of relationships is often remarkable, organised crime groups are characterised, perhaps more than anything else, by their focus on the connections between their members, their associates and their victims. They are people-centred networks, in addition to being profit-making ones.

In recent years, some writers have directed their attention to what Scott (1992) refers to as 'open systems' organisations. Such organisations are characterised by a high level of interdependence between themselves and the environment within which they operate. They are also characterised by contingency within their structures and relationships. Here, 'contingency' means that there is no one model of relationships within the organisation. There is no one way in which they may be organised. The best way to organise depends on the nature of the environment within which the organisation operates. Lawrence and Lorsch (1967) coined the name 'contingency theory' to describe this syndrome. It highlights the adaptability that such organisations may need to exhibit in attempting to meet the demands of their changing environments. Open systems' organisations, in this sense, are characterised by their variable structures, by their network arrangements, and by their ability to change to meet the challenge of new circumstances (Scott 1992: 76–94).

What has this analysis to do with organised crime? The first point to make is that analysts of organised crime groups should not expect to find bureaucracies of the kind that Max Weber described, with well-defined structures or highly specified goals (Gerth and Wright Mills 1948: 196–8). Although Reuter (1983) was right to say that the industrial model of organisation was not evident in his analysis of crime groups in illegal markets, observers are entitled to ask whether he has shot the wrong fox. Although crime groups rarely meet the rigorous expectations of the rational systems' model, they may well exhibit some of the features of natural and open systems organisations. Natural systems' crime groups are likely to adopt a range of highly personalised approaches to ensure solidarity among their members. Such groups will also be characterised by goal complexity. Promoting loyalty and avoiding betrayal are likely to be as important to criminal entrepreneurs as is the control of cartels to maximise profit. Open systems' crime groups are characterised by adaptability, which enables them rapidly to meet the changing demands of their environment. New markets, such as cyber crime and new types of fraud, may prove alluring. Indeed, it is this very adaptability that makes organised crime so durable and so difficult to contain. However, it is unlikely that organised crime will follow one single model of organisation of those set out above. Contra Reuter (1983), the rejection of industrial organisation as the working paradigm for organised crime does not mean that it is simply 'disorganised'.

Indeed, as early as 1977, A.K. Cohen had argued that a broader social analysis of criminal organisation is required (Cohen 1977). The claims of writers such as Ianni and Ianni (1972), who had focused primarily on internal relations in Mafia families, were in this sense quite limited. For Cohen, it is necessary to map the interactions, processes and patterned relationships both within and outside organisations in a more holistic way. It is necessary to establish the social context of the criminal activities of 'organised criminals', as well as the structure of their associations. Cohen points out that criminology has done little work on the nature of organisational processes in crime groups. It has overlooked such things as recruitment, socialisation of members within organisations, and the way in which subcultures are developed and maintained. It has also to a large extent ignored such things as the protection and insulation of participants from the impact of conventional moral definitions. This remains largely the case. For Cohen, criminal groups should be subject to assessment of their internal structures and to analysis of all societal activity as it bears upon the production of their criminal behaviour. It is necessary:

> to show that the functional problems of human systems take a distinctive form in criminal enterprise and that this distinctiveness provides a justification for the specialised study of criminal organisation.
>
> (Cohen 1977: 111)

Chapter 2 will return to these themes in the analysis of gang life.

Recent developments in thinking about the nature of organisations place less emphasis on the establishment of meaning through analysis of their functions and structure than has hitherto been the case. Even in the case of legitimate organisations, it is possible to detect a shift in 'the mode of administration'. According to Heydebrand (1989), a postmodern organisation:

> would tend to be small or be located in small subunits of larger organizations; its object is typically service or information, if not automated production: its technology is computerized: its division of labour is informal and flexible: and its managerial structure is functionally decentralized, eclectic, and participative, overlapping in many ways with nonmanagerial functions... [it] tend[s] to have a postbureaucratic control structure even though prebureaucratic elements such as clanlike personalism, informalism, and corporate culture may be used to integrate an otherwise loosely coupled, centrifugal system.
>
> (Heydebrand 1989: 327, quoted in Clegg 1990: 17)

Although Hydebrand did not have organised crime in mind when he made this claim, many of his points are relevant to that phenomenon, especially in its recent adoption of the internet as a means of communication and control.

Building on this theme, Lippens (2001) rightly argues that organised crime has arrived in a phase of transition. Contemporary criminal organisations no longer conform to the models predominant in the previous 'bureaucratic' age. The functionalist structures of industrial bureaucracy discussed by Gouldner (1954), which had Weberian thought as their basis, are no longer the viable model for most forms of organisation. Highly formalised rule systems, in any case, were rarely evident in criminal organisations. According to Lippens (2001), labyrinthine clusters of networks are more likely to be the characteristic mode of organisation in the post-bureaucratic age. As later chapters will show, the demise of the recognisable 'underworlds' of the pre- and immediate post-Second World War eras is reflected in the growth of new types of crime group organised in new ways, often in networks of networks.

Criminology has not yet concluded this debate. On one hand, Van Duyne (1996) is right to maintain that organised crime is diverse, varied and contestable. On the other hand, there is certainly empirical evidence to suggest that we can regard much of the criminal activity discussed in this book, in some significant sense, as 'organised', or at least subject to the organising abilities of sentient beings. At both the theoretical and practical levels, however, a less rigid, more informal networked model of 'organising' may be appropriate to a satisfactory evaluation.

As later chapters will suggest in considering substantive examples, a number of 'organising' features may be evident. Indeed, many theorists are rightly suspicious of the tendency to reify the idea of 'organisation', preferring to rely on identifying the organising role of people and events, rather than of structures. According to Weick (1974):

> The word, organization, is a noun and it is also a myth. If one looks for an organization, one will not find it. What will be found is that there are events, linked together, that transpire within concrete walls and these sequences, their pathways, their timing are forms we erroneously make into substances when we talk about an organization.
>
> (Weick 1974: 358, quoted in Scott 1992: 90)

It seems highly likely that this is the real problem of 'organised' crime. Indeed, some analysts specifically refer to it in terms of the 'organising' activities of criminal groups, rather than the structural term 'organisation' (Block and Chambliss 1981; Block 1983). Therefore, instead of seeking the invisible 'substance' of a controlling organisation, analysts should look for what Reuter (1983) has called the 'visible hand' of violence and corruption which affects persons and events as evidence of an organising force behind 'organised crime'. The extent to which this is evident in the operation of criminal gangs will be the subject of a more detailed discussion of the role of gang violence in Chapter 2 and in the substantive examples in later chapters.

The loci of organised crime

Many of the definitions set out above encourage us to regard organised crime as present if it meets the criteria that they provide. This is so, even if the activities in question are restricted to a single jurisdiction. For example, although they may have affiliations elsewhere, many organised crime groups virtually confine their activities to the USA, including outlaw motorcycle gangs and some corporate crime, such as that which the Savings and Loan scandals of the 1980s revealed. Many of the cases of organised crime in Britain that Chapter 8 discusses were also limited mainly to the domestic jurisdiction. However, many of the major organised crime networks that other later chapters discuss do not confine their activities in this way. They have become increasingly international in their scope.

It is surprising that many of the definitions discussed above do not emphasise the international aspects of organised crime. Nor do they focus much upon the ways in which the activities of criminal groups have changed in recent decades. Some recent official definitions, however, do insist that organised crime is international in its character. For example, the explanation adopted by European Commission and Europol cited above, suggests that for organised crime to be regarded as such, it should 'operate at an international level' (European Commission 2001). However, simply to assert that this is so says very little about the real geographical distribution of the phenomenon.

Identifying where the offences are committed is an important factor in trying to establish the locus of any criminal activity. The legal locus of offences, generally speaking, is the place where investigators find them. In this sense, offences relating to organised crime are always located within the territory of a particular state. Currently, there is no international court capable of trying offences resulting from organised crime. Although the International Criminal Court (ICC) appears to be truly transnational, its remit extends only to dealing with persons accused of offences against humanity, such as genocide. It does not extend to dealing with international organised crime or to 'transnational' offending. More recently, however, as Chapter 9 indicates, co-operation between states in this field is increasing, in response to the internationalisation of the activities of criminal groups. Many states have ratified international treaties making it easier to bring organised criminal groups to justice. As a result, the outreach activities of some countries, in particular the USA, has been notable.

Given these legal limitations, to what extent can analysts draw meaningful distinctions between local, international and transnational crime? They can argue with some justification that an organised crime group such as the Japanese Yakuza is local, national and international in character. Although it may have gang members who reside outside the country, it has its origins in one jurisdiction: Japan. Most of its members reside there. In addition to its domestic activities, it draws upon its connections in other countries to generate profit. It may seek to commit offences in other jurisdictions or to profit from the offences that its associates commit there. In this way, it extends its influence beyond its home territory. The internationalisation of organised crime of this kind increased during the twentieth century in parallel with the globalisation of transport and communications. In recent years, however, the phenomenon has fostered criminal networks whose activities seem truly global.

Are such organisations involved in what official sources and the media increasingly describe as 'transnational' organised crime? Mueller (1998) points to the fact that the term 'transnational crime' is over a quarter of a century old. The UN Crime Prevention and Criminal Justice Branch coined the term during the 1970s:

> in order to identify certain criminal phenomena transcending international borders, transgressing the laws of several states or having an impact on another country.
>
> (Mueller 1998: 13)

However, he also points out that the term did not (and still does not) have a juridical meaning. It is largely a criminological term indicating that the activities concerned transcend the jurisdiction of any particular state. Some commentators regard this concentration as mistaken, pointing to the local focus of much of what some observers might regard as 'transnational' organised crime. Hobbs (1998), for example, suggests that much of the activity that some regard in this way in the UK is essentially localised. It presents social and economic challenges to local communities within specific jurisdictions, as where local drug markets impact upon an estate, a town or an area of a city. Local or national law enforcement agencies are capable of dealing with such challenges, although some criminal groups may require intervention in more than one jurisdiction. Similarly, Van Duyne (1996) argues that although organised criminal groups in Europe may carry out their activities across national borders, this does not mean that they are truly transnational in their structures or their span of authority. Nor does it mean that only supranational institutions can tackle them.

Criticisms of the tendency to use the term 'transnational crime' as shorthand for organised criminal activity that may have international links but is essentially local or national in its nature are well founded. Some commentators have gone so far as to suggest that the concept of transnational organised crime is a construct intended primarily to provide justification for the actions of the international community, prominent individual states and their law enforcement agencies. According to Woodiwiss (2003a, 2003b), the USA has been a primary mover in promoting this trend, mainly for political purposes connected with its foreign policy. Sheptycki (2003a) suggests that the term 'transnational organised crime' did not derive from genuine analysis by criminologists or political scientists. It is a term that serves the stereotypes generated by enforcement agencies and governments, who use it to suit their policies in several fields. Drawing on the work of Bigo, Sheptycki says, 'the problematics of immigration, terrorism and drugs have been fused together in the discourse of transnational organised crime' (Sheptycki 2003a: 131; Bigo 2000: 89). As such, it is little more than a 'protection racket', which aims at promoting law enforcement agencies as the arbiters and providers of public safety (Sheptycki 2003b).

These criticisms of the use of the term 'transnational organised crime' should caution analysts to make sure that their use of it is meaningful. If a network operates primarily from one jurisdiction and carries out its illicit operations there and in some other jurisdictions it is 'international'. It may be appropriate to use the term 'transnational' only to label the activities of a major crime group that is centred in no one jurisdiction but operating in many. Someone who adopted this approach might regard the activities of the Mafia in this sense, as both transnational and international. However, because the term 'transnational organised crime' remains problematic, and to avoid confusion, the current text will use the preferred term 'international organised crime' to label the activities of criminal groups whose activities extend beyond a single jurisdiction.

Despite the semantic and empirical difficulties in assessing the 'transnational' or 'international' nature of organised crime, it is certainly the case that there is a radical mismatch between the ability of organised crime groups to act with flexibility and the constraints that international law places on the law enforcement agencies of individual states. The increased ability of criminal groups to operate in extra-territorial ways, using the internet and other means, is one of the key features of a new generation of crime groups. The globalisation of commerce, transport and communications systems provides an important opportunity for organised crime groups to extend their influence. This has led to a situation where individual nation states and their disparate systems of justice have not kept pace with the risks and challenges presented by international organised crime. As Chapter 9 will show, law enforcement and international regulation is only now beginning to come to terms with these advances and to bring the locus of their operations into line with those of organised crime groups themselves. Institutions such as Europol and (in the UK) the Serious and Organised Crime Agency, should be at the leading edge of new measures to deal with these challenges.

The locus of organised crime, however, is not only about its spatial location or about its distribution across the world. It also relates to its logical location within particular worlds of experience. As the definitions set out above show, organised crime operates in the social, economic and political domains. In the social domain, it may seek to develop social control in relation to particular communities. This is the case, whether they are located in single states or dispersed globally. For example, Chinese criminal groups often seek to exercise a degree of social control over populations of Chinese origin who live within host states. Similarly, in the economic domain, criminal groups seek to exert influence by means of corruption and by coercion of legitimate and illicit business. They do this to consolidate their financial base and their profitability. For example, the activities of the corrupt Bank of Credit and Commerce International (BCCI) affected the economic domain on a worldwide scale (Punch 1996). In the political domain, criminal groups use corruption and violence to attain power and status. The control of illicit drug production in Afghanistan and in Colombia by warlords and by organised criminal groups has severely affected the political stability of those countries (see Chapter 4). Each of these arenas (social, economic and political) provides an important logical locus for the activities of organised crime groups. They enable them to exercise their power and influence in ways that transcend simple profit maximisation under conditions of competition, although that remains an important economic objective.

Recent trends show that not all organised crime follows the traditional patterns of activity that commentators have fostered upon the Mafia and similar groups. In parallel with the internationalisation of organised crime, a more varied collection of crime groups has come to the fore in recent years. This applies both to the USA and elsewhere. As Ianni (1974) has shown, an increasing number of Hispanic and black groups have become involved in organised crime in the USA. In addition, outlaw motorcycle groups, youth and prison gangs, and 'posses' of Afro-Caribbean origin have become active. Lyman and Potter (2004) describe the development in the USA since the 1980s of these non-traditional types of organised crime:

> Just as traditional organized crime is associated with Italian-American and Sicilian crime organizations, non-traditional organized crime is associated with new and emerging crime groups, such as the Chinese Triads, outlaw motorcycle gangs, and California-based youth gangs. Probably the most glaring descriptor of this category is that groups associated with it are typically involved with the drug trade.
>
> (Lyman and Potter 2004: 51–2)

Although Lyman and Potter focus on the USA, the phenomenon of pluralisation is evident also in the development of organised crime in Europe, Russia, Asia and elsewhere. For example, Europe has seen the growth of a large number of new groups. Factors leading to pluralisation in Europe include the war in the Balkans, expansions of criminal group activity from the states of Eastern and Central Europe and the Baltic Sea region in the wake of political changes, changes to the activities of indigenous groups and groups migrating into Europe from outside the region.

The rationality associated with illicit enterprises of this kind is very different from that of traditional Mafia-style groups. An important factor in these changes is the tendency away from centralisation of power and reliance upon family ties towards a fragmentation of structures and informality of relationships in crime groups. With some exceptions, such as local youth or street gangs, the 'new wave' of organised crime is likely to be international in scope, rather than focused upon one jurisdiction. Conflict between factions and striving for status are the concepts most likely to characterise such organisations. They often keep themselves small or in cellular groups to ensure self-protection. Where such groups are involved in drug dealing, as is highly likely, they may exhibit little by way of permanence or centralisation of structure.

For all these reasons, it is important to locate the debate about organised crime in the contemporary discourse about risk. The very fact of the internationalisation and pluralisation of organised crime means that it poses a diversity of threats to the political, economic and social stability of communities. The risks that organised crime presents, however, are not static. They present an ever-changing panorama of problems. Alongside changes in structure, as Chapters 3 and 4 will show, the political economy of organised crime shows an ever-increasing focus upon 'enterprise' crime, including white-collar and corporate crime, drug dealing and people smuggling. These changes to both structure and substance of organised crime have considerably modified the landscape.

However, before discussing the political and economic effects of organised crime in Chapter 3, it is necessary to say more about the ways in which goals and objectives of crime groups are developed and to examine their organisation and the variety of risks that their activities entail. In particular, it is necessary to explore how and to what extent organised crime groups use violence and coercion to further their goals. Although not all organised crime is gang related, the gang provides an important logical and empirical construct in our understanding of the subject. In order to develop these themes, it is to the analysis of criminal organisation represented in gang life that this debate will now turn.

Chapter 2

Criminal organisation: the gang as a violent way of life

In Chapter 1, the temptation to plunge straight into the study of organised crime through the study of substantive cases and examples was resisted. A preliminary analysis of concepts was required in order to provide an explanatory framework through which to make sense of such cases in the later chapters. It is equally tempting to say that the study of organised crime does not require an understanding of the origin and nature of criminal gangs. Although the criminological literature often regards the two subjects as separate, there are good reasons for including a discussion of gang life at an early stage in the debate on organised crime. The study of gang life and the violence that it often entails can provide a useful insight into other forms of organised criminality and to the risks that organised crime may pose to specific communities and to the public at large.

As the discussion of economic crime and drug trafficking in Chapters 3 and 4 will show, gang life is not the only way in which organised crime makes itself manifest. However, although corporate fraud and drug trafficking may occur without typical gang activity, a distinctive gang culture does underpin many organised crime groups. Members of such groups often learn the mores of this culture through early exposure to gang life. This chapter, therefore, considers aspects of organised crime through an examination of gangs and gang culture. In particular, it examines youth and street gangs and the social conditions that make them a fertile recruiting and proving ground for organised crime, especially in providing the 'foot soldiers' for more established groups.

The chapter is set out in three parts. First, it examines the research on the social contexts within which gangs develop. It discusses the way in which gang activity influences both the lives of their members and the society within which they operate. Using the already extensive research on gang life, it examines the socialisation of gang members and the role played by delinquency in encouraging and developing gang membership. Secondly, the chapter discusses a typology of gangs, to provide an insight into the way in which some organised crime groups develop. This includes their structure and organisation, their degree of cohesive activity or otherwise, the extent to which they may pursue rational objectives, and their relationships with local communities and with the authorities. It also examines the effect of interventions by law enforcement and other agencies into gang activity. Thirdly, the chapter examines the role of strategic and tactical violence and coercion in providing discipline for client groups and gang members, and in dealing with threats from rivals. It suggests that of all the characteristics of gang life and organised crime, violence and coercion are predominant. The research on gangs points towards some of the substantive issues that later chapters discuss in relation to criminal groups in Europe, the USA and elsewhere.

What is a gang? Context and socialisation

Criminologists have studied gang activity for many years. Not surprisingly, given the prevalence of gangs in that jurisdiction, much of the research is American. There are, however, a number of studies of British and other European gang life, mainly in the context of research into delinquency. Most of the studies in Europe and the USA refer to the activities of youth gangs or street gangs, many of which have increasingly become involved in drug dealing in recent decades. Developments in gun crime in the UK have brought the activities of some youth drugs gangs into the mainstream of issues relating to organised crime. Because of their crack-cocaine dealing and use of firearms by such gangs, some law enforcement agencies now regard their activities as of primary importance alongside those of more established organised criminal groups. However, it is necessary to enter a caveat on making assumptions about the nature of gangs and their relationship to organised crime without first reviewing the research. Because gangs are sometimes a resource and sometimes a platform from which more sophisticated criminal operations are developed, research on gangs provides a useful insight into the growth and operation of organised criminal gangs more generally.

What is a gang? Decker and Van Winkle (1996), who have carried out extensive studies into gang life, provide an extensive overview of the American literature. According to their research (1996: 2), Sheldon first made academic use of the term during the late nineteenth century (Sheldon 1898) to refer to predatory associations of people involved in violence and property crimes. Other early studies explored the effects of immigration and of the urbanisation and poverty associated with cities on the development of gangs. Riis (1902) argued that for a young man joining a gang was a natural outcome of slum life. The gang equipped him to deal with his surroundings and to generate self-esteem. New York in particular found itself with a considerable level of gang activity in the 1890s. Much of this involved Irish, Jewish and Italian immigrants. This gang activity, which appeared to be a response to the need for social and economic provision that was lacking from other sources, continued throughout the early part of the twentieth century in many American cities (Decker and Van Winkle 1996: 2–4).

Most early criminological studies of gangs focus upon the problem of delinquency and on the growth of collective activity from adolescence onwards, mainly among groups of young men. Thrasher's study of gangs followed the Chicago School of Criminology in seeking to understand gang life as part of the ecology of local neighbourhoods (Thrasher 1927). According to Thrasher, gangs were most likely to develop in deteriorating neighbourhoods that had shifting populations. A neighbourhood of this kind, labelled as a 'zone in transition' by Burgess (1925), had high rates of delinquency and was characterised by conditions that the Chicago School regarded as a form of social disorganisation (Shaw and McKay 1942).

For Thrasher, it was the high mobility of people in these areas of cities and the disorganisation of slum neighbourhoods that allowed gangs to flourish. He argued that gangs were likely to develop from adolescent associations in these conditions. Conflict between groups, fighting and theft served to produce a kind of solidarity within such gangs and to give them some cohesion. Thrasher was not alone in studying gang life during this period. Zorbaugh (1929), who studied and compared areas on the north side of Chicago, drew heavily on Thrasher's work. Following the ecological thesis of the Chicago School, he maintained that such gangs were the product of conditions in the deprived 'zone of transition' of the city. He also claimed that these areas provided many of the recruits for the more sophisticated organised gangs. According to Zorbaugh, referring to the late 1920s when he carried out his studies, 'the underworld kings of today are the products of gang life of the Jewish and Italian slums' (1929: 154–8, 174).

Criminological opinion varies on the validity of the claims of scholars such as Thrasher and Zorbaugh. Despite the extent of Thrasher's insights into a large number of gangs (apparently he investigated over 1,300!), some commentators regard his work as of very limited utility for the analysis of gang life today (Pearson 1994). On the other hand, writers such as Decker and Van Winkel (1996: 6) acknowledge that much of Thrasher's work on gang culture remains important for understanding gang life. The work of Zorbaugh has apparently been of relevance to (as yet unpublished) work on gang-related gun crime in London. As a whole, however, the work of the Chicago School has been the subject of considerable criticism. Although it has some advantages over individualistic theories of the causes of criminality, the extent to which the ecological theory espoused by these scholars can provide an adequate explanation for crime more generally and for the rise of gangs in cities remains controversial (Downes and Rock 1988: 70–5; Bottoms 1994: 591).

Gangs in Britain also have a long history, the basis of which may have been in the criminogenic conditions of inner city and dockland life and in the opportunities that centres of vice and unregulated money exchange (such as at racecourses) afforded to criminal groups. The Second World War and its economic consequences affected the types of gangs that operated during the 1940s and thereafter. In wartime Britain, gang activity was associated with the black market in goods and services that existed during the period of rationing and austerity. Such gangs were not primarily youth gangs; they were loose collections of individuals who were engaged in a variety of wartime criminal activity. Although many were avoiding military service, they frequently colluded with military personnel to obtain goods that were not freely available to the public. Chapter 8 will examine the growth of organised criminal groups in Britain in more detail.

Gangs whose basis was in cultural or social forms of solidarity began to re-emerge in the 1950s and 1960s in both the USA and the UK. They emerged, however, in very different conditions to those that had attracted the attention of criminologists such as Thrasher in the 1920s. In the USA in the post-war period, social and ethnic divisions produced conflict between youth gangs seeking to establish their own territories. In Britain, in the 1950s, the growth of cosh and razor gangs led to the enactment of legislation to prohibit the use of such offensive weapons. Although most of the so-called 'Teddy boys' of this period or the later 'mods' and 'rockers' were not extensively involved in criminality, many of those who did become involved in gangs were young people who were beginning to rebel against the austerity of the post-war era. A preference for specific kinds of music and fashion was often the cultural adhesive that bound them together into identifiable groups, not unlike the more recent phenomenon of so-called 'gangsta rap', which is discussed in more detail in Chapter 6.

In the post-war period, a number of criminologists carried out research to identify why many of these youths became involved in gang activity. In general, their claims related more to aspects of social and economic relations in specific environments than to the ecology of the environments themselves. Cohen (1955) argued that working-class adolescents became involved in gangs because of their frustration with their inability to achieve the status and attain the goals of the middle classes. Cloward and Ohlin (1960) also emphasised the importance of blocked opportunity as a factor in the membership of gangs. They suggested, however, that the effects of this were not uniform. Uneven distribution of opportunities across the population had the effect of creating different types of gang. Types of gang included those that focused on robbery and property theft, those that focused on fighting and conflict, and those that were 'retreatist', focusing on such things as drug taking. Yablonsky (1962) also emphasised that there were variations in types of gang. In particular, he identified the violent gang as a 'collective structure', situated somewhere between the disorganised group or mob, and the better organised delinquent or social gangs.

The concept of delinquency also influenced a number of criminologists who carried out research into gang life in the USA in the late 1960s and early 1970s. Some studies of gangs evaluated the intervention programmes set up by law enforcement and other agencies. These studies produced useful insights into the social context of gang activity. For example, Spergel (1966) carried out studies of the practical problems of social workers in Chicago intervening in gang activity. His work encouraged the study of the reasons for the delinquency that lay behind gang membership. In fact, Spergel was one of the first criminologists to focus upon what analysts might now refer to as 'evidence-based practice'. For Spergel, evidence rather than a reliance on intuitive approaches should drive any intervention into gang life and culture. Klein (1971) also studied a number of social work projects aimed at reducing the effects of gang membership. He found that interventions by social workers actually made gangs more attractive to their members. This increased the levels of delinquency among gang members by promoting group solidarity and by encouraging violence. He concluded that external pressures were more likely to produce strong bonds of gang membership than were interactions between members within the gang itself. Later work by Klein also confirmed the importance of external influences in consolidating gang culture. In this way, gangs emphasise their opposition both to communities and to institutional pressures (Klein 1995).

Other research, however, suggests that the concept of delinquency is only of limited utility in analysing the factors that consolidate gang membership. For example, Short and Strodtbeck (1974) found that many of the factors that researchers had previously thought to produce gang-oriented delinquency were no different from those that operated upon non-gang members. Their research showed that status as a gang member played a far more important role than other social factors in determining the membership of a gang and its relationship to others and to the community in general. The gang, in this sense, is a collective solution to threats posed by these relationships. Detailed accounts of the US research are set out in Decker and Van Winkle (1996), Huff (1996) and Miller et al. (2001).

Although research on youth gangs in Europe is not as prolific as that in the USA, there are a few important studies. In his highly respected ethnographic study of youth groups in Liverpool, for example, Parker (1974) illustrated the problems of applying the concepts of culture and subculture to the explanation of delinquency. Parker, who studied the groups concerned for three years, showed the detail and complexity of adolescent development in such circumstances. Downes and Rock (1988) point out the richness of Parker's analysis as an example of the way in which accomplished analysts can bring a number of criminological theories to bear on the complexity. They say of Parker's work:

> Theoretically, the study shows affinity with strain theory (the 'good times' must be wrung from a penny pinching society); with labelling theory (the subjective shift from a sense of apartness to a sense of alienation results from first hand experience of the police and the courts); with control theory (the 'streetwise' involvement in trouble from early childhood and the eventual decision that the costs outweigh the benefits); and conflict

theories (the 'iron cage' which ultimately clamps down on their horizons and life chances).

(Downes and Rock 1988: 151–2)

Fine-grained analysis of the kind that Parker provides should certainly warn readers not to expect simple resolution of the problems of gang delinquency, nor an easy ride to establish a viable theory of gang formation and culture.

Gang-related research in Europe shows that gang life there has both parallels and contrasts with that in the USA. Klein *et al.* (2001) and Klein (1996) provide a comparative study of gangs in the USA with those in a number of European cities, including The Hague, Manchester, Oslo, Copenhagen, Frankfurt, Brussels, Bremen, Stockholm and Kazan. Only in the cases of England, Norway, Denmark and Russia were indigenous gangs reported. In most cases, European gangs derive from refugee or immigrant populations:

The list is very long: Afro-Carribean, Algerian, Antillian, Croatian, Filipino, Iranian, Italian, Moroccan, Pakistani, Russian, Somali, Surinamese, Turkish and Vietnamese. Such a list makes it abundantly clear no one ethnicity is more or less prone to gang formation. Rather it is the status of being marginalized, alienated or rejected that makes some groups more vulnerable to gang formation.

(Klein *et al.* 2001: 135)

However, the lack of co-ordinated research points to a fragmented understanding of the gang phenomenon in Europe. The paradox that derives from this is the tendency to deny the existence of gangs in Europe because they do not fit the stereotype derived from earlier studies, especially media stereotypes of US gangs as highly organised, stylistic and violent (Klein *et al.* 2001: 3). In contrast, widespread publicity about gangs in The Hague that have emulated those of the US cities, including the adoption of the names, signs and clothing of the Los Angeles 'Crips' and 'Bloods', have placed the street gang phenomenon clearly in the Dutch experience (Klein *et al.* 2001: 69).

Despite the criticism of the work of the Chicago School noted above, there remains a wide consensus among criminologists in both the USA and Europe that social and economic conditions are an important factor leading to the development of youth gangs. Young (1999) rightly points to the role that social exclusion plays in this tendency. Many young people would not resort to joining gangs if the social conditions in which they found themselves were different. However, later field research into gangs in American cities departs to some extent from the delinquency debate, although it shows a similar degree of respect for the complexity of the gang phenomenon and the environmental conditions that produce it (Moore 1978, 1991; Padilla 1992; Decker and Van Winkle 1996). Moore showed the specific role of Hispanic and prison cultures in the development of gangs in the Mexican-American areas of Los Angeles. The gangs Moore studied had their bases in specific territories, had an age-graded structure of cohort groups and were strongly characterised by fighting and drug abuse. Prison experience played a major role in the formation of these gangs. Alongside the social and economic isolation of those who were the subject of the study, prison experience served to increase ethnic solidarity and to promote gang cohesion.

Similarly, Padilla (1992) studied ethnic Puerto Rican drug-dealing gangs in Chicago. His methodology focused on the cultural rejection of gang members and their exclusion from mainstream social institutions of the predominant Anglo-American culture. Again, as was the case in the studies of gangs by Moore and others, social exclusion had the effect of increasing gang solidarity. Paradoxically, exclusion from school, as part of a disciplinary framework, may be counter-productive in the sense that it may help to drive individuals towards destructive forms of association. This may be the case particularly for youth from ethnic groups. According to Padilla, membership of a gang is rational for ethnic youth because they see it as a solution to the problem of their marginalisation and the problems they experience in conventional society.

For Decker and Van Winkle (1996), who themselves carried out detailed field research into gangs, understanding the gang means understanding gang culture and its context. This includes the symbols, values and traditions of the gang. Values, in particular, play an important role. Unable to rely on formal rules, institutions or authority, the gang creates its own identity, which is recognisable by non-gang members and by the community at large. They note that colours, in particular red and blue, have symbolic significance for many gangs in the USA, including the Crips and the Bloods, which are the predominant street gangs (Decker and Van Winkle 1996: 1). Gang members also use tattoos to indicate gang affiliations. Although it may be tautologous to include it, alongside the other means through which gang members identify themselves, criminal activity plays an important role in defining gang membership and in separating the gang from the community within which it operates. Bringing these factors together in their working definition, Decker and Van Winkle say:

> a gang is an age graded peer group that exhibits some permanence, engages in criminal activity, and has some symbolic representation of membership.
>
> (1996: 31)

In summary, the research on the culture and social context of the gang shows that it is a complex phenomenon. Analysts can explain it by reference to the social and economic barriers that affect its members and to the way in which it creates its own world with values that stand in opposition to those of local communities and wider society. In addition to allegiance to the group, overt signs, such as the use of tattooing and symbolic rituals of initiation, may also serve to reinforce cultural solidarity in the gang. This solidarity, and the violence that sustains it, enables the gang to define and maintain itself against threats from other gangs, from the police, from mainstream social institutions and from the communities within which they operate. Although much of the research described in this chapter relates to youth, street and ethnic gangs, as substantive examples in later chapters will show, many of the factors that influence the solidarity and social location of street gangs are similar to those that apply to more sophisticated organised criminal groups. As Zorbaugh (1929: 174) suggests, recruitment into more established organised criminal gangs is not accidental but is the culmination of these social and environmental factors.

The research on delinquency, exclusion and other factors, following the approach prevalent in mainstream criminology, is therefore an important part of debate about gangs and their social context. Readers who are interested in why individuals turn to crime should refer to the long-standing criminological debates about its causes. In particular, they might refer to the work of Hirschi (1969), who sets out the way in which social bonds through attachment, commitment, involvement and belief operate to control (or fail to control) the potential for an individual to participate in criminal activity. However, a detailed study of the causes of deviance is beyond the scope of this current text. Readers who wish to pursue this aspect should refer to standard texts on the subject including Downes and Rock (1988), Coleman and Norris (2000) or Hopkins Burke (2005). For more insight into the contemporary debate on the role of environmental criminogenic factors as determinants of crime, see Bottoms (1994) and Bottoms and Wiles (2002).

Gang structures, goals and organisation

Chapter 1 discussed the degree of organisation that is evident in the phenomenon of 'organised' crime. This question has also claimed the attention of researchers into gang life, who examined the extent to which a degree of organisation was present in street and drug gangs. Central to the question of whether street and drugs gangs are organised are whether such groups have formal structures, whether they have clear hierarchies and leadership and whether they are rational in the pursuit of their goals. In fact, there are conflicting research findings in this area, pointing to a continuing controversy over the way in which analysts should interpret the organisational rationality present in gangs.

The research findings tend to divide into two contrasting schools. On one hand, some researchers have concluded that gangs do in fact have rational structures. For example, Skolnick *et al.* (1990) examined the life of street gangs that came into being specifically for selling drugs. Their research concluded that the structure and behaviour of such gangs exhibited a degree of organisational rationality. According to their findings, such gangs required organising in order to be effective in drug dealing. Members often explicitly saw themselves as 'organised criminals'. Sanchez-Jankowski (1991) carried out an ethnographic study of thirty-seven gangs in New York, Boston and Los Angeles over a ten-year period. He drew similar conclusions to those of Skolnick *et al.*, claiming that the gangs he examined were formal-rational organisations. Evidence for this included strong organisational structures, and well-defined roles and rules that guided members' behaviour. They also had highly specified and regular means for generating income, both legal and illegal. Padilla (1992) also suggested that the ability of the gang to make money was an important factor indicating the presence of organisational rationality. According to Padilla, gang members carried out specific criminal tasks to achieve this end. He argued that this showed that a degree of rationality was present in the activities of such groups in pursuing their goals. The findings of this research tend to support the claims of Cressey, which Chapter 1 explored in some detail.

On the other hand, a number of researchers took a different view. For example, Klein *et al.* (1991) concluded that many of the drugs gangs they investigated were loose confederations rather than well-defined organisations. They were lacking in persistent focus. There was comparatively low cohesion between members, who defined their goals expressively rather than instrumentally. Klein *et al.* (1991) also found that they had little effective organisational structure and few shared goals. These criminal groups also had a disproportionate representation of black members whose crack-cocaine sales often involved the use of firearms. For Klein and Maxson (1994) it is a misconception to suggest that the structures of gangs mirror those of business organisations with well-defined hierarchies:

> Only in *West Side Story* is control wielded effectively by the few: in real street gangs, multiple cliques, dyads, and triads are common units of companionship, each responsive to its own peers rather than to powerful (or older) leaders.
>
> (Klein and Maxson 1994: 45)

Accordingly, they found little evidence of cohesiveness, shared norms, values or organisational loyalties.

In their extensive study of gang members based upon three years' fieldwork, Decker and Van Winkle (1996) concurred with the research that suggested a less organised gang world than that observed by Skolnick *et al.*, Sanchez-Jankowski and Padilla. They found that gang structures were often chaotic. Sub-groups set objectives, rather than the gang as a whole. There was little role differentiation and most gang members operated as generalists, fulfilling a variety of roles. Although gang members regarded gang values and loyalty as paramount, gangs were relatively ineffective as institutions in the enforcement of their own rules and values (Decker and Van Winkle 1996: 274–5).

Analysts might account in part for the divergence between these two schools by differences in the way in which they carried out the research and differences in the types of gangs and activities that they studied. For example, Skolnick *et al.* based their work on interviews carried out in prison. Their respondents might have been engaging in *post hoc* rational reconstruction of their activities, thus giving the impression that their actual operations were rational and well structured. In any case, given their opportunities to plan, prison gangs may well be better organised than are street gangs. In contrast, much of the field research that this chapter has discussed, including that of Decker and Van Winkle, focused on gangs involved in chaotic crack-cocaine dealing and other drug markets. Not surprisingly, the methods that they discovered in gang activity were themselves somewhat chaotic (Decker and Van Winkle 1994).

The question of the relationship between gang life and organised crime is an important one. Organised crime groups do not simply come into being without antecedents. Some have their origins in local crime. In many cases, members graduate from youth gangs to more highly developed criminal groups. Examples of this include the Italian-American street-corner gangs of the 1920s and 1930s, who later evolved into more sophisticated and complex forms of organisation (Ianni and Ianni 1972: 53–4). In the UK, examples include the Kray gang, whose early criminal careers involved petty crime with other local youths in London's East End (see Chapter 8). Of course, some of the more recent gangs, such as the Hell's Angels, those of the West Coast of the USA and the Afro-Caribbean posses of New York, have their own ethos. They exist in their own right without necessarily leading to other forms of association or criminality. The development of such groups is part of the pluralisation of organised crime discussed in Chapter 1.

There is certainly some evidence of the affiliation of local street gangs to larger gangs or groupings, although the research is sometimes conflicting and inconclusive. Sanchez-Jankowski (1991) observed street gangs that were already in touch with organised crime syndicates and, as such, may well have been adopting structured methods to emulate or rival them. Some Chinatown youth gangs have links to adult organised crime groups, although their violence does not appear to support the protection rackets, political intimidation and drug trafficking activities of the older groups with which they are associated (Chin 1996a: 181). According to Fagan, in many cities, in addition to scavenger gangs and those who seek control of neighbourhood 'turf', organised or corporate gangs exist which mimic businesses in their group dynamics (Fagan 1996: 43). Although such gangs mainly comprise young people, they are often similar in their structure and goals to more sophisticated organised crime groups.

Decker *et al.* (1998) examined the extent to which street crime gangs are becoming organised crime groups. Taking examples from two American cities (Chicago and San Diego), they found that only Chicago provided evidence that gangs were assuming the attributes of organised crime groups. The Chicago case, however, is interesting. Decker *et al.* chose the Gangster Disciples and Latin Kings gangs for the research because they were reputed to be the most organised gangs in the city. The research findings showed that the Gangster Disciples had moved well beyond the rather disorganised groups that were characteristic of gangs in San Diego and elsewhere in the USA. Their drug dealing produced large sums of money, although it was not clear how the gang used or invested the profits. In many cases, however, members of the gang owned legitimate businesses in addition to their illegal drug dealing. In contrast, the Chicago Latin Kings represented a model of the cultural gang, where elements of the Hispanic culture assumed the central role in the gang. According to Decker *et al.* (1998), there was little evidence of penetration into traditional organised crime groups by either group. The San Diego gangs (the Calle and the Syndo Mob) were even less well connected. The gangs investigated were not durable and ceased to be central players on the street within a year of identification.

Decker *et al.* concluded that there is no universal determinant of a linkage between gangs and traditional organised crime groups. In addition to the neighbourhood characteristics that previous gang studies had identified as relevant, city-level differences were important factors in defining the types of gangs that might develop in particular locations (1998: 91). In a later paper, however, Decker argues that the presence of organised criminal groups in a city will lead to more organised gangs: 'This as much reflects the availability of organised crime opportunities as it does the penetration of organized crime groups by gangs' (Decker 2001: 38). Clearly, the organised crime history of a particular city plays a role in determining the kinds of gangs that operate there. Whether cases where gang life emulates organised crime (such as the Gangster Disciples of Chicago) indicate an emerging trend remains unclear. More research is undoubtedly required in this field.

As Cohen (1977) suggests, the question of the extent of criminal organisation in crime groups is not one that criminology can settle without reference to their specific social relationships. This applies as much to extensive and sophisticated crime such as the Mafia and the Chinese Triads as to the youth and street gangs discussed above. In terms of their structure, no single organised crime group is archetypal. In some cases there may be well-defined patterns, such as vertical integration where criminal groups attempt to control both the supply and demand, as in the case of drugs trafficking. There is often (but not always) a cellular structure for concealing identity and profits and serving to protect the leaders (Lyman and Potter 2004: 52–3). Partnerships are common, although it is perhaps too early to predict the eclipse of 'family firms' (Hobbs 2001).

As Mars (1999) shows, it is important not to assume that criminal organisations are all of the same type. It is, however, possible systematically to disaggregate types of organisation and to assess their diverse value systems. Using the methods of cultural theory developed by Mary Douglas and discussed by Thompson *et al.* (1990), Mars compares the values and attitudes of different approaches to criminality in criminal groups and reflects upon their organisational structures. He identifies four archetypal categories or 'ideal types' of criminal organisation:

- criminal individualists;
- criminal isolates;
- organised criminal hierarchies; and
- criminal ideologues.

According to Mars (1999), *criminal individualists* are freebooting, innovative schemers, fixers and opportunists. Their way of life is characterised by networking, aspiration and competition. However, their very flexibility makes them vulnerable to agents provocateurs and to a lack of planning. Their tendency towards conspicuous consumption or accumulation of wealth and their rivalry with other criminals makes them more visible to law enforcement agencies. Because they are individualists, they may cause resentment when they abandon network members as of no further use. A striking example (although not one cited by Mars) is that of Curtis Warren, whose activities are discussed in Chapter 8.

In contrast, *criminal isolates* lack membership in a significant group. Because they lack social and material resources, Mars regards them as the lower-level petty criminals who are more likely to act as 'fall guys' for their more organised colleagues. Owing to their isolation, they are vulnerable to manipulation by law enforcement officials and by other criminals.

Organised criminal hierarchies are distinguished by the strong boundary that differentiates those inside the organisation from those outside. They often operate with set procedures and prefer established routines to innovating activity. They are vulnerable when a lack of resources makes the organisation difficult to run. They are sometimes over-reliant on external specialists when expertise does not exist within the group. They are also vulnerable to conflicts between the higher and lower echelons and often have succession crises in their leadership. Examples cited by Mars include the Italian and US Mafia.

Criminal ideologues are likely to be committed to a more egalitarian outlook. According to Mars, where such groups cohere they do so by mobilising a unifying opposition to malign influences outside their own organisation. Their lack of administrative continuity means that they have to make every decision from scratch. They are vulnerable because of their internal fault lines and factionalism. A good example cited by Mars is that of the IRA active service units.

The methodology of cultural theory deserves to be more widely known as a means of disaggregating criminal activity. Although Mars concedes that the four categories are essentially archetypes and rarely exist in their pure forms, they present a plurality of risks and require different methods of regulation and control. The differences in risk that these archetypes provide appear rarely to inform the strategies and tactics of regulatory and enforcement agencies.

In summary, as the above discussion suggests, analysts should not interpret gangs and other criminal organisations only in terms of their compliance with the rational systems' model. While some gangs and criminal groups exhibit aspects of organising activity, there is continued doubt over the extent to which they are formal-rational organisations in the Weberian sense. To reinforce the need for a high level of specificity in this analysis, it is necessary to return to the point made by Cohen (1977). Interpretation of gang and crime group activity depends upon the detail. It is difficult to construct an overarching theory of gang life because of the diversity of activities and circumstances. In the longer term, ethnographic and case study methodologies are likely to be of most benefit in disaggregating the nature of crime group and gang life.

Violence and coercion

There is perhaps less controversy among criminologists over the importance of violence and coercion in the life of gangs and organised crime groups. The use of the term 'violence' here does not refer to the violence of one individual against another for personal or sexual reasons or its use in the furtherance of crime such as robbery. It refers to the use of violence in circumstances that are specifically associated with the membership of a gang or organised crime group. In most cases, this violence is not simply gratuitous. Gang members carry it out for some purpose, although in some cases it may occur because of the nature of the group criminal activity with which it is associated (such as in protecting illicit drugs manufacture and distribution).

Thrasher (1927) noted that gangs come into being through violence. Conflict, he suggested, is endemic to their existence. More specifically, groups of youth form gangs to deal with threats from existing gangs or in response to pressures from the community or the police. Violence is an integral part of the means through which they protect themselves and their members. Klein (1971) observed that violence has a mythic nature for gangs. They constantly refer to it and many members join gangs to find the protection they need to survive in difficult social conditions. In such cases, the source of gang cohesion is external to the gang. It grows in proportion to the external threat. Violence and the threat of violence therefore strengthen the ties between gang members. Gang members arm themselves with firearms in the belief that members of other gangs have guns. They obtain increasingly sophisticated weapons to avoid a shortfall in firepower with their rivals (Horowitz 1983).

Many gangs are territorial and are therefore highly aware of the importance of their location. This is especially the case in relation to the pursuit of their major revenue producing activities. For this reason, they are very sensitive to incursions onto their 'turf'. Gangs defend their territory against other gangs who may have ambitions to take over lucrative business within their boundary. The relation between violence, territory and particular kinds of lucrative business is common to much gang activity. Loftin (1984) suggests that the growth in gang violence of this kind results from 'contagion', producing 'spikes' in violent (often gun-related) crime. Contagion occurs when there is a spatial concentration of violence, when it becomes reciprocal and when it begins to escalate. This perpetuates the 'myth' of violence and makes it real. The substantive evidence in later chapters shows that these points are as appropriate to well-established organised criminal groups as they are to youth and street gangs.

Decker and Van Winkle have illustrated the aggregate effect of these 'push–pull' factors as shown in Figure 2.1, providing a theoretical perspective accounting for group and individual activities inside and outside the gang. In this schema, the threats from the neighbourhood gang itself interact with threats from the outside or from rival gangs. Violence and the use of weapons increase; the threats from both the gang and its rivals induce more members to join, thus disrupting the socialising power of local institutions such as the family, school or job. Violence also tends directly to isolate gang members from the labour market and from other social institutions. Acts of extreme violence (such as drive-by shootings) are very threatening to non-gang members and to communities.

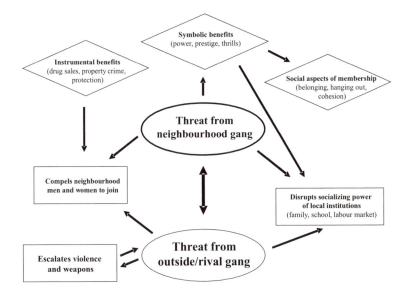

Figure 2.1 Factors affecting gang activity
Source: S.H. Decker and B. Van Winkle (1996) *Life in the Gang*, Cambridge: Cambridge University Press, 25

The primary effect of violence, therefore, is that of estrangement. According to Decker and Van Winkle:

> As gang members are involved in violent events, both as perpetrators and as victims, members of the community attempt to distance themselves from relationships and contacts with gang members. It is within this context that life in the gang must be understood. Life in the gang is an existence characterized by estrangement from social institutions, many neighbourhood groups, and, ultimately, conforming peers and adults.
>
> Decker and Van Winkle (1996: 23–4)

This also makes it difficult for the authorities to help reintegrate gang members into legitimate roles. It is difficult for members to leave the gang for much the same reasons. The cumulative effects of this separation, however, are paradoxical. In one sense, the community has gang life embedded within it. In another sense, the community has gang life radically distanced from it.

Decker and Van Winkle apply this model to neighbourhood gangs, but it is possible to define similar claims in relation to more established criminal networks. Although it is necessary to avoid conflating youth gangs with more sophisticated crime groups, in both cases the symbolic benefits of power, prestige, excitement, belonging and solidarity play as important a part as do the instrumental benefits that relate to making profit from illicit markets.

It is clear from substantive examples in later chapters that violence and coercion are endemic in organised crime as in other gang life. However, in both cases it is necessary to make a distinction between tactical and strategic violence. The difference between tactical and strategic violence is often a matter of scope and extent. Organised crime groups use tactical violence and coercion to achieve short-term, specific goals. If the objective is to secure particular financial or other benefits in the short term, the use of violence or coercion is likely to be at the tactical level. It is used to persuade groups and individuals to conform to particular courses of action in support of gang objectives: to encourage them to part with money or to provide services that they would not otherwise have provided if violence or the threat of violence were not present. Examples include using direct violence or threats to extort money, to secure resources or co-operation from officials or from supposedly 'legitimate' business, or to defend particular operations from predators.

Strategic violence is administered to consolidate longer-term goals. If the objective is to secure the growth or survival of the group, the violence is likely to be strategic. This includes the use of violence to protect the group from rivals or from law enforcement agencies who seek to destroy it, or to extend territory by taking over a particular market. As the examination of substantive examples in later chapters shows, violence of this kind includes such things as the killing of a rival leader to disrupt or destroy the competition or the killing of a law enforcement official or magistrate as an example to others. Although it may apply to street gangs, the use of strategic violence is often a characteristic of more sophisticated or well-established crime groups.

In some cases, a reputation for violence rather than its actual application is sufficient to coerce a gang's victims. In such circumstances, it may be enough simply to exhibit a presence in order to discipline syndicate members, to intimidate victims or to deter competitors. The mere mention of a name may be enough to bully the community at large into compliance. Theorists have long recognised the importance of the nexus between power and reputation. As Thomas Hobbes claims, 'The reputation of power *is* power: because it draweth with it the adherence of those that need protection.' (Hobbes 1651 in Oakeshott 1947: 56). Coercion based upon reputation, therefore, is an instrumental form of illegitimate power.

An examination of the use of instrumental violence and coercion for tactical or strategic ends does not exhaust the analysis. As Decker and Van Winkle (1996) have shown in relation to youth gangs, the instrumental effects are not the only issues that analysts should consider in understanding the relationship between gangs and violence (see Figure 2.1 above). For Decker and Van Winkle, it is also necessary to note the effects of a number of affective factors, including the symbolism of certain kinds of violent behaviour, its effect on the status of gang members, and its role in illustrating their toughness and resilience. Violent gang activity is often symbolic in its character, rather than purely instrumental in the pursuit of particular ends, represented in three ways. First, the use of violence has an important role in defining the ethos of the gang to itself and in expressing its power to its rivals and to the community. Secondly, it demonstrates the status of individual gang members and makes this clear to others, both within the gang and outside. Protagonists use weapons in a symbolic way and the type of weapon they use tends to define gang members. This is necessary in order to maintain the position of individuals within the gang hierarchy, including establishing their rights to rewards and their claims to make decisions affecting other members. Thirdly, it is aimed at sustaining the myth that gang members are 'hard for hard's sake'. This underlines the supposed courage and toughness of the gang as a particular form of life, rather than as a group that exists only for the sake of profitability. The basis for the claim that a crime group is capable of making 'offers that can't be refused' stems as much from the status and reputation of those who make them as from the possibility that direct tactical violence may be offered in the short term. In cases of reluctance, of course, the severed head of a horse at the foot of one's bed may serve to concentrate the mind: as illustrated in Mario Puzo's *The Godfather* (Puzo 1969).

For Gambetta (1996), who analysed the so-called 'protection' of certain markets by the Mafia in Sicily, the gangster must have a real capacity for violence in order to be effective – only the 'reliably tough' character is likely to have success in such rackets:

In order to reassure our clients that we can supply credible protection, we also need strength, both physical and psychological. The capacity to command respect, to inspire awe, has frequently been attributed to *mafiosi* of stature. But above all the *mafiosi* must be able to resort to violence; the ability to inflict punishment is crucial to the role of guarantor.

(Gambetta 1996: 40)

The linkage between such toughness and the limits that the *mafioso* sometimes places on actual applications of violence is not entirely clear. In some cases, a rule of economy of violence may apply. In this sense, the actual use of violence, according to Gambetta, must be something which is not too costly to the *mafioso*.

Judge Giovanni Falcone, who in 1992 paid with his life for his challenge to the Mafia in Italy, identified the notion of respect as one of the keys to the *persona* of the real *mafiosi*. Respect is something that strongly configures their attitudes to power and violence. Falcone says:

The members of the Cosa Nostra demand respect. And only respect those who display towards them a minimum of consideration.

(Falcone 1993: 32)

The many killings and vendettas that Falcone describes are as much the result of failures to accord the respect that the Mafia demands, as of failures to support illicit profit-making ventures. To those whose thinking cannot conceive of this way of life, this appears simply as gratuitous violence. To the *mafioso*, however, the relationship between violence, respect and status is simply an inescapable part of a form of life into which his family inducted him at an early age.

The prohibitions that promote illicit markets may themselves be criminogenic where violence is concerned; for example, where dealing in illicit drugs is encouraged by competition and high levels of profitability. In this environment, in defending himself against law enforcement and against the competition, the gangster (in the cases that Gambetta discusses, the *mafioso*) has 'a very strong incentive to show his ruthlessness and to invest in his military skills' (Gambetta 1996: 42). Where such skills are highly developed and suitable weaponry is routinely available, violence is perhaps an inevitable consequence. In such circumstances, the fact that violence is endemic in gang life is almost certain to come to the surface.

Of course, not every contact between gang members, competitors and client groups leads to violence, although the possibility is ever-present. Again, there are push–pull factors. On one hand, the informal rules of gang life do not soften the capability for violence. On the other, stable relationships between criminal competitors may ameliorate it. Similarly, although the giving of respect may also attenuate the need for violence, observers may regard compliance as simply allowing organised crime to operate as it pleases.

In summary, it is probably right to regard violence and coercion as essential properties of most gang life, rather than as accidental or contingent. The constant presence of violence or the threat of violence in many gangs shows that this is empirically true in a large number of cases. Analysts can argue with justification that such groups would not be what they are without the use of violence and coercion. The Sicilian Mafia and the Japanese Boryokudan have violence embedded in their very fabric. In the cases of corporate crime and other organised criminal activity where overt violence is not immediately evident, however, the picture is less clear. Nevertheless, as the murder of the Italian banker Robert Calvi following the collapse of Banco Ambrosiana shows, it is unwise to assume that corporate crime does not involve violence and coercion (Punch 1996: 180–98). Again, it is necessary to re-emphasise the contested and variable nature of organised crime and to understand it through detailed examination of examples. It is not viable to build overarching general theories, even when their basis is such a widespread phenomenon as that of violence.

Chapter 3

Dirty business: the political economy of organised crime

Chapter 2 examined the nature of gangs and discussed their relationship with other forms of organised crime. It assessed aspects of their social impact, including conflicts with their competitors and their effect on communities but did not comment upon forms of organised criminal activity which could not strictly be said (in the sense in which Chapter 2 used the term) to be gang related. In contrast to Chapter 2, in this chapter we begin to move away from the focus on gangs per se to examine the wider range of activities of criminal groups and to assess the threats they pose in economic and political domains.

In 1994, the UN identified eighteen activities that it regarded as being endemic in 'transnational' organised crime (Mueller 1998: 14). These included such activities as money laundering; corruption of officials; protection rackets; kidnapping; terrorism and maritime piracy; trafficking in drugs, arms, illegal immigrants, and nuclear materials; trafficking in women and children, protected animals and birds, stolen art and cultural objects, body parts, and stolen vehicles. Theft and violent offences such as robbery, hijacking and kidnapping may also figure in the activities of some organised groups, alongside lucrative activities such as counterfeiting, loan-sharking and those connected with illegal gambling and prostitution. Table 3.1 lists these activities, distinguishing the primary categories from activities such as instrumental violence and corruption that enable criminal groups to achieve their goàls and to make a profit.

Table 3.1 Organised crime: table of activities

Primary activities	Enabling activities
Arms dealing	
Counterfeiting	
Drug trafficking	
Extortion and protection rackets	
Fraud and corporate crime	
Illegal vice: gambling and prostitution	
Labour racketeering	Corruption of officials
Loan-sharking	
Marine piracy	Violence, threats and intimidation
Smuggling of nuclear materials	
Smuggling of other contraband	Money laundering
Smuggling illegal immigrants	
Smuggling women and children for sex	Internet and other 'cyber' crime
Smuggling stolen vehicles	
Smuggling body parts	
Smuggling protected animals and birds	
Smuggling art and cultural objects	
Terrorism*	
Theft, robbery, hijacking and kidnapping	
White-collar and corporate crime	

*Whilst recognising that there may be a linkage between terrorism and organised crime, as is the case in Northern Ireland, this text does not examine terrorism, which is the subject of its own specialised literature.

This list is not exhaustive; nor does it represent all the possibilities for the future. However, the choice of these activities by organised crime groups is not accidental. Both primary and enabling activities are concerned with making money and with power.

Relating organised crime only to violent activity of the kind perpetrated by gangsters fails to grasp the range of actors involved in these activities. Albini (1971) and Haller (1990) argue that syndicated crime often goes beyond those who are core group members to include politicians, government officials and business people. Business has always been important to organised crime. As Chambliss suggests:

One of the reasons we fail to understand organised crime is because we put crime into a category that is separate from

> normal business. Much crime does not fit into a separate
> category. It is primarily a business activity.
>
> (Chambliss 1978: 53, quoted in Hobbs 1994: 461)

Punch (1996) rightly refers to the actually illicit activities of ostensibly legitimate forms of business enterprise as 'dirty business'. This term accurately captures the corruptness of certain ways of making a profit where moral and legal scruples are abandoned. The term 'organised crime', therefore, may not only be of application to the activities of gangsters or traditional organised criminals. If writers such as Chambliss (1978) and Punch (1996) are right, it is important to understand the activities associated with organised crime in terms of their status as 'business enterprise', although it is equally important to establish the proper sense in which we can use this terminology.

Given these preliminary distinctions and caveats, this chapter examines the activities associated with organised crime from four perspectives. First, it examines the economic and political impacts of organised criminal activities on individual states and on the international community as a whole. This includes an assessment of the roles that greed, bribery and corruption play in enabling criminal groups to penetrate legitimate economic and political systems. The second part of the chapter examines enterprise crime in its many forms. It compares the objectives and activities of organised crime groups with those of legitimate business and suggests ways in which organised crime is similar to legitimate business activity and ways in which it differs from it. Thirdly, the chapter discusses so called 'white-collar' crime and corporate fraud, questioning whether we should regard these activities as part of organised crime, or as phenomena in their own right. Drawing upon the work of Ruggiero (1996), Slapper and Tombs (1999) and Croall (2001), it raises the question of the symbiosis between organised crime and white-collar or corporate crime. Finally, the chapter reviews laundering as the primary means that enables criminal groups to convert the proceeds of their criminal activities into resources that can safely be used for their own purposes.

The economic and political impact of organised crime

During recent decades, theorists and policy makers have increasingly turned their attention to the ways in which organised crime affects the nation state and world trade. Its adverse effects on democracy and economic development in Colombia and on some aspects of the Italian polity are well known (see Chapters 4 and 5). Concerns about these effects increased in the wake of the political changes in Russia and in Eastern and Central Europe in the late 1980s (see Chapter 7). However, perhaps the most problematic aspect of organised crime is the challenge that it provides to the viability of national economies. Such concerns are evident not only in relation to developing states where controls over organised crime are difficult to achieve. They apply to a greater or lesser extent to all economies and political systems in both the developed and the developing world. The adverse effects of organised crime have certainly encouraged governments to take the subject seriously.

How may we assess these effects? As is the case with terrorism, some criminal groups deliberately seek a direct political impact. Some may even try to dominate the economies of states. Even where no such intention is apparent, the activities of criminal groups have indirect impacts. Indeed, there is always a link between organised crime and the political, economic and financial systems within which it operates. In particular, organised crime requires established financial systems in order to operate effectively and to convert the proceeds of criminality into usable funds. In general, therefore, it seeks to make a profit within such systems, not to undermine them. There is little point in seeking political or economic power while destroying the very systems that will sustain profitability.

What is the economic impact of organised crime? It is paradoxical that in liberal societies the free-market economy that many argue provides the best chance of success for legitimate business may also provide the most fertile ground for the growth of illicit enterprise. For those who argue from the perspective of economics, organised crime is a clandestine economy. There is no doubt that the financial stakes involved in organised crime are high. Reports suggest that organised criminal activity produces a turnover of around $500 billion per year. It could be as high as $1,000 billion (*Financial Times*, 14 February 1997). The 1997 *World Drugs Report* estimated that organised drug trafficking alone was worth around $400 billion annually or about 8 per cent of world trade. This is equivalent to the world's textile industry (United Nations 1997). Slapper and Tombs (1999: 67) estimate that the cost of consumer and personal fraud, tax fraud and corporate financial crime in the USA could be as high as $715 billion annually. However, despite these estimates by well-informed analysts, it is impossible to be accurate about the impact of economic crime on the global economy.

In addition to the economic burdens it generates, corporate malpractice has the effect of reducing the confidence of the public in financial institutions. This is especially the case where fraud involves banks or the stock markets. For example, the results of major corporate failures such as the Bank of Credit and Commerce International (BCCI) secured very high financial rewards for professional crooks and company officers by misleading the public and the regulators. The Pakistani financier Agha Hasan Abedi set up BCCI in Luxembourg in 1972. According to Punch (1996), a number of forces pushed BCCI towards crime and enabled it to continue unchecked. These included: Abedi's leadership style; the use of Asian *hundi* and *hawala* banking practices (see below); a personalised style of operating which drew in unscrupulous operators, crooks and security services; a cavalier attitude to paper accounts; and a fragmented, opaque structure that was hard to oversee and which guaranteed almost complete power to Abedi. The collapse of BCCI was the largest bank closure in history. The Bank of England, with the co-operation of banking regulators elsewhere, closed the bank in 1991. The extent of the fraud was considerable; the New York indictment spoke of a $20 billion swindle (Punch 1996: 9–15; Passas 1996). Whatever else in the way of criminal activity that it involved, the BCCI collapse was a breach of the trust that is necessary for banking and other forms of commerce to operate. Both a degree of trust between those involved in commerce of all kinds and effective systems of regulation and contract law are the basis for legitimate business. Where trust and regulation break down, it becomes impossible to find a clear boundary between legitimate and illicit enterprise. Economies where this happens quickly become havens for organised crime. In such jurisdictions, organised crime brings all business and commerce into disrepute.

In addition to its effects on the global economy, organised crime generates political problems. These appear at both the national and the international level. The effects of organised crime upon democracy are widely debated (Allum and Seibert 2003). In securing their business goals, criminal groups undermine the rule of law by the coercion and corruption of public officials. Intimidation of government and the assassination of public figures serve to undermine the stability of civil society. They are an affront to human rights. If this kind of activity continues unimpeded, it could affect international security (Berdal and Serrano 2002). According to Shelley, there are severe dangers in ignoring the problem:

While the world focused on such highly visible problems as the superpower conflict or regional hostilities, the increasingly pernicious and pervasive transnational crime that now threatens the economic and political stability of many nations was ignored. Long term neglect of this problem means that the world now faces highly developed criminal organizations that undermine the rule of law, international security and the world economy and which, if they are allowed to continue unimpeded, could threaten the concept of the nation-state.

(Shelley 1995: 464–5)

Perhaps the most dangerous aspect of these developments is the extent that organised crime groups may penetrate or control the organs of state. Again according to Shelley (1995):

This is evident in Italy, where for more than a century a symbiotic relationship has existed between crime and politics. The seven-time prime minister Giulio Andreotti – the stalwart of the pre-eminent post war social democratic party – has twice been deprived of his parliamentary immunity for charges of collaboration with the *Mafia*. Another former prime minister, Bettino Craxi of the Socialist Party, has been officially charged with corruption.

(Shelley 1995: 469)

Shelley points to similar examples in Colombia, where the relationship between the government and the drug cartels has undermined democracy and the rule of law. Some regions of Russia and the newly independent states have also fallen under the influence of criminal organisations. These trends have an effect on the global economy, especially on the financial and commodities markets. Unless there is concerted international action, no government is immune from these incursions. No legal system seems able fully to control them. No economic system seems able to resist a level of profit that is substantially higher than that which the licit system affords (Shelley 1995: 485).

Lupsha (1996) also provides a model of the growth of organised crime in terms of its potential to affect the nation state. According to Lupsha (1996: 30–3), organised crime includes predatory gangs and groups such as smugglers and bootleggers, who are parasitic on legitimate commerce. Some have symbiotic relationships with legal business or with the holders of state power. For Lupsha, this is an evolutionary process. In the predatory stage, criminal groups are rooted in particular territories, over which they attempt to maintain a monopoly of the illicit use of force. In this phase, the criminal gang gains recognition among legitimate power brokers, which use the gang's violence and skill for their own ends. In the parasitic phase, organised crime develops a corrupting nexus between itself and the power brokers. This builds on particular 'windows of opportunity', such as during the prohibition era or during the growth of widespread drug trafficking (as in Colombia). There are also other 'triggers':

> war, conflict, historical alienation and ethnic identity, have created either black market opportunities, or allowed (in anarchy and the breakdown of civil society) criminal gangs, as in Bosnia, to emerge as power brokers and/or nationalist spokesmen.
>
> (Lupsha 1996: 31)

Corruption is the 'glue' that binds this together. By this means, criminal networks extend into the economic and political sectors. In this way, organised crime increasingly becomes an equal, rather than an opponent, of the state.

In the final, symbiotic stage, the bond between organised crime and the political system becomes one of mutuality. Lupsha cites the Cali drug cartel's influence over Colombia's legislative and judicial system and, in Italy, the forty-year relationship between the Mafia and the Christian Democrats as examples. The political involvement of the Yakuza in Japan provides another example. In this phase, organised crime is no longer simply a law enforcement problem:

> The traditional tools of the state to enforce law will no longer work, for organized crime has become part of the state; a state within a state.
>
> (Lupsha 1996: 32)

As will be evident from the discussion in Chapter 7, developments in organised crime in the former Soviet Union and in some parts of Eastern and Central Europe have followed this model. The dangers of instituting a system of privatisation and free market capitalism without the stabilising influence of the institutions of civil society and the rule of law are all too obvious (Lupsha 1996: 33). Only drastic action by the states concerned, supported by the international community, will be able to remedy these situations.

Enterprise crime: organised crime as business

The empirical evidence in cases such as the collapse of the BCCI shows the virulence of the links between organised crime and business. As the debate about corporate crime set out below shows, the relationship is a two-way street. According to Lupsha, it is not difficult for organised crime to entice the 'suckers' of the business world into its web of operations. Greed is an important factor. He says:

> given the extent of planetary avarice, transnational organized criminals do not have to be geniuses, for smart, supposedly legitimate businessmen and entrepreneurs beat a path to their door with new ideas, technologies, techniques and investment opportunities to enrich themselves while furthering the business of transnational organized crime.
>
> (Lupsha 1996: 34)

When comparing organised crime with legitimate business, scandals involving bribery and corruption in the latter may incline an observer to think that there is little difference between them. There are certainly similarities between them in their use of global networks of contacts and dubious associations that aim towards profit at any cost. However, there are also a number of qualities that organised criminal groups seem uniquely to possess. These include:

- high levels of adaptability and responsiveness to change;
- the threat and use of violence to achieve ends;
- the use of terminal sanctions to remove inefficiency; and
- secrecy and the routine use of covert methods.

Sceptics are right to be suspicious about the extent to which some of these attributes might also apply to supposedly legitimate businesses. However, in most cases they should serve to convince even the most sceptical that there is some degree of difference between much legitimate business and organised crime (Lupsha 1996: 35).

Given the clear differences between the best of legitimate business practice and the worst of organised crime, how much further can an impartial analysis take the business analogy? What is required to support the claim that organised crime is a form of business is an explanatory theory that sets out a rationale for the business model of organised crime and distinguishes it from legitimate business. This chapter explores two important approaches to understanding organised crime in terms of dirty business: Smith's enterprise model and the theory of the criminal organisation as a firm.

Smith (1975), like many others, was critical of Cressey's Cosa Nostra model of organised crime. For Smith, it is important to draw attention away from such stereotypical models and direct it towards the dynamics of the marketplace. The proper point of departure is the concept of enterprise. According to Smith, illicit enterprise exists in the same dimension as does legitimate enterprise:

> Illicit enterprise is the extension of legitimate market activities into areas which are normally proscribed – i.e., beyond existing limits of the law – for the pursuit of profit and in response to latent illicit demand.
>
> (Smith 1975: 335)

In this sense, it is a mistake to assume that the marketplace ends at the edge of legitimacy. The law does not bring an end to demand, as experience of the prohibition era in the USA illustrates. Analysts should regard enterprise under such conditions no less as enterprise because illegal markets provide the means through which it operates.

For Smith (1975), entrepreneurial transactions form the basis of all enterprise. It is possible to assign every entrepreneurial transaction to a place on a continuous scale according to the degree to which they are legal or illegal. Legitimate business activities cover a wide range of goods and services above the legal limit. Those of illicit enterprise cover the provision of goods and services below the legal limit. The limit itself may change from time to time, as was the case with prohibition in the USA, creating new illicit markets. It is therefore possible to rank entrepreneurial transactions on a scale that reflects their levels of legitimacy within a specific marketplace. For example, a commercial bank with low interest rates and low collateral risk is firmly in the legitimate sector. A usurer (loan shark) with very high interest rates may be beyond the legal limit, especially where the activity involves coercion or violence (Smith 1975: 336).

Smith further argues that the theory of illicit enterprise leads to better ways of responding to the phenomenon of organised crime. Agencies can respond better because they do not have to deal with it as an alien structure or conspiracy that survives on violence and bribery. For Smith, what observers regard as organised crime is only the illicit aspect of two widespread entrepreneurial technologies: the mediating technology of power brokering and the service technology of security and enforcement (Smith 1975: 343). The former is a series of mechanisms through which individuals or groups are able to exercise a right or to redress a wrongful application of governmental or corporate power. It is possible to rank these mechanisms on a scale of legitimacy. For example, a civil claims court is at the high end of legitimacy in enforcing a contract. A briber is at the low end, beyond the legal limit of legitimacy (Smith 1975: 343).

The mediating power of security and enforcement is a series of mechanisms through which individuals are able to obtain security of the person or of property, enforcement of rights and regulation of the behaviour of groups or individuals. As with power brokering, it is possible to rank security and enforcement on a scale of legitimacy, in this case, the scale that reflects the extent of sanctions governing the exercise of force and the detention and confinement of persons. Criminal justice agencies are at the high end of legitimacy in this respect. Vigilante groups or the 'underground policeman' are at the low end. They are below the legal limit, unless they have regulatory or oversight mechanisms that ensure their legitimacy (Smith 1975: 344–5).

The activities of the briber and of the vigilante are all forms of illicit enterprise. Their activities result either in extortion or in the assumption of a private monopoly of public rights. Victims and officials only attribute power to them because of their association with violence or threats of violence. The provision of illicit goods and services by this means enables the successful entrepreneur to exert a profound effect on a community. For Smith therefore:

> The task ahead is to understand the scope, characteristics, and functions of illicit enterprise in all its manifestations, because it is only through that process that we can learn how to preserve the legitimate threads in the fabric of … society.
>
> (1975: 346)

It is important to recognise that Smith does not claim that legitimate business is identical with illicit enterprise. The activities of legitimate business cover a wide range of goods and services above the legal limit. Those of illicit enterprise cover the provision of goods and services below that limit. Among others, the arms trade fits well into this continuum.

As the above argument makes clear, there are differences in the degree of legitimacy and the type of activity. However, the themes of power brokering and of the technology of security and protection are common to both legitimate and illicit enterprise. While some legitimate enterprises may sit outside this framework, for example, in businesses that specialise in supplying food or accommodation, most fall within these two themes. Therefore, although all organised crime is like legitimate business in some respects, the reverse does not follow. Not all legitimate business is like organised crime.

The extent to which organisations comply with the law provides an important means of comparing legitimate business with illicit enterprise. In general, although they may not always act ethically, most legitimate businesses try (or are forced) to keep within the legal limits that states place upon their actions. Criminal organisations have no such legal or ethical limits. They have the ability, through corruption of officials, to act and acquire influence, to gain access to rule makers and rule enforcers and to deal with opponents. Although legitimate business may resort to these ploys in some environments, the international community and regulatory authorities do not regard these strategies as the norm, nor as being desirable.

Firms of all kinds depend on a potential or an existing market within which they can deliver their products or services. A pre-existing economic system is necessary for this to be successful. Neither legitimate business nor organised crime can exist in conditions of anarchy. The cost of a 'war of each against all' is too high. Both legitimate and illicit enterprise, therefore, rely upon money, commerce and political order to sustain their efforts. In their original form, traditional organised crime groups may differ in this respect. An unstable local socio-political order was the original basis for groups such as the Mafia. Similarly, the development of criminal gangs whose origins are in the Balkans was almost certainly a by-product of political changes in the former Yugoslavia and Albania. However, without fruitful ground upon which to develop, such groups would remain primitive. The successful modern firm (criminal or otherwise) requires social, political and economic conditions that encourage the growth of particular markets.

In his classic introduction to the theory of the firm, Coase (1937) argued that analysts should conceive of a firm as an entity the existence of which is justified only in terms of the relation of the costs of its transactions to its overall costs of production. As the above argument suggests, firms (whether they are licit or illicit enterprises) cannot thrive in conditions of anarchy. Firms only exist because their agents find this way of organising a useful means for minimising transaction costs. Such firms aim to maximise profits and to minimise such transaction costs, whether they are in a monopoly situation or whether they have competitors. As Chapter 1 implied, it is not necessary to adopt the bureaucratic model of industrial organisation to recognise the relevance of a wide range of transaction costs.

According to Williamson (1981: 552), exchange of goods and services between persons or across boundaries of any sort incurs a transaction cost. Transaction costs apply both to legitimate business and to illicit enterprises. They include the costs of conflicts and misunderstandings that lead to delays, to breakdowns and to other malfunctions. They can include such things as the costs of incentives, of ensuring co-ordination and the enforcement of regulations, rules or customs. In the case of a criminal organisation, controlling transaction costs is necessary to keep it protected from betrayal and from prosecution. This includes the need to protect the organisation from informers and from others (such as law enforcement agencies) who threaten its profits and stability. For such organisations, the use of violence and coercion is often the most effective way of reducing transaction costs.

Anderson sets out the effect of transaction cost analysis in relation to the activities of the Mafia in Sicily and in the USA (Anderson 1997: 33–54). Anderson regards the Mafia as a diverse governance structure made up of competing families rather than as a single firm. Mafia groups consider the costs of each transaction in estimating the risk involved in their drug dealing operations. Betrayal of the group by informers leading to disruption of operations, seizure of drugs and arrest of group members is the predominant transaction cost in such cases. Analysis of transaction costs is also relevant to other aspects of the operations of organised crime groups. For example, Dick (1995) has drawn upon transactional cost analysis to predict which illegal goods and services organised crime will supply in the marketplace. Although transactional cost analysis remains controversial, with further research it could provide a useful tool to explain the use of violence, coercion and corruption by organised crime groups.

Using the theory of the firm enables analysts to compare aspects of legitimate business with those of organised criminal groups across a number of dimensions that generate transaction costs. These include their organisation, boundaries, goals and objectives, competition and rent seeking (see below). Each of these involves transaction costs, which vary according to the extent to which an enterprise is licit or illicit. Table 3.2 sets out a comparison of legitimate business and organised criminal groups across these dimensions. This listing is not exhaustive. Readers should be able to add their own categories (see Chapter 8 for discussion of criminal 'firms' in Britain).

Table 3.2 Analytical table comparing organised crime groups with legitimate business

Dimension	Legitimate business	Organised crime groups
Enterprise	Activities cover the whole range of goods and services above the legal limit. May be involved in licit forms of power brokering or security/protection.	Illicit; only covering a limited range of goods and services below the legal limit. These often involve illicit forms of power brokering or security/ protection based on threats and violence.
Transaction costs	Apply to all transactions, including incentives, co-operation and enforcement. There is a tendency to minimise such costs to support profits.	Apply to all transactions, including incentives, co-operation and enforcement. In particular, they are relevant to the security and survival of the group.
Organisation	Generally hierarchical; sometimes bureaucratic in structure but now less so. Exceptions to this in some specialist fields, where structures are less well defined. Transaction costs because of organisational structures may be somewhat higher than they are in organised crime groups.	Hierarchical, non-bureaucratic, in loose confederation, often with partners. Organisational transaction costs may be lower than in legitimate business, although applying too many draconian sanctions may increase them.
Boundaries	Legal and ethical boundaries. Businesses may impose strategic boundaries by choice. Multinational organisations have only limited jurisdictional boundaries.	No jurisdictional, legal or ethical boundaries. Transaction costs comparatively low in this dimension.
Goals and objectives	Generally accessible, although some business strategies are kept con-	Clandestine to protect the group and its leaders. Except in 'expressive' gangs,

Table 3.2 continues on facing page

Table 3.2 continued

Dimension	Legitimate business	Organised crime groups
	fidential for commercial reasons. Goals are often multiple to satisfy a range of constituencies within the firm.	goals generally are limited to those that maximise profitability. Transaction costs are minimised in this respect.
Profitability	Optimising 'satisficing' behaviour, depending on the type of business, the multiplicity of its goals and the character of its executive and stakeholders.	Generally maximising, although personal generosity is not unknown.
Competition	Competitive edge preserved through technology, research, marketing and intellectual property rights. Not adverse to corruption to achieve their ends in some environments. Transaction costs more predictable than they are in a firm pursuing illicit enterprises.	Competitive edge preserved by means of coercion, violence and use of capital resources for corruption on a regular basis. These may appear to reduce transaction costs but there may be a long-term price to pay.
Rent seeking behaviour	Some rent-seeking behaviour to achieve specific goals. It is rarely immanent in the functions and purposes of the business.	Almost constant rent-seeking behaviour, which is often immanent in the functions and activities of the group.

Chapter 1 has already discussed the structure and organisation of crime groups. Although there are differences between crime groups and legitimate businesses in terms of the rationality of their structures, there are also certain similarities. Both are to some extent hierarchical, sometimes with divisions of function between members. However, reasons for allegiance to the group differ greatly between crime groups and legitimate businesses. Legitimate business sets out formal rules that regulate the conduct of members. There are transactional costs, but regulations serve to define their scope. In organised criminal groups, the costs involved are unregulated except by the informal rules or oaths that apply to that organisation. When a member or client 'steps out of line', a criminal group will apply sanctions to regulate their behaviour. These are often of a violent kind. Profit is generally the real objective, hence the cliché that often precedes the violence, 'it's nothing personal, just business'. However, it is the routine threat or use of violent sanctions that marks an important boundary between legitimate and illicit business.

According to Schelling (1967), the fact that an organised crime group is a type of firm specialising in providing illegal goods and services to buyers serves to consolidate the goals and objectives they will pursue. The same is not the case for legitimate business. The behavioural theory of the firm postulated by Cyert and March (1963) suggests that although profit always predominates organisations often have a variety of objectives, some of which may be in conflict. Because there is no single objective, they balance their efforts by means of 'satisficing' rather than 'maximising' behaviour. Satisficing behaviour is that which is satisfactory to the organisation, to its members and to its customers. It suffices to make profit, although not necessarily to maximise it.

There are a number of differences between legitimate business and illicit enterprise in respect of their goals and the means they use for management and control. In legitimate business, workers, unions, executives and customers all have views about the goals of the firm and about the way in which it should try to achieve them. In public companies, where there is a separation of ownership and control, shareholders exercise a degree of oversight of the business in order to protect their investment. Some businesses are subject to scrutiny by bodies appointed for regulating conduct and maintaining standards. Companies in the financial sector, including banks and insurers, are increasingly subject to scrutiny by such regulatory bodies. Legitimate business therefore adopts an approach that both suffices to make it profitable and satisfies the diverse needs of a wide range of stakeholders. Illicit enterprise has no constraints of this kind. Transaction costs are therefore lower in this respect for organised criminal groups than for legitimate enterprise, which learns to live with a higher degree of goal ambiguity.

Both legitimate businesses and criminal groups indulge in a variety of 'rent-seeking' behaviours. Rent-seeking behaviour is that which improves the welfare of one person at the expense of another. An extreme example of rent-seeking behaviour is that of a protection racket, in which one particular group betters themselves without creating any welfare-enhancing output at all. Not all examples of rent-seeking behaviour are criminal. Organisational analysts also describe the behaviour of a business that tries to improve its own share of turnover without increasing the total volume of turnover in the market as 'rent seeking' (Bannock *et al.* 1998).

The idea of a criminal 'firm' engaged in enterprise crime which follows some aspects of legitimate business provides a tentative working model for much of what many analysts recognise as 'organised crime'. Indeed, without a great deal of difficulty, it is possible to conceive all of the activities in Table 3.1 in terms of enterprise crime. In some cases, as in the Mafia activities in Sicily observed by Gambetta (1996), this will be gang related, including involvement of gang members from a variety of socio-economic backgrounds. In other cases, as in the groups observed in the USA by Chambliss (1978) and Haller (1990), broader partnerships are at work. In the case of white-collar and corporate crime, however, it is necessary to extend the analysis to assess the extent to which such 'dirty business' is an integral part of organised crime.

White-collar and corporate crime

Many commentators have drawn attention to the extent to which so-called 'white-collar' crime, corporate crime and fraud are forms of organised crime (see Croall 1992, 2001; Hobbs 1994; Ruggiero 1996; Slapper and Tombs 1999; Naylor 2002; Levi 2003). Crimes of this type are not new. We can regard the scandals of the eighteenth century, such as the investment fraud perpetrated by the South Sea Company and other 'bubble' companies, as forms of corporate crime. According to Woodiwiss, their combination of fraud and violent coercion, 'serve as spectacular antecedents of modern organized business crime.' (2001: 23). Modern examples of white-collar or corporate crime include the deaths resulting from organisational negligence at the Union Carbide Company in Bhopal, India, the collapse of BCCI, depredations of pension funds in the Maxwell Group, the US Savings and Loan scandal and the collapse of Barings Bank brought about by the activities of 'rogue trader' Nick Leeson (Punch 1996: 5–38). Each of these cases has generated a substantial corpus of debate and discussion.

Compared with the supposedly glamorous world of the gangs, white-collar and corporate crimes have not caught the public imagination. As far as the writer is aware, apart from the film *Rogue*

Trader (1999) about Leeson, there are very few films and absolutely no musicals about white-collar crime. The public does not regard it with the same degree of seriousness as they do street robbery or burglary or with the same amount of interest as they do the activities of gangsters. White-collar and corporate crimes have not figured as prominently as high volume offences such as burglary or street crime in public policy. In the USA and the UK, the vast majority of white-collar and corporate crimes have not attracted high levels of investigative and legal resources. The exceptions are a number of long-drawn-out (often flawed and frequently unsuccessful) fraud trials. These include the 1990–3 trials relating to illegal share dealings associated with the takeover bid by Guinness of the Distillers Company, which cost around £30 million, the 1992 Blue Arrow fraud trial, which cost around £40 million, the 1994 Brent Walker trial, which also cost around £40 million, and the 1996 Maxwell pensions trial, which cost around £25 million. A recent spectacular failure was the trial relating to alleged corruption over contracts for building London's Jubilee underground railway line. This lasted two years and cost around £60 million. In each case, the majority of the expenditure related to legal and court costs.

Sutherland coined the term 'white-collar crime' in 1939. He defined it as 'a crime committed by a person of respectability and high social status in the course of his occupation' (1983: 7). His claim that business managers and executives were more likely to commit such crimes than were the socially deprived working classes broke new criminological ground. Unfortunately, Sutherland's claims did not resolve the many questions that subsequently arose about the nature of white-collar crime. Legal positivists such as Tappan (1947) argued that Sutherland was mistaken to describe people as 'criminal' unless the law could take action to prosecute them. White-collar crime contained many acts and omissions, which although they were unethical, were not always unlawful. As such, they might not merit prosecution. As is the case with 'transnational crime', white-collar crime is a term that has had no juridical meaning in national and international law.

Croall believes it is best to define and conceptualise white-collar crime as 'abuse of a legitimate occupational role which is regulated by law' (1992: 9; 2001: 17). Nevertheless, white-collar crime includes a wide variety of offences, possibly too many for the term to have any real legal utility. For Croall (2001), white-collar offences include fraud; public sector, commercial and political corruption; health and safety offences; consumer offences; offences concerned with food labelling and poisoning; and environmental crime, such as dumping toxic waste and causing pollution. In considering these offence types it is also necessary to draw attention to the distinction between 'occupational' crimes, which are often committed by individuals or small groups, and 'organisational' crimes, which corporations perpetrate. Croall argues that some types of organisation may be more criminogenic than others. Like Punch (1996), she suggests that the search for profitability at the expense of business ethics provides an important causal link (Croall 2001: 85–6).

Croall also examines the debate about whether white-collar crime is a crime and points to its ambiguous status, although conceding that the difference between legal and social representations of crime can explain some of the ambiguity (2001: 13–14). Other problems also bring into question the explanatory power of the concept. For example, it is not clear whether the offence or the offender should be the basis for analysis. Neither is it always clear who its victims are, although the list can include company shareholders, managers and employees, as well as the public as consumers. Similarly, Nelken (2002: 847–59) identifies a number of ambiguities in relation to white-collar crime. These include problems of defining it, difficulties in explaining its causes and dilemmas in regulating and handling the phenomenon.

Although it has wide usage in criminological discourse, the concept of corporate crime also entails similar problems relating to its meaning and extent. Indeed, it is far from clear where white-collar crime ends and corporate crime begins or if there is an overlap between them. According to Slapper and Tombs (1999: 16–19), corporate crime includes acts and omissions by corporations designed to increase their revenue and profit. Some of the examples they adduce are similar to those mentioned by Croall (2001), who includes organisational or corporate offences in her discussion of white-collar crime. In such debates, impartial analysts are to some extent confronted with a distinction without a difference, making discrimination between the concepts difficult.

Nevertheless, Slapper and Tombs provide an extensive and detailed review of corporate crime, setting out the different types of corporate offences. They include examples of their historical and contemporary forms. These can include actions ranging from serious fraud, to the dumping of toxic and other waste products and ignoring health and safety legislation (Slapper and Tombs 1999: 42–9). The debate set out in Slapper and Toombs accounts for the existence of corporate crime, the ways in which the state responds to corporate crimes and the way in which the discipline of criminology treats the subject. For Slapper and Tombs, the shift in criminological discourse from a primary focus on crimes committed by working people, the basis of whose criminality was in social and economic deprivation, to those committed by the bourgeoisie was long overdue. They note that within the capitalist system the profit imperative has predominance over both law and normative business ethics. The downside of this is that it has been to the advantage of capitalist societies to give more attention to working-class crime than to the crimes of those who are engaged in business. Corporate crime, in this sense, is one of the structural necessities of capitalism. The arguments set out by Slapper and Toombs (1999) draw on a large range of sources, although there is an evident debt to those who have promoted study of the crimes of the powerful, especially Pearce (1976) and Box (1983).

Croall (1992, 2001), Slapper and Tombs (1999) and Nelken (2002) have succeeded in analysing white-collar and corporate crime and in showing its essentially contested nature. However, for the purposes of this current debate it is necessary to ask how and to what extent analysts can legitimately apply these terms to the activities of criminal groups who are engaged in various forms of 'enterprise crime'. The latter expression has acquired a particularly important meaning that might serve to place much of the activity of such groups within the domain of 'dirty business', not just within the broad but somewhat unhelpful category of 'organised crime'.

According to Hobbs (1994), thinking in terms of 'professional crime' may be more useful than over-reliance on organisational theory when considering the activities of organised crime groups. The business orientation of many such professional crime groups is likely to exacerbate the blurring of lines between types of business activity and the very idea of illegality itself. He says:

> In the near future, it will become impossible to distinguish for any other than academic purposes between the categories of white collar crime and organized crime...Legality will be increasingly irrelevant in an international market immune to any moral perspective other than profit.
>
> (Hobbs 1994: 459)

Similarly, Ruggiero (1996) has argued that analysts should analyse corporate and organised crime as conjoined phenomena. Business and the underworld, in this sense, are not separate arenas:

The impact of white collar crime is global and local and many crimes involve what people see as an increasing tendency for the 'upperworld' to be increasingly involved in the 'underworld' because many activities involve partnerships between organised crime, legitimate organisations and government officials.

(Ruggiero 1996, in Croall 2001: 43)

Here, as the arguments of Albini (1971) and Lupsha (1996) make clear, the fulfilment of mutual (essentially capitalist) goals aimed at profit is the origin of the symbiosis between organised crime and business. In examining substantive cases, therefore, it is always worth establishing the extent to which they demonstrate the existence of relationships between members of criminal groups and other actors from commerce and politics. This is not just an academic point. As Chapter 9 suggests, it increasingly affects the ways states tackle organised crime. According to Ruggiero (1996: 22), it is also the view of law enforcement agencies, who see the demarcation between corporate and organised crime as increasingly blurred.

In the light of contemporary developments in corporate fraud, such as in the Savings and Loan scandal in the USA, the collapse of BCCI and artificial inflation of company profits to boost stock market values as in the Enron case, it is necessary to take this seriously. Although the differences between legitimate business and organised crime in most cases are clear, sceptical criminologists are far from sanguine about the separation. The idea of enterprise crime as 'dirty business' expresses a new kind of rationality for organised crime that is not simply parasitic but is in deeper symbiosis with 'legitimate' business. As Lyman and Potter claim, the Savings and Loan scandal in the USA illustrated three truths about organised crime that are often ignored:

- There is precious little difference between those people whom society designates as respectable and law abiding and those people whom society designates as hoodlums and thugs;

- The world of corporate finance and corporate capital is as criminogenic and probably more so than any poverty wracked slum neighbourhood;

- The distinctions between business, politics and organized crime are at best artificial and in reality irrelevant. Rather than being dysfunctions, corporate crime, white-collar crime, organized crime and corruption are mainstays of US political-economic life.

(Lyman and Potter 2004: 476)

When the analysis takes into account the potential for violence the risk increases. Of course, these are large generalisations, about which more can be said. Perhaps, as already argued, it is preferable to provide a more discerning model through which accurate comparisons can be made. However, as Hobbs argues, where organised crime groups get involved in legitimate business enterprise, their use of violence becomes an important resource for the assertion of a new kind of market sovereignty (1994: 461).

Money laundering

Organised crime groups generate large amounts of money by activities such as drug trafficking, arms smuggling and financial crime. This money, however, is of little use to them unless they can disguise it and convert it into funds that are available for investment in legitimate enterprise. Money laundering is important because of the scale of the problem and the damage it causes. The methods that organised crime uses for converting its 'dirty' money into 'clean' assets encourage corruption. They tarnish the reputation of the banking industry and the financial world more generally. Money laundering is also important because of the opportunities for survival and expansion that it affords to organised criminal groups. If they were unable easily to convert the proceeds of their activities into legitimate funds, they would be less profitable and therefore more vulnerable. Unchallenged money laundering is bad for domestic and international trade, bad for the reputation of the international banking industry and bad for effective government and the rule of law.

A number of factors have sustained the rapid growth of money laundering. First, the sheer scale of illicit enterprise precludes organised crime being a cash business. The vast amount of money now available to criminal groups makes it imperative to render it into other, more usable forms. Apart from using some cash for living and other expenses, they have little option but to convert the bulk of the proceeds into legitimate funds. They achieve this by means of investment, by developing legitimate businesses and by purchasing property of various kinds. The second factor in the growth of money laundering is the globalisation of communications and commerce. Technology has made the rapid transfer of funds across international borders much easier. Although this means that the funds may become evident to the authorities during the conversion process, criminal groups continually develop new techniques to keep them ahead of the investigators. A third factor in the growth of money laundering activity has been a trend towards a lack of effective financial regulation in some parts of the global economy. The continuing existence of a number of havens that protect financial secrecy has also served to facilitate money laundering by transnational groups. Although the authorities act to close loopholes wherever possible, it is perhaps inevitable that criminal groups will continue to convert a considerable bulk of their criminal proceeds into legitimate funds.

There is little doubt that money laundering has now become a global problem of vast proportions. In 1995, the US Congress Office of Technology estimated that money generated annually by organised crime and other profit-motivated crime in the USA was around $300 billion (Lyman and Potter 1997: 174). According to Robinson (1996), money laundering each year deals with from $200 billion to $500 billion. He suggests that it is the third largest business in the world, after foreign exchange and oil. The UN's estimates of the amount of money laundered in one year have ranged between $500 billion and $1 trillion. Although the margin between these figures is huge, even the lower estimate underlines the seriousness of the problem (United Nations Office for Drugs and Crime 2002).

How do criminal groups carry out money laundering? The so-called 'laundry' or 'wash cycle' operates to cover the money trail and to convert the proceeds of crime into usable assets. The 1994 Courmeyer Conference, a meeting of experts which preceded the 1994 UN Naples Conference on organised crime, discussed a number of conceptual and practical issues relating to money laundering (Savona 1997: ix). The key issue was not simply that of law enforcement; the objective was to help promote international policies for its control by regulating the financial markets themselves. According to Savona, who described the Courmeyer Conference and its policy outcomes:

> The main goal of these policies is to make the financial markets transparent, minimising the circulation of criminal money and its influence upon legitimate industries.
>
> (Savona 1997: x)

Savona and De Feo (1997) discuss the extent of the problem and set out a typology of money laundering. They cite evidence and examples from a number of jurisdictions to support their arguments. According to Savona and De Feo, money laundering is a three-stage process that requires placement, layering and integration.

Placement is physical disposal of the money by moving funds from direct association with crime and putting them into the financial system. Robinson (1996) refers to this part of the laundry cycle as 'immersion'. Criminal groups sometimes achieve this by 'smurfing': moving small amounts at a time to avoid raising suspicion. Placement or immersion may also involve bank complicity, the mixing of illicit with licit funds, cash purchases and the smuggling of currency to safe havens (Savona and De Feo 1997: 23–4).

Layering disguises the trail to foil pursuit. Robinson (1996) refers to this part of the cycle as 'heavy soaping'. It involves the creation of false paper trails, conversion of cash into monetary instruments and the conversion of tangible assets obtained by means of cash purchases. The use of electronic methods to facilitate the layering process is increasing. According to Savona and De Feo, electronic processes:

> are probably the most cost effective layering method available to money launderers. They offer criminals speed, distance, minimal audit trail, and virtual anonymity amid the enormous daily volume of electronic transfers, all at minimal cost.
>
> (Savona and De Feo 1997: 27)

Integration makes the money available to the criminal again with its occupational and geographical origins hidden from view. Robinson (1996) refers to this as the 'spin dry' part of the laundry cycle: repatriating the money in the form of clean, often taxable, income. This is achieved by means of real estate transactions, front companies and sham loans, foreign bank complicity and false import and export transactions.

Savona and De Feo provide a number of examples of currency exchanges of money laundering by means of money transmitters, black money markets and the 'cleansing' of cash from heroin sales by purchasing goods, changing cash through gambling and other means. They note a trend towards increasing complexity in the money trail and towards internationalisation, possibly as a conscious strategy to minimise law enforcement risks. The number and complexity of criminal transactions involving BCCI, for example, raised money laundering to an almost 'industrial' scale (Savona and De Feo 1997: 55).

Robinson also sets out a number of examples of money laundering, many of which include the use of parallel or 'underground' banking. These methods, known variously as *fei ch'ien* (literally, 'flying money'), chop, *hundi* or *hawala*, involve a system of clandestine 'bankers' around the world. Although people may use these arrangements legitimately, many underground bankers are willing and able to cash promissory notes for criminal groups. Robinson cites one case in the UK where an underground banker laundered over £120 million (1996: 15).

Robinson also points out that the boundaries of dirty business in relation to money laundering are far from clear. Not only criminals are involved in these processes. Apparently, legitimate corporations also carry out money laundering. And as the Iran-Contra affair indicated, agencies of the state have not always been innocent in respect of money laundering activity. According to Levi:

> When the CIA move money via BCCI, the Americans call it facilitating the national interest; when the Mafia do the same thing, we call it money laundering...
>
> (1997: 259)

In this respect, money laundering is to some extent tolerated by the liberal democracies, who find it convenient to have channels to transmit illegal money. Bringing 'illegal' cash into circulation may also serve to boost an economy.

Money laundering is no longer a 'do-it-yourself' project. Savona and De Feo (1997) note the increased professionalisation of money laundering by:

(a) progressive separation between criminal activities and money laundering activities;

(b) more professional launderers such as accountants, lawyers, private bankers;

(c) provision of money laundering services to a wide range of criminals and to more than one criminal organisation.

They provide a number of examples to support this contention, including the provision by professionals of money laundering services to both the Colombian drugs cartels and to organised crime groups in the USA. In this case, the launderers were not direct cartel employees or gang members but independent financial specialists (Savona and De Feo 1997: 13–15).

The international community has become increasingly aware of the threat that money laundering poses. According to Savona (1997: 259), states do not find the downside effects of economic interdependence and globalisation only in such things as organised crime and money laundering. They span issues in public welfare more generally. The fact of the involvement of states and of legitimate corporations in 'dirty business' points to a wider need for regulation of the financial world. The contemporary development of new measures to combat money laundering includes systems for ensuring the disclosure of financial transactions and electronic and other forms of surveillance. Chapter 9 will examine in more detail the anti money-laundering strategies that followed the 1994 Naples conference, within the wider context of measures to tackle organised crime.

Chapter 4

The magic roundabout:
traffic in the global village

Organised crime is an industry that panders to human dissatisfaction. Much of its illicit output is about satisfying the needs of people who want to be somewhere else, either mentally or physically. It serves a mental need by providing the means to achieve altered states of consciousness for the end-user of products of the illicit drugs industry. It serves a physical need in providing an illicit means through which people can move to some place other than their current domicile. Both are forms of enterprise crime. In each case, organised crime provides desired goods or services that are beyond the legal limit permitted by a state: in the case of drugs, goods that are beyond the legal limit for the purposes of therapy or recreation; in the case of people smuggling, services that are beyond the limit of official permission to enter or to remain in a country. In cases such as enslavement for labour or trafficking in women for the sex industry by means of force or coercion, it provides services that are required by third parties but which, nevertheless, remain forms of enterprise crime.

This chapter examines the role of organised crime in relation to drug trafficking and people smuggling. The chapter consists of four parts. The first part discusses the history and scope of the illicit drug trade and the efforts of Britain and the USA to contain and control drug misuse. It explores the extent of the trade with reference to assessments by the UN and other drug control bodies. The second part examines the activities of criminal organisations engaged in the illicit drug trade. This includes the powerful cartels that control illicit drug production in some parts of the world and other organisations that are further down the supply chain. It also reviews the involvement of terrorist groups in drug trafficking. The third part of the chapter discusses models of trafficking. It compares the different types of drug traffickers and relates the means for their control to their particular vulnerabilities. Business models such as supply-chain theory can provide a useful means of modelling the different aspects of such trafficking. The final part of the chapter discusses the nature and rationale of people smuggling, including the distinction between the smuggling of immigrants and trafficking in people for the sex trade. It examines the groups involved in this traffic and discusses specific types of activity that are typical of their work.

The illicit drug industry: corner shop or supermarket?

This chapter explores drug trafficking as a key activity of organised crime, providing an overview of a subject that has tended to dominate the activities of many criminal groups since the 1960s. Although the chapter deals with it as a discrete entity, most observers rightly do not regard it as separate from other aspects of international organised crime. As later chapters show, in relation to the activities of organised crime groups in various parts of the world, it is an important part of a range of highly lucrative activities that such groups have adopted as a means to produce profit. Although it is perhaps the most notable contemporary example of enterprise crime, it is worth remembering that drug trafficking is a two-way street. Its products, although beyond the legal limit, are highly sought after by large sections of the public, particularly in the West. Critics may rightly condemn organised drug producers and traffickers for satisfying this demand, but it is necessary to remember that the market is as much 'made' by drug users to satisfy their needs and desires as by the profit motives that drive the traffickers. It is also 'made' by the limits that the state prescribes for a wide variety of licit and illicit substances. Although this chapter focuses primarily on the supply end, a comprehensive analysis of the trade would include aspects of both supply and demand and the role of states and the international community in setting boundaries to the legality of drug use.

Drug misuse and drug trafficking in their current forms are of great sociological and psychological interest. However, it is necessary to recognise the historical development of the problem, including the part played by organised crime and by states themselves in its growth. The growth of the international drug trade has been progressive, with its origins in international trade between Europe, the USA, the

Far East and South America. Rising consumer demand for drugs and the opportunities this has provided to organised crime groups have created a market on a massive scale. International crime groups have facilitated the refinement and smuggling of larger quantities of drugs to feed the retail market. The rapid growth of small drug-dealing groups or individual dealers at the local and national level has enabled effective distribution to consumers.

The drug control policies that developed nations have adopted have also affected the growth of the illicit drugs industry. In particular, the different control policies adopted by Britain and the USA are significant in this respect. During the nineteenth century, British companies made substantial profits out of the drug trade, especially with China. The use of opiates was widespread and largely uncontrolled in both Britain and the USA, especially among the poor (Berridge 1984; Woodiwiss 2001: 91–4). A growing belief in the danger and damage caused by drug misuse, however, led to measures to control the problem. The British government took an active role in the development of the international control system for the misuse of drugs that emanated from the Shanghai Conference of 1909 and the Hague Convention of 1912. Parliament enacted domestic legislation to restrict both import and use.

In the USA, Congress passed the Harrison Narcotics Act in 1914, after accepting the principles of the Shanghai Conference and the Hague Convention. The Federal government progressively introduced drug misuse controls thereafter. The main thrust of the Federal drug campaign was to close the addiction clinics that doctors and public health authorities had opened. In 1923, the US Supreme Court ruled that it was an offence for any person, including doctors, to administer narcotic substances, so forcing addicts to turn to the illegal drug market for supplies. Rigorous enforcement by the US Narcotics Bureau shaped the penal nature of US drug misuse policy for the next forty years. This encouraged, rather than reduced, the opportunity for organised crime to create new enterprises based upon drug trafficking.

Britain adopted a very different approach to the problem of drug misuse. In 1926, the Rolleston Committee recognised that drug addiction was a disease that the medical profession should treat, like any other. This approach, however, placed very little emphasis upon any criminal activity that might be associated with the misuse of drugs. Until the 1960s, the British government continued to emphasise the importance of the medical approach to the problem. In 1958, the Brain Committee recommended that the government should continue to pursue its existing policies on treatment and rehabilitation of drug users (Wright *et al.* 1993: 12–13).

During the late 1950s and early 1960s, however, drug misuse spread rapidly in Europe and the USA. In Britain, there were large increases in the consumption of cannabis, amphetamines and heroin, alongside new synthetic drugs such as LSD. Although the government retained some aspects of the previous medical approach, in 1971 Parliament enacted legislation that recognised the scale of the problem. In 1985, in the face of rising drug misuse and trafficking, the UK government published the first edition of its strategy *Tackling Drug Misuse* (Home Office 1985). This shifted the emphasis from the pre-1965 focus on treatment to a battery of measures, including enhanced enforcement and reducing supplies from abroad. Successive governments have amended this strategy since 1985, but they have continued to emphasise action at both the demand and supply ends. At the demand end, measures to deal with education, treatment and rehabilitation were put into place. At the supply end, enforcement continued against importers and dealers (Wright *et al.* 1993: 21).

In 1986, the Association of Chief Police Officers (ACPO) initiated measures to consolidate the enforcement response to drug trafficking at all levels. It had become evident that organised criminal gangs were switching their operations from robbery and other crime to drug trafficking. New police units (Regional Crime Squad Drugs Wings) came into being in 1987, with a special remit to work in conjunction with HM Customs and Excise to deal with 'high level' traffickers. Combating lesser dealers within their jurisdictions was the task of individual police forces. Local (divisional) police would tackle 'street level' dealers and users (Association of Chief Police Officers 1986: The Broome Report).

The Broome Report assumed that drug trafficking operated very much like a 'pyramid' of distribution, with illicit products passing from higher-level dealers to the lower and on to the users. Research carried out in the wake of implementation of the report showed that this was not always the case. The actual network of distribution was more complex than the report had assumed (Wright and Waymont 1989; Wright *et al.* 1993; Dorn and South 1990; Dorn *et al.* 1992).

In effect, the assumption that trafficking was pyramidal simply followed the shape of the 'tiered' control structures that were already in place to deal with it. This did not give recognition to the complexity of drug trafficking, which often had quite different characteristics. More recently, however, developments in policing and crime intelligence in the UK have recognised the complexity of the crime groups engaged in this trade. Law enforcement agencies have adapted their responses to meet the realities of the environment in which they work. However, despite the clarification of roles which came about from the formation of a National Crime Squad (NCS) in the UK and the adoption of a National Intelligence Model (NIM), the problem of fitting the investigative strategy to the target environment remains.

In terms of overall strategies for tackling drug misuse, at the demand end recent iterations of the UK government's strategy have recognised the need for harm reduction among addicts. Partnership between agencies has been encouraged to promote treatment, rehabilitation and education. Referral schemes have been set up to deal with users who come into police custody for other offences. Treatment and rehabilitation processes, by means of assessment, drug testing, personal action plans and agency support, are in operation through local Drugs Action Teams and the Probation Service.

Continued controversy about the recreational use of so-called 'soft' drugs has raised arguments for a degree of decriminalisation. In 2002, the UK government introduced measures to reduce the classification of cannabis to a lower level (Class C). This follows the model in parts of the Netherlands, which condones the consumption of cannabis in private or in designated premises. In the UK however, the strategy of downgrading cannabis appears only to have raised the level of trafficking and the level of use. The government has also considered measures to enable more addicts to receive heroin under the supervision of doctors. Although this would mark to some extent a return to pre-1965 measures, it is difficult to assess whether this approach would be effective in the current climate. Overall, however, the government intends these measures to help reduce demand, thereby loosening the grip of organised crime on the trade and reducing acquisitive crime by addicts to pay for their habit. Police and HM Customs and Excise continue to pursue traffickers in an attempt to control the supply end. Despite these attempts to rationalise the response to drug supply and demand, controversy remains. For example, the appointment in 1998 of Keith Hellawell (the former Chief Constable of West Yorkshire) as the national 'Drugs Czar' did not satisfy those who thought that such a move would 'solve' the problem. Eventually, confusion and disagreements over policy made Hellawell's position untenable and he resigned in June 2001 (Hellawell 2002).

In the USA, both the problem and the measures that the US authorities have adopted for its control have developed differently.

Following the Harrison Act of 1914, opiates rapidly became difficult to obtain. Many middle-class drug users switched to cannabis (marijuana). However, throughout the 1940s and 1950s, the use of cannabis and cocaine slowly gained popularity. The first US president to declare a 'war on drugs' was Richard Nixon in 1971. At that time, there were around 1.5 million heroin addicts in the USA. During the 1980s cocaine gained popularity and was easy to transform into crack-cocaine, a smokable form of the drug. By 1992, US Bureau of Justice statistics estimated that there were 6.4 million cocaine users in the USA (Lyman and Potter 1997: 186).

The 'war on drugs' model has long been the defining characteristic of US drug policy. This is because many American cities are the target of organised crime groups from Colombia, the Far East and elsewhere. In 1973, the US Federal government created the Drugs Enforcement Administration (DEA), with responsibility for enforcing drug laws. This agency also collaborates with other law enforcement and intelligence agencies across the world. Following Nixon's earlier declaration, President Reagan declared his own war on drugs in 1982. He gave the US military the authority to aid anti-drugs efforts during the 1980s. They undertook many operations, including some in South America. However, according to Siegel:

> Enormous sums of money were poured into interdicting illegal drugs entering the country. But billions of dollars and thousands of drug seizures later, the government was forced to concede that 'Despite interdiction's successful disruptions of trafficking patterns, the supply in illegal drugs entering the United States continued to grow'.
>
> (1991: 102)

When President George Bush entered office in 1989, US drug control strategy had already begun to shift from supply reduction to demand reduction. To consolidate this, he appointed a 'Drugs Czar' to oversee demand reduction efforts (Drucker 1991: 102). Zero tolerance of drugs, including the 'just say no' campaign which was promoted by Nancy Reagan, President Reagan's wife, had already been a feature of anti-drugs campaigns in the USA during the 1980s. The strategy of blaming the user continued throughout the Bush administration (Siegel 1991: 102–3; Lyman and Potter 1997: 186).

In effect, however, at the demand end, the 'war on drugs' model has often meant harm maximisation rather than harm reduction. Siegel (1991) provides a number of examples, including the case where a court found a pregnant mother guilty of supplying cocaine to her newly born child through the umbilical cord at the moment of the child's birth. Although there have been positive campaigns in the USA, the public representation of the drug problem has continued to be that of prohibition rather than of public health (Drucker 1991: 81).

Despite the considerable efforts of national governments and international bodies such as the UN and the EU, the problem of drug trafficking continues on a massive scale across the world. According to the UN 2004 *World Drug Report*, around 3 per cent (185 million people) of the world's population had abused drugs within the previous 12 months. Nevertheless, there are some grounds for optimism. Although there has been an epidemic of drug abuse over the last half-century, its diffusion into the general population has been contained and its spread may be losing momentum (United Nations 2004: 7–9). The UN report, however, concedes that drug abuse continues to be a global problem. It affects the lives of many people in terms of health, crime and exploitation by criminal organisations, in both developed and developing countries. The problem continues on a large scale, but the international community has made significant progress in relation to the two main problem drugs, cocaine and heroin. These are responsible for most drug-related deaths and treatment demands. They are also responsible for much of the drug-related violence, especially that which is associated with the involvement of organised crime.

The 2004 *World Drug Report* provides detailed estimates of cultivation, production and seizures. According to the report, there was a reduction of coca cultivation between 1999 and 2003 of around 30 per cent, reversing the massive upward trend of the 1980s. The report estimated that global illicit cocaine manufacture was down from around 800 tonnes in 2002 to 655 tonnes in 2003, with Colombia, Bolivia and Peru as centres of the majority of production.

There was also a reduction in opium cultivation, which was 40 per cent less than in the 1990s, reversing the previous upward trend. However, the distribution of cultivation has changed over the past decade, with a decline in the low opium yield areas of South-East Asia and an increase in the high opium yield areas of Afghanistan. In 2003, more than 90 per cent of the illicit cultivation of the opium poppy took place in Afghanistan, Myanmar and Laos. However, an increase in cultivation in Afghanistan in the wake of the war ousting the Taliban and a higher yield in South-East Asia resulted in an increase of 5 per cent in global illicit opium production between the years 2002 and 2003. In 2003, the 3,600 tonnes of opium produced in Afghanistan (the second highest opium production in Afghanistan's history), provided more than three-quarters of the world's illicit opium supply. The Russian Federation appears to be the world's largest heroin market (United Nations 2004: 14–15).

The production and use of cannabis is less concentrated than that of the opiates, with over 142 countries reporting seizures over the period from 1992 to 2002. Global estimates suggest that cannabis production has been rising and may have reached some 32,000 tonnes in 2002. In contrast to the opiates, which are either stable or declining, the consumption of cannabis appears to be spreading at an accelerated pace. It has again reached the levels experienced in the 1980s. Cannabis products (herb and resin) remain the most trafficked drugs worldwide. The most cited source countries in Europe were Albania and the Netherlands (United Nations 2004: 19). The levels of amphetamine type stimulants also remain high, with around 38 million users, among them 8 million users of ecstasy (United Nations 2004: 20–21).

That there has been a degree of containment of the illicit drug market is due to a number of factors. The 1990s saw the dismantling of some of the world's main drug cartels involved in cocaine and heroin trafficking, notably in South America and Asia. Growth in both heroin and cocaine trafficking fell during the 1990s, compared with the 1980s. The most significant increase worldwide in the 1990s was in the consumption of amphetamines, peaking around 1996/7, although the recent increases in cannabis production and misuse have emulated these earlier patterns. There have also been reductions in opiate misuse in many developed countries. There is increasing evidence that both prevention and treatment play a significant role in reducing drug demand (United Nations 2004: 10–11). However, although there are some grounds for optimism, this does not mean that international organised crime groups are no longer interested in drug trafficking.

Indeed, some analysts are sceptical about the optimistic picture that the UN report describes. For example, in its annual report for the year 2000, the Observatoire Géopolitique des Drougues (OGD) cites counter evidence suggesting that drug trafficking in many regions continues unabated (Observatoire Géopolitique des Drougues 2000). Although there are continuing difficulties in estimating the extent of the problem, there is little doubt (even allowing for the degree of optimism expressed in recent UN *World Drug Reports*) that drug trafficking continues at a comparatively high level. Much of this appears to be a consequence of the ability of organised crime to adapt to new challenges from law enforcement agencies and from international drug control policies. Chapter 9 will examine further the measures that the international community has adopted for controlling drug trafficking.

Cartels, caterers and narco-terrorists

So far, in setting out the extent of the problem, this chapter has concentrated on the growth and scope of drug cultivation and production. This part of the chapter, however, begins to focus on trafficking in more detail, especially on the supply end of the market. In particular, it examines the activities of those organised crime groups that have adopted drug production and trafficking as a major part of their business enterprise. Examining the trade in terms of different drug types as set out below is somewhat arbitrary. Owing to the complex and dynamic nature of organised crime, such classifications are little more than a convenient way of organising the explanatory text.

The main areas of production of heroin have been under pressure in recent years from war and from enforcement efforts. However, the areas of the so-called 'Golden Crescent' of the mountain valleys of Iran, Afghanistan and Pakistan and the 'Golden Triangle' of the border area of Thailand, Mynamar (formerly Burma) and Laos continue to provide the greatest sources of production. Other sources, including Turkey, have also been contributors. OGD continues to regard them as such, despite 'official' estimates to the contrary by the UN (Observatoire Géopolitique des Drougues 2000: 8).

Drug production in the Golden Crescent has continued unabated, reaching a peak during the Soviet campaign in Afghanistan. For example, in 1986 the Dutch authorities in Rotterdam searched a Soviet cargo ship and found 220 kg of pure heroin aboard. The origin of the heroin was Kabul. The traffickers transported it by truck overland from Afghanistan across the Soviet Union, where they placed it on a ship bound for the West. This was the first time that western security services had hard proof that the Soviet occupation forces in Afghanistan were directly involved in the drug trade (Steinberg 1995).

According to Steinberg (1995), while some of the opium-producing areas were under the control of the Soviet Army during their occupation, the majority were under the control of the *mujahideen*.

During the mid-point of the Afghan/Russian war, laboratories in the Northwest Frontier Province were producing over 1,000 tonnes of heroin per year. After the Soviet Army left Afghanistan, opium warfare broke out among the *mujahideen*. A number of factional disputes and assassinations took place in Afghanistan itself and in Pakistan. After the defeat of the Taliban by coalition forces in 2001/2, Afghan warlords appear again to be seeking control of the lucrative drug trade. As mentioned above, the 2004 crop was at record levels. It produced a glut of low-priced heroin for western and Russian markets.

The extent of seizures in Iran throughout the 1990s and into the new millennium provides evidence of the continued level of production of opium and refined heroin emanating from the Golden Crescent. Although Iran has its own serious heroin problem, much of the material is bound for the West, especially Europe. The West rarely gives credit to Iran for seizures of opiates amounting to 80 per cent of the total seizures across the world. Traffickers have killed many Iranian enforcement officials who have attempted to stop this traffic (Muir 1999).

Drug production in the Golden Triangle is also extensive, although production may have declined in recent years compared with Afghanistan. Chouvy (1999, 2002) has provided a useful analysis describing the drug sources and routes in South-East Asia. Much of the refined heroin is smuggled through the jungles of Thailand and in some cases through Hong Kong or via India. According to Chouvy (1999: 5) and to Lyman and Potter (1997: 281; 2004: 237), the Burmese trafficker and revolutionary Kuhn Sa transports large quantities of opium to Laotian refineries by donkey caravans.

Although the heroin produced in this region reaches most of South-East Asia, India, Australia and the USA, only a comparatively small amount of South-East Asian heroin ('China White') reaches Europe. However, Cambodia extensively exports cannabis to western markets. Almost as important as heroin to the region is the production in Mynamar of methamphetamine known as *Yaa Baa* ('mad pills'). These are mainly destined for the consumer markets of Thailand and Laos (Chouvy 2002).

As already described, Asian organised crime in the West has traded extensively in drugs emanating mainly from the Golden Triangle. The American Tongs maintain connections with others in Hong Kong, who obtain their heroin from there or Bangkok. The Triads smuggle opium out of the Golden Triangle, refine it and sell it on to wholesale buyers in North America and Europe. During the

1980s, large quantities of heroin were smuggled through Sicily by an alliance between Chinese criminal groups and the Sicilian Mafia. According to Lyman and Potter (1997: 280) one Sicilian operation had scheduled the delivery of 1.5 tonnes of heroin.

Heroin has also provided a lucrative source of income for Colombian and Mexican organised crime groups. Lyman and Potter (1997: 200–4; 2004: 239–243) maintain that entry into the heroin market by the Colombian cartels is strategic; to diversify their efforts from cocaine and in an attempt to capitalise on a growing market. Mexico plays an important role in the production of 'Mexican brown' heroin, cannabis and methamphetamine, most of which is smuggled into the USA by the Mexican drug cartels. This is also the main route for the importation of Colombian cocaine into the USA.

In summary, the trade in heroin continues to be extensive, despite the degree of optimism expressed in the 2004 *World Drugs Report* (United Nations 2004). Organised crime groups continue to dominate the trade. Although they sometimes collaborate, there are continual struggles between them. It is not the case that one cartel or faction has a monopoly of the world heroin trade.

The growing of narcotic coca leaves in Bolivia, Peru and Colombia has a long history. Since the 1970s, Colombia has emerged as the foremost cocaine producing country in the world. Numerous laboratories process the coca leaves from Colombia itself and from the other South American growers into cocaine base and thence into cocaine hydrochloride. A limited number of production and trafficking organisations control these laboratories. The drug industry in Colombia is very substantial. Cocaine is the main product, but Colombia also produces cannabis and heroin on a large scale. The DEA estimates that the drug business has an annual value of $1.5 billion to the Colombian economy.

The Colombian drug industry has been characterised by the operation of 'cartels', which control production and distribution. In 1992, the US government credited the Colombian cartels with supplying up to 90 per cent of the world's total cocaine consumption (US Bureau of Justice 1992). The DEA still regards Colombia as responsible for most of the world's cocaine-base production and wholesale cocaine-hydrochloride distribution. The USA is Colombia's most important target market, although there is increasing trade through European and Russian crime groups.

It is possible to trace the origin of the cartels from the era of the 1970s, when Pablo Escobar-Gaviria and the Ochoa brothers developed a cocaine trafficking alliance. This became known as the 'Medellin cartel' because of its location. From his drug trafficking activity, Escobar became a very rich man, with a personal fortune estimated at $2 billion. The Medellin cartel was involved in many political assassinations and in the murder of rivals and informers. Between 1983 and 1993, the authorities credited it with the assassination of the Colombian attorney-general, a justice minister, three presidential candidates, more than 200 judges, thirty kidnapping victims, many journalists and an estimated 1,000 police officers. In 1986, the US authorities indicted Escobar for importing 60 tonnes of cocaine. Thereafter, he was a fugitive. The Ochoa brothers surrendered to the Colombian government in 1991. In 1993, law enforcement officers shot Escobar dead while trying to apprehend him. After this, the Medellin cartel broke up and lost its hold on the cocaine market (Lyman and Potter 1997: 139–42).

The death of Escobar and the demise of the Medellin cartel did not mean the end of the cocaine trade. During the time Escobar was a fugitive from the police, the rival Cali cartel expanded its operations considerably. By the mid-1990s the Cali cartel was reputed to be the source of most of the cocaine consumed in the USA. All of the cartels made extensive use of aircraft, high-tech computer equipment and communications to give them a competitive edge over their rivals and to evade the enforcement authorities. But the capture in 1995 of Gilberto and Miguel Rodriguez Orejuela and the deaths and capture of their close associates brought the domination of the trade by the large cartels to an end.

However, other groups have expanded their operations to fill the gap left by the demise of the Medellin and Cali cartels. According to threat assessments carried out by the DEA, the Colombian cocaine industry is now more decentralised and fragmented than hitherto. Action by the Colombian national police with US assistance has accelerated the fragmentation. Consequently, no one group of traffickers dominates all aspects of the trade. Groups from Peru are beginning to produce cocaine hydrochloride, again emphasising the degree of decentralisation. According to the DEA, however, despite this fragmentation, Colombian drug trafficking organisations will remain the dominant players in the international cocaine trade. They are increasingly self-sufficient in cocaine-base production and dominate Caribbean smuggling routes and wholesale markets in the USA and Europe (US Drug Enforcement Administration 2001). Whether the premature release of the Orejuela brothers, which took place in November 2002, will reverse this fragmentation is a matter for conjecture.

Trafficking from the major centres of production in the Golden Crescent, Golden Triangle and Colombia is extremely important. However, independent international organised crime groups also carry out a considerable amount of drug trafficking, either as a speciality or as part of a wider portfolio of criminal activities. Chapter 5 will discuss the involvement of the Sicilian Mafia with Chinese organised crime and with the Colombian cartels in this respect. It will also discuss the activities of Asian organised crime and the alliances that the major producers and other organised crime groups sometimes arrange between themselves.

Here, it is worth distinguishing between drug trafficking *as* international organised crime and the involvement *of* international organised crime in drug trafficking. In the former, using the example of the cartels, the illegal drug business is run using many of the same methods as legal businesses. Paradoxically, those who produce drugs need to conduct their business in a predictable way. A system to transport the drugs is required along with the ability to extend credit to potential buyers. As is the case with legitimate business, associates such as accountants, lawyers and bankers are required to facilitate the drug-trafficking enterprise. The involvement of other organised crime groups in drug trafficking is a 'downstream' activity, a kind of credit-based or 'cash and carry' supermarketing. Such groups facilitate distribution to other wholesalers and retailers (Lyman and Potter 1997: 194) who provide (depending on particular cases) distribution at local street or 'corner shop' levels.

Shelley (1995) provides an interesting example of the complexity and international nature of organised crime in relation to drug trafficking. In the case to which she refers, the network that was unmasked involved criminals from Pakistan, Africa, Israel, Eastern Europe and Latin America. The drugs (cannabis – *hashish*), originated in Pakistan and were delivered to the port of Mombasa (Kenya). Here they were added to a cargo of tea and reshipped to Haifa (Israel) via Durban (South Africa). At Haifa, the gang put the cargo onto a ship of a company with departures for Constanza (Romania) every fifteen days. From there, an Israeli-Romanian company was to ship it to Italy, via Bratislava (Slovakia). The head of the network was a German citizen of Ugandan origin who worked for the Romanian company. Law enforcement officials only discovered this complex network because they arrested the perpetrators in Constanza (Shelley 1995: 472–3).

Shelley also gives an example of the seizure of 517 kg of cocaine at a Polish port. This seizure linked Poles with Ecuadorians who were members of the Cali cartel of Colombia and members of Italian organised crime. This drug network illustrates the complexity of the supply chain. It also illustrates collaboration between three important international organised crime groups: Colombian, Italian and the recently emerged Eastern and Central European (Shelley 1995: 473). Such cases are typical of those which law enforcement uncovers. There are many others; indeed, too many to list. However, these cases reinforce the point that international organised crime is dynamic and fragmented. It is an extensive distributed network system. Even in the times of the Colombian cartels and their association with the Mafia, it was not one totally controlled by super-syndicates.

In recent years, the growth of terrorist groups has posed a serious problem for all states, both in the developed and developing world. Terrorist groups have become increasingly involved in drug trafficking, often to secure the funds through which to pursue their political activities. Social disruption may also be an end in itself. The clandestine nature of drug trafficking, and more particularly of terrorism, makes the extent of the problem difficult to estimate. There are, however, a number of examples of such narco-terrorism. First, there is a considerable amount of terrorism involved in some forms of drug trafficking. As suggested above, this was certainly the case in relation to the Medellin cartel and Pablo Escobar. The campaign of violence they orchestrated went further than that of drug-related violence against rivals. It is possible to distinguish the terrorist violence of the Medellin cartel from simple drug-related violence in the sense that it was both premeditated and politically motivated (US Drug Enforcement Administration 2002).

The second category of narco-terrorism is that where terrorist groups turn to drug trafficking to support their political goals. Examples include the Revolutionary Armed Forces of Colombia (FARC), the Kurdistan Workers Party (PKK) and the Provisional IRA. The former, which is in armed conflict with Colombian government forces, controls large coca producing regions in Colombia. It manages cocaine processing, sells drugs for cash and negotiates arms deals with international drug-dealing organisations including Russian organised crime. The extent of the involvement of the PKK in drug trafficking remains controversial. However, the Turkish press has reported that the PKK produces 60 tonnes of heroin per year and receives an income of around $40 million per year from drug-trafficking proceeds (US Drug Enforcement Administration 2002). IRA involvement in drug trafficking in Northern Ireland has been evident since the 1980s (Boyce 1987; Bean 2002: 111).

The third category of narco-terrorism is that where the state itself is involved. Afghanistan is a relevant example; narco-terrorism there was not limited to terrorist organisations. As the above arguments show, Afghanistan was the major source of the world's heroin in the late 1990s. Consequently, illicit drugs became a major source of the state's income. According to the DEA, it was through this drug income that the Taliban was able to support and protect Osama Bin Laden and the al Qaeda network. In this case, drugs and terrorism share the common ground of geography, money and violence (US Drug Enforcement Administration 2002).

Typologies of traffickers and supply chain theory

Although it is possible to draw some general conclusions from the examples set out above, they do not provide a conceptual framework that helps us to understand how the drug trade operates. Without theoretical models on which to base our judgements, describing crime groups or merely listing cases, sources and routes will not enable us to understand how drug trafficking is structured and sustained. As shown in Chapter 1, however, there are dangers in over-rationalising these structures where organised crime is concerned. Picking the wrong model leads to choosing the wrong strategies to deal with the problem. Three contrasting approaches to understanding the structure of drug distribution include:

- the pyramidal model set out in the above discussion;
- a typology of traffickers that recognises their diversity; and
- the supply- or value-chain model, which recognises that drug trafficking is very much like any other business enterprise.

The assumption often made by law enforcement practitioners, that drug trafficking and distribution networks are pyramidal in structure, was included in the Broome Report, which recommended a restructuring of the enforcement response to drugs trafficking in England and Wales (Association of Chief Police Officers 1986). Subsequent research showed that this was not the case, and that law enforcement practitioners in the field did not operate as if it were (Wright and Waymont 1989; Wright et al. 1993).

According to Dorn et al. (1992), it is a mistake to see drug trafficking as a pyramid of this kind with large organisations such as the Mafia or the Colombian cartels controlling the market. They say:

There is no person, no *Mafia*, no cartel organising the market overall. Rather, a large number of small organisations operate fairly autonomously of each other in a manner that may be described as disorganised crime.

(Dorn *et al.* 1992, quoted in Bean 2002: 108)

This follows the thesis already discussed in Chapter 1 (see Reuter 1983). It is certainly the case that most drug-trafficking enterprises are dynamic and fluid, operating without the existence of a top-level executive group or a 'Mr Big'. Crime groups are 'organised' but are not organised bureaucracies of the kind that enforcement agencies sometimes postulate to support bids for resources and funding. Of course, this does not deny that there are important and influential figures in international organised crime in general and in drug trafficking in particular.

In contrast to the pyramidal model, which sets out a strict hierarchy of dealing, Dorn and South (1990) and Dorn *et al.* (1992) identified a variety of trafficker types operating within the British drug market. In their approach, different types of trafficker 'cater' for different sectors of the market. As 'caterers', they have different kinds of objectives, different modes of operation and different vulnerabilities from those that would be evident in a pyramidal structure. There are seven categories in their typology as follows:

1. **Trading charities** are enterprises involving an ideological commitment to drugs with profit as a secondary motive;

2. **Mutual societies** involve friendship networks of user dealers who support each other and sell or exchange drugs amongst themselves;

3. **Sideliners** are licit business enterprises that begin to trade in drugs as a sideline;

4. **Criminal diversifiers** are existing criminal enterprises that diversify into drugs;

5. **Opportunistic irregulars** are those who get involved in a variety of activities in the irregular economy, including drugs;

6. **Retail specialists** are those enterprises with a manager who employs others to distribute drugs to users;

7. **State sponsored traders** are those enterprises that operate as informers and that continue to trade.

(Dorn *et al.* 1992)

Although the empirical work that is the basis of this typology relied mainly on British research, the principle is of wider application. It illustrates the point that the pyramidal version of drug distribution is flawed. The reality of drug trafficking is more fluid and fragmented which 'official' accounts of the trade often postulate at the higher strategic levels. Interestingly, however, practitioners working in intelligence or operations at lower levels in law enforcement are very well aware of the complexities and tend to rely on empirical evidence of complex connections. As mentioned above, they do not rely on preconceived pyramidal models of drug distribution (Wright and Waymont 1989; Wright *et al.* 1993).

Models that recognise this complexity are more likely to be useful than those that oversimplify it. One way to gain an understanding of the illicit drug trade is to apply models of business competitiveness. Supply-chain theory is a useful example. Business analysts have long been aware that there is only limited value in regarding the process from production to delivery to the customer as a linear chain of events and agencies. The degree of complexity in manufacturing and distribution is such that more accuracy is required in the models that might properly explain the process. In 1985, Michael Porter described a model of the chain through which a business adds value at each stage of its enterprise. Figure 4.1 shows the relationship between each part of the chain.

Readers will note that the 'value' or supply chain encompasses both the support activities of the firm and the primary activities that produce its final products. Support activities include the infrastructure of the business, its financial and planning systems, human resources and technology. Its primary activities include its 'inbound logistics'. These consist of materials, money, time and information. The business operates on these to generate its products. Outbound logistics take the products to the customers, aided by the activities of marketing, sales and service. The effective working of both support and primary activities produces a profit margin for the business.

Figure 4.2 applies this model to the illicit drug industry as a whole. Only in the case of small enterprises, such as minor amphetamine manufacture and distribution, might all these activities be limited to a single business. It is more often the case that distributed organised

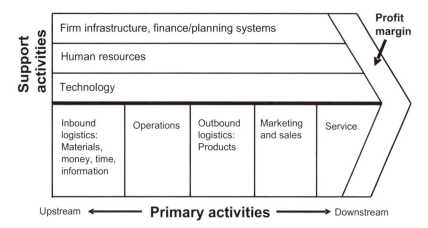

Figure 4.1 The business value chain
Source: Adapted from M.E. Porter (1985) *Competitive Advantage: Creating and Sustaining Superior Performance*, New York: Free Press

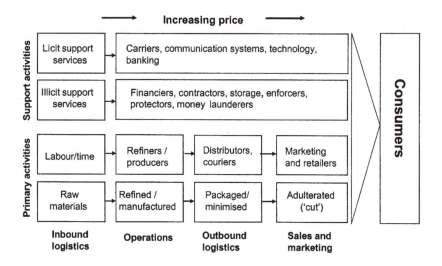

Figure 4.2 Illicit drug industry simplified supply chain
Source: A. Wright (1998) 'The Illicit Drug Industry', *Lectures on Drug Trafficking*, Bramshill: National Police College (unpublished)

crime networks provide the support and primary activities. These range from working partnerships to uneasy alliances between crime groups, which only survive because of their mutual interest in profit.

In the case of the illicit drug trade, one part of the network might provide the primary activities. Some members of the network provide the labour and time to harvest or obtain the raw materials. Producers and refiners make the basic product and convert it into a usable commodity. Outbound logistics include distributors and couriers ('mules') who may or may not be a permanent part of the crime group that is organising the trade. Minimisation of the size of the product is an important function to make it suitable for concealment. Each stage adds value to the product, thus enhancing profitability. Marketing and retailing are separate from the wholesale element. Wholesalers or retailers may adulterate the product with other substances at this stage, again to maximise profitability.

Interestingly, both primary and support activities include legal and illegal services. For example, licit support services such as banking, airfreight, communication systems and technology all provide (generally unwittingly) services without which most drug trafficking would be impossible. Illicit support services, such as finance, safe storage, violent enforcement and protection and money laundering, serve to complement those that are licit. Organised criminal groups may sometimes subcontract all or part of illicit services to people who are not strictly part of their 'core' group. The important issue, however, is that the drug trade rarely operates as a strict hierarchy. It does not do so either in the organisation of its business or in making and distributing its illicit products.

As is the case with the groups identified by Dorn *et al.* (1992), this is an example of a distributed organisation or of a network that is characterised by 'organising' groups and individuals. The various elements of the supply chain have different vulnerabilities to the actions of the police or customs authorities. In some cases, law enforcement policies can disrupt operations by means of structural measures. For example, formal limitations on bank transfers may serve to render money laundering or payments to contractors more difficult. Restrictions on the issue of aviation licences in Colombia have been a useful weapon against the cartels.

Although distributed networks of the kind described above do not have strict hierarchical control, they are sensitive to the opportunities that public policy itself provides in facilitating the growth of new markets. As Chapter 3 noted in its examination of the logic of Smith's enterprise model, there is a relationship between the means of control of an illicit market and the growth of the market itself. In cases where the state prohibits the use of a commodity that large numbers of a population demand, organised crime has little difficulty in making a market. It has little difficulty in setting up an illegal enterprise as a vehicle through which to maximise its profits. The public policy dilemma in the case of drug misuse, however, is that of liberalising the availability of drugs to deflate the market versus physiological danger and adverse social consequences. This will remain a dilemma for politicians, whether they choose to legalise drugs or not. The illicit drug industry, in this sense, provides a key example of the flexibility of enterprise crime. As for organised crime, if the drug market declines, it will merely seek another. Until this happens, drug trafficking will continue as a central activity of organised crime groups.

People trafficking: travel agents or new slave traders?

Alongside drug trafficking, the smuggling of economic and political migrants has become an important form of 'business' activity for organised criminal groups. In recent years, such groups have taken advantage of the opportunities presented by the need for illicit services in this new market. Many of the criminal groups that later chapters discuss have people smuggling as an important part of their operations. Some specialise in this field, including the movement of women and children for sexual and other purposes. Criminal groups from Eastern and Central Europe and the Balkans are particularly active in this field. The final part of the chapter examines this important area of activity in more detail: including defining the factors that encourage the provision of services in this illicit market. Chapter 9 discusses the measures that the international community has instituted to control this trade.

Migration has a long history. During their evolution, most societies have experienced it to some degree, through invasion, through commerce or through pressures brought about by economic and political displacement of other populations. Since the nineteenth century, however, the pace of migration has accelerated. Political upheaval, wars, economic opportunity and improvements in the means by which large numbers of people can move between countries and continents have fuelled the drive for migration. Both 'push' and pull' factors are evident. 'Push' factors include political persecution and repression. 'Pull' factors include the possibility of economic improvement. Freilich *et al.* (2002) identify six reasons for the international movement of people. These include:

1. Geographic differences in supply and demand for labour which encourage decision to move to make more money in the new 'host' country;

2. Benefits of additional markets and other benefits in the target country;

3. Demands by developed countries for cheap labour;

4. Feedback: perpetuation of migration by existing networks of immigrant families in the host countries and by organisations there which promote migration;

5. Environmental degradation, where the physical or agricultural environment in the home country no longer proves acceptable; and

6. Involuntary migration produced by civil war or oppression.
(Freilich *et al.* 2002: 4–5)

The effects of large-scale immigration are to be found in the both countries of origin and of destination. In the countries of origin, the reduction of human capital may have a long-term effect on their development. This is especially the case where skilled labour is lost, perhaps permanently. The effects on destination countries are highly variable. In some, immigration may produce considerable economic benefits by providing additional labour and a richer mix of cultures. In others, the diverse cultures of immigrant groups may alter the character of the host country to a considerable degree. Immigrant groups may also resist changes to their allegiances or avoid the assumption of a new national identity by maintaining separate communities for mutual support. Such communities often seek to retain the cultural identity associated with their former domicile, including language and the characteristics of their shared heritage. The study of these effects is beyond the scope of this book. It is right to say, however, that immigration has both positive and negative aspects.

Much of this migration is a popular movement not orchestrated by organised crime. For example, the attempt in December 2001 by over 500 refugees to storm the Channel Tunnel in Calais does not appear to have been the result of activity by organised criminal groups. Indeed, during the first half of 2001, Eurotunnel claimed that it had turned back over 18,500 refugees trying to reach Britain. Most of these came from the Sangatte refugee camp (CNN News report, 26 December 2001). It may also be the case, however, that some human smuggling is 'crime that is organised', rather than the product of organised crime. Koslowski (2001) rightly points out the dangers of assuming too much about the involvement of well-established groups. Whether or not migrant smugglers are gangsters who are moving into another line of business or business people moving into illegal activity to help people across borders varies by regions and by the particular migrant flows involved. In some cases, well-established crime groups may traffic both in migrants and in narcotics. In others, as in the case of some Chinese migrant smuggling, smuggling rings may be loose networks of relatives and friends who organise transportation and border crossings as a lucrative sideline (Koslowski 2001: 348).

Despite the self-generated character of much of the migration, there is evidence that some organised criminal groups have taken advantage of the potential illegality involved to generate a market in people smuggling and trafficking. The failure of the international community to recognise a legitimate market in the mobility of labour and effectively to regulate it has only served to promote illicit enterprise. According to Arlacchi:

> The lack of common regulation…and the inadequacy of state regulations has created a large and profitable illegal market which has become a new source of income for transnational organized crime. There are two overlapping variants:
>
> 1. The *smuggling* of migrants, that is the procurement of illegal entry into a state of which the migrant is not a national, with the objective of making a profit.
>
> 2. *Trafficking* in human beings, that is the recruitment, transportation or receipt of persons through deception or coercion for the purpose of prostitution, other forms of sexual exploitation or forced labour.
>
> (2002: 17)

The difference between smuggling and trafficking is an important, but often overlooked, distinction. Sheptycki points out the extent to which it is sometimes blurred:

The 'human smuggler' may cheat migrants of their money and merely dump them ashore, or may continue to extort money subsequent to successful passage, thus blurring the boundary with 'human trafficking'. Human trafficking is sometimes no more than facilitating travel arrangements and providing travel documents; the sort of job a travel agent might do.

(2003a: 144n1)

Graycar (2002: 30–2) describes the methods through which criminal groups carry out the smuggling of immigrants and trafficking in individuals. Human rights abuses are frequent, especially where migrants are unable to provide the money that they are committed to pay the gang. Drawing on unpublished work by Scholenhardt (1999), Graycar suggests that the spectrum of traffickers includes:

Amateur traffickers: who provide occasional, sometimes single services for crossing a border or locating an employer in a host country;

Small groups of organised criminals: who specialise in leading migrants from one country to another using recognised routes; and

International trafficking networks: who can respond wholesale to the needs of immigrants, including the provision of stolen or altered documents and provision of accommodation and employment contacts. The routes such groups use are often well-tested by other transnational activities, such as drug trafficking.

(Graycar 2002: 31)

Graycar, who reported on people trafficking activity in Australia, found that groups involved in this illicit enterprise included Chinese Tongs and Triads, the Japanese Yakuza, Korean gangs and the Russian Mafia.

People smuggling in the USA and Europe involves these groups, although it may also involve indigenous gangs. It is also important to recognise that people smuggling and trafficking are not entirely separate from drug trafficking and other illegal enterprise. Although a degree of specialisation may be evident in some cases, people smuggling and trafficking are part of a range of activities that characterise organised enterprise crime more generally. Many of the groups involved in smuggling and trafficking activity have often diversified their criminal operations, combining smuggling with other organised crime, illegal commodities and services.

As is the case with the drug-trafficking supply chain, people smuggling and trafficking involve a range of people, each of whom may have particular vulnerabilities to investigation. According to Graycar, these include:

- *Arranger/investors*: who direct and finance the operations;
- *Recruiters*: who arrange the customers;
- *Transporters*: who assist the movement of immigrants at departure and destination;
- *Corrupt public officials*: including law enforcement officers, who obtain travel documents or overlook illegal transit;
- *Informers*: who provide information on border controls and other factors;
- *Guides/crew-members*: who move immigrants between transit points;
- *Supporting personnel and specialists*: who provide accommodation/assistance;
- *Debt collectors*: who collect trafficking fees in the destination country;
- *Money movers*: who launder the proceeds of transactions.

(2002: 34)

The dangers that some immigrants run in trusting their lives to criminal gangs in trying to get into Europe is evident. In 2000, 360 people died attempting to cross the sea from Morocco to Spain. Chinese so-called 'snakehead' gangs have provided facilities for the smuggling of immigrants to the USA and into Europe from Hong Kong, mainland China and other parts of South-East Asia (Chin 1999). Police ascribed the tragic deaths of fifty-eight Chinese immigrants who police and immigration officers found asphyxiated in a truck at Dover Eastern Docks in June 2000 to snakehead organisation of the chain of transportation. Each of the immigrants had apparently paid tens of thousands of dollars to the snakeheads for the chance of a new life in the West. Only two survived the trip from the Netherlands. The English courts sentenced Lorry driver Perry Wacker and interpreter Ying Guo to fourteen and six year's imprisonment, respectively. The Dutch authorities also arrested several people in Holland. Two defendants, Goursel Ozcan (of Turkish nationality) and Haci Demir, a Dutch resident of Turkish origin, each received from the Dutch court nine-year sentences and a substantial fine for their involvement. The authorities believed that the sixty immigrants left China early in June 2000 and travelled via Yugoslavia, Hungary, Austria, France and Holland before starting the fatal leg of their journey to the UK (CNN News report, 11 May 2001). The fact that the chain of transportation involved a number of nationalities and transit countries points to the complexity of the relationships that are often involved in human smuggling.

Immigration into the USA has also been a long-term phenomenon. Although criminal gangs sometimes facilitate it, there is also a considerable amount of self-generated popular immigration by economic migrants, especially across the Mexican border. The military and law enforcement authorities have heavily resisted such immigration. On the California-Mexico border, Operation Gatekeeper has provided 2,200 armed paramilitary border guards to deal with extensive immigration attempts into the USA. This, together with other operations such as Safeguard in Tucson and Hold the Line in El Paso, have combined elements of the US Army, Marine and Air Force personnel, National Guard and local sheriffs' departments in a concerted effort to stem the tide. The dangers are evident. An estimated 1,600 accidental migrant border crossing deaths took place on the US-Mexico border between 1993 and 1997. The authorities killed over 500 people from 1994 to 2000 in the California-Mexico border area alone. The activities of the authorities mean that migrants attempt to cross in ever more dangerous areas. The involvement of organised crime does not explain the extent of military and paramilitary operations. Many commentators have been sceptical about the motives behind such operations. The high degree of 'mission creep' (in the sense that the original objectives may have been greatly overstepped) may also be due to anti-drug-trafficking activity (Dunn 2001; Nevins 2001). The reasons are primarily political and economic. According to Huspek:

> Gatekeeper has used immigrant resistance practices of its own making to promote a build-up of its legal and policing apparatuses and to facilitate the regulation and control of documented and undocumented labour...
>
> (2001: 63)

Of all the smuggling activities where organised crime is involved, people smuggling appears to be the one where there is a degree of sympathy with the motivation of migrants. On the other hand, there is also resistance by some states who are concerned to protect their economic power and territorial integrity.

The other side of Arlacci's distinction, people trafficking rather than people smuggling, often involves the trafficking of women and children for sexual purposes. Most commentators have rightly dismissed the extent to which some women may initially be willing parties to this trafficking as a substantial misconception of the problem. The trafficking in women for sexual purposes is often overtly coercive and, in any event, is always exploitative. Often, women are trafficked into conditions of sexual slavery, although similar exploitation for domestic work is also common. Kelly and Regan (2000) have carried out extensive research into this phenomenon in the UK. International estimates suggest that 500,000 women were trafficked into the EU in 1995. The early discussion of trafficking in women centred on abuses in South-East Asia, but now virtually every continent has sending and/or destination countries. According to police sources, the first contemporary signs of trafficking into the UK were evident in Triad-controlled brothels. Information concerning women from South America, Thailand and most recently, from Central and Eastern Europe has followed this (Kelly and Regan 2000: 16–17).

Because it remains largely a hidden problem, the actual UK figures are probably several times greater that the number that the researchers could document with certainty. Accurate estimates of the numbers of women involved are not available either nationally or internationally. However, Kelly and Regan believe that as many as 1,400 women could have been trafficked into the UK for sexual purposes during 1998, which was the year of their fieldwork (Kelly and Regan 2000: *v*). Gangs often use the UK as a transit country, especially where they move women via UK airports. Other women reportedly from Albania and Kosovo have come to the UK 'possibly in hundreds'. Criminal groups use mail order 'bride agencies' as a front for trafficking women for the purposes of prostitution. Recruitment includes outright abduction, deception by promises of employment, deception through half-truths suggesting a role in the entertainment industry, and coercion of women who know they are coming to the UK for employment as prostitutes but without awareness of the extent to which they will be intimidated, exploited and controlled (Kelly and Regan 2000: 24).

Current intelligence suggests links between international networks that traffic in drugs, money and human beings. The gangs provide false documentation to facilitate entry, together with an escort for the journey. On arrival, the trafficking gang transfers control of the woman to brothel owner or pimp, at which stage they take away the false documentation. The brothel owner now fully controls the woman. With debts mounting, her coercion into compliance is complete. Although Kelly and Regan concede that the problem of trafficking women for sexual purposes into the UK may not be of substantial proportions, it is yet another example of the lucrative market that the illicit sex industry provides as part of a broader picture of illicit trafficking enterprise (Kelly and Regan 2000: 24–6).

The academic literature on this form of trafficking is comparatively sparse; however, readers who wish to pursue further study of aspects of immigration crime should refer to Kyle and Koslowski (2001), Freilich *et al.* (2002) and Troubnikoff (2003), who provide a number of critical papers on the subject.

In summary, the forms of enterprise crime represented by trafficking activity of whatever variety provide ready-made vehicles for criminal groups of all kinds to make exceptional profits. Paradoxically, because the levels at which states set the limits of legality define these markets, public policy is never entirely free of complicity in determining the extent to which criminal groups and individuals can take advantage of this 'magic roundabout' of opportunity. As we shall see, in examining organised crime in the USA in Chapter 6, too many legal prohibitions may simply enable organised crime to develop its more virulent forms. Drug trafficking and people smuggling provide the most salient contemporary examples of this phenomenon. A parallel situation exists in relation to the other great example of enterprise crime – the provision of illicit types of security beyond the legal limit – and it is to the role of traditional organised crime groups in providing protection as one of their original activities that we shall now turn.

Chapter 5

Organised crime: its 'traditional' forms

Chapters 5 to 8 contain comparative case studies focusing on prominent examples of international organised crime. This chapter initiates the debate about different genres of organised crime and sets out a discussion of the activities of a number of so-called 'traditional' organised crime groups. These include the Sicilian Mafia, Chinese Triad and Tong groups and the Japanese Yakuza. The use of the term 'traditional' to prefix the contents of this chapter may appear contentious. However, the term conveys the fact that the criminal groups discussed here have developed over many years, often from secret societies or warrior groups whose earlier goals were as much social and political as criminal. Gathering them together in this chapter is a response to the degree of similarity, albeit limited, in their origins and in their continuity of tradition and structures. However, the chapter also compares them in relation to their preference for distinct kinds of enterprise activities, in particular to the provision of illicit forms of 'protection'. These groups are also traditional in the sense that they have their own mores, customs and rites of passage the origins of which are in the historical conditions surrounding their inception. Their traditions are also subject to a degree of continuity, although they are now at the service of criminal objectives.

When discussing this topic it is necessary to preface the debate by pointing to a tendency that is prevalent in the popular literature of organised crime: to use the term 'Mafia' to represent any kind of gangsterism. There is also a trend, albeit one that has a sociological rationale, for some analysts to use the term as a generic label for the activities of any group that meets market demands for extra-legal protection (Gambetta 1996: 252–4; Varese 2001; Hill 2003: 13). These authors apply the term variously to Sicilian organised crime groups, to Russian organised crime and to the Japanese Yakuza. However, despite the exemplary degree of detailed examination of the groups studied, the use of the term in relation to syndicated crime across such a wide spectrum does little to help to discriminate between the historical differences in types of protection, and the more recent drug dealing and assorted enterprise crime that these groups carry out. Although protection may have been a frequent activity in their earlier days when such groups provided alternatives to the state in the settling of debts, enforcement of contracts and crime control, there are dangers in combining them in a wider sociological 'movement' or 'tendency'. The alternative to this is to accept that the term 'Mafia' has a specific history, one which misunderstandings of the nature, organisation and activities of the real *mafiosi* often confuse. In the context in which the arguments of this chapter use it, therefore, the term Mafia refers to the form of social organisation that developed in the south of Italy under some very specific social and cultural conditions. Initiated gang members themselves often appear to have referred to it by the title Cosa Nostra, although even this may have developed from American usage (see Gambetta 1996: 138–9 and 266–8).

Although there are good arguments for examining Chinese or Japanese organised crime first, the opening part of this chapter discusses the rise of organised crime in Europe. This reflects the fact that Chinese and Japanese groups have only become more active outside their own territories comparatively recently. The first part of the chapter therefore focuses upon the characteristic activities of the groups emanating from southern Italy, including their early role in providing social control in the absence of effective government. In particular, it examines the growth and activities of the Sicilian Mafia, the Camorra and similar groups, especially their role in providing illegal protection and the growth of their activities in a range of illicit markets. It examines the later development of such groups and the Mafia diaspora, whereby their activities have spread beyond their original roots.

The second part of the chapter examines organised crime of Chinese origin. In particular, it explores the activities of Triad and Tong groups, whose operations have extended to Europe, to the USA and elsewhere. This includes people smuggling by so-called 'snakehead' gangs, and participation in every level of the illicit drug trade from production through to local distribution. The third part of the chapter discusses Japanese organised crime, particularly the activities of the Yakuza, including their involvement in political corruption and drug trafficking. It also discusses the activities of the Yakuza in developing their financial interests in the USA and elsewhere.

Having rejected the claim that international crime networks such as these are centralised organisations, it is important not simply to regard them as regional phenomena. The analysis is concerned with activities that go far beyond their origins. A balance must be struck that recognises both the importance of continued activity at their geographical roots and the impact of their activities within a global diaspora. The divisions based on origin set out here only provide a convenient way of studying a more extensive phenomenon. Because it is necessary to distil the character of these examples, it is not possible to discuss every type of organised crime in each genre in very extensive detail. Readers may wish to explore some of the quoted literature to develop a more detailed understanding of these networks.

European origins: the rise of the Mafia and other groups

Although it is usual to regard organised crime as a modern phenomenon, it has a long history. If we regard it as systematic criminal activity for money and power, it is as ancient as the first systems of law and government and as international as trade itself (Woodiwiss 2001: 3). It arose in the very formation of European states in the pre-modern era and often deeply involved monarchs and rulers. Speaking of its origins in classical Rome, Woodiwiss says:

> Criminal enterprise was itself deeply embedded in the machinery of Roman law and government, particularly during and after the rule of Tiberius (AD 14–37). There are well-documented examples of the rich and those in positions of administrative power breaking the law to cheat, intimidate, and steal from the general population and the poor in particular.
>
> (2001: 16)

In medieval European society, the feudal system provided similar opportunities for the abuse of power. Until the seventeenth century, kings only differed from the robber barons in that their plundering was greater. English monarchs such as Elizabeth I regarded the activities of privateers and pirates as legitimate when it suited their political and financial goals.

Although the formation of modern nation states began to make inroads on large-scale banditry, by the nineteenth century this still existed in places where state authority remained weak (Woodiwiss 2001: 20–1). It is against this background of variability in state power that groups based on crime and the provision of local 'protection services' began to arise in Southern Italy. These groups, of which the Sicilian Mafia and the Neapolitan Camorra were the most prominent, became an alternative to the state and to the law in obtaining the settlement of debts and enforcing contracts.

The south of Italy, the Mezzogiorno, is Mediterranean and rural in character, compared with the European and industrial north. Whereas the north seems to accept the largely capitalist ethic that power comes from wealth, the southerner accepts the largely medieval tradition that wealth comes from power. Although the Mafia may have changed in recent years, it is the primacy of the family, the juxtaposition of church and state and the ascendancy of personal honour over statutory law that help to explain why the Mafia and other secret societies developed as they did in the south of Italy (Ianni and Ianni 1972: 15–17).

Of the three imperatives of family, church and the ethic of personal honour, that of the family is predominant. The southern businessman runs his business as he does his family: in a mixture of respect, fear and affection. These, not just profits, are his rewards. This pattern extends beyond the nuclear family into a network of related families. *Compareggio*, the practice of establishing fictitious (godparental) kin roles and the taking of oaths further extends the family. Although these are rites of passage, they are nonetheless binding on family members in terms of moral obligation (Ianni and Ianni 1972: 18–19).

It is necessary to contrast the establishment of these strong social traditions with the weakness of the Italian State, which allowed the development of bands of brigands throughout the Mezzogiorno. According to Ianni and Ianni (1972: 21), these bands sprang 'from the same cultural sources which produced the *Mafia* and other criminal secret societies and are in many ways ancestral to them'. Although the true origins of the word 'Mafia' are lost in history, it is against this social and cultural background that the Sicilian Mafia developed. They may have begun during the occupations of Sicily by Saracen, Norman or Spanish invaders. They may have had their origin in the private armies that which were set up to protect the lands of absentee feudal landowners.

The collapse of the feudal system after the rise and fall of Napoleon in the early nineteenth century marked the emergence of the Mafia into a *società* (society) of families that mediated between the landowners and the masses. The former sought their help in obtaining protection for their estates, whereas the peasant classes sought their help to protect themselves against the landowners. In such cases, Mafia leaders became judges in interpersonal conflicts and, as such, provided a source of order that was an alternative to the weakness of the Italian state (Ianni and Ianni 1972: 27–8).

The apportionment of controlling interests between the various Mafia families often led to feuding and violence. However, both before and after the First World War, there was a balance of power, attributed by commentators to the controlling genius of Don Vito Cascio Ferro, who brokered order among competing power groups. According to the Iannis:

> Under Don Vito, all crimes became organized and the *società* controlled them all directly or through licencing arrangements. He devised the *Mafia* system of demanding tribute – of *fari vagnari a pizzu* ('wetting the beak') by dipping into every business venture. He also maintained rigid discipline.
> (Ianni and Ianni 1972: 31–2)

The rise of Fascism in Italy resulted in driving the Mafia underground, as much from reintegration of political and social systems as from police action. The police and courts were no longer responsive to Mafia pressure. There were no more deals into which the *mafioso* could dip his beak (Ianni and Ianni 1972: 33).

According to Gambetta (1996), in a society where trust is scarce and democracy is weak, the aim of the Sicilian Mafia is to provide protection for those who are engaged in commercial transactions. However, because the Mafia sells protection, it cannot tolerate the provision of this commodity by other agencies, especially by those for whom ideology is the motivating factor (Gambetta 1996: 93). It is as opposed to the protection provided by socialist trade unions as to that provided by the state through a police that claims a monopoly of coercive force.

The Allied occupation of Sicily during the Second World War resulted in a resurgence of Mafia influence. Between 1943 and 1945, the Allied military government appointed *mafiosi* as the mayors of a number of communes in western Sicily and in Regio Calabria (Arlacchi 1988). Despite this, however, the power of the

Mafia as an agency for protection has progressively diminished, following the blows it had already suffered before the Second World War under Fascism. A combination of trade unionism, left-wing political militancy and a reassertion of the role of the police were the causes. The Italian government set up an Anti-Mafia Commission in 1963, after a national outcry when a bomb killed seven police officers.

Changes to social and political conditions in Sicily also brought about changes to the nature of the Mafia itself. After the 1970s, Mafia families followed the trend of competing for wealth on a massive scale. The 'New Mafia' marked the rise of the *Mafia Gansteristica*, the name of a new more power-oriented gangster capitalist, set on discouraging the competition, holding down wages and corrupting large commercial firms and political rulers alike. No longer does the Mafia entrepreneur seek the mediation of government or political representation in his crooked dealings. He seeks actually to control them (Arlacchi 1988: 88–9). According to Arlacchi, during the 1970s, the *cosca* (the extended Mafia family) became a truly international organised crime gang:

> it is only in quite recent times that an entrepreneurial and capitalist outlook has come to play the leading role in determining the *coscas* activities – with the result that the *Mafia* ceased during the 1970's to carry out its ninety-year-old role of political, economic and cultural mediation between the central state and the periphery.
>
> (Arlacchi 1988: 219)

Unlike the old Mafia, which resisted involvement in 'dishonourable' crimes such as international trafficking in drugs and prostitution, the new Mafia became embroiled with other international organisations, such as the Colombian cartels and Chinese organised crime. Even the familial basis of the Mafia began to change. The 'Old Mafia', where everyone was a blood relative or *compare*, gave way to looser affiliations. Vertical integration drew other (non-family) criminals into their operations.

The cumulative effect of these changes is a shift from a traditionally-based network of organised crime groups to one that is more distinctively modern, characterised by:

- a shift away from protection activity towards more diverse goals;
- horizontal financial integration ('gangster capitalism');

- control of political/economic clients: not using them for mediation;
- vertical integration by inclusion of extra-familial members;
- violence used for tactical control, rather than for strategic coercion.

The Mafia also appears to have moved into other activities that go beyond protection of the kind identified by Gambetta (1996), although that remains as a cornerstone. Specific projects include the infiltration of the wine and citrus industries and assumption of control of hospitals and soccer teams. Maintaining a grip on public sector contracts is the largest and most lucrative activity, although extortion of small business to pay protection money continues. Perhaps most important is the increased involvement in the global heroin trade, although even this may have diminished in recent years (Lyman and Potter 1997: 294–5).

The Sicilian Mafia, although of great importance, is not the only criminal network to emerge from southern Italy. The Neapolitan Camorra and the Calabrian 'ndrangheta are also of major significance. In recent years, the Sacra Corona Unita (United Holy Crown) from Apulia has added its activities to those of the longer established networks (Jamieson 1995: 152).

According to Behan (1996), the origins of the Camorra precede those of the Mafia. The Camorra came into being around Naples at the end of the eighteenth century in the failure of the Neapolitan Republic and the power vacuum that followed it. The growth of the Camorra follows the model of the alternative state described by Lupsha (1996). Control of the impoverished and alienated masses was a service that the Camorra could offer local rulers. Later, during the unification of Italy under Garibaldi, an alliance between the police and the Camorra for the maintenance of order showed the extent to which they inhabited the corridors of power (Behan 1996: 11–18).

There were efforts to curb the Camorra's growth during the nineteenth century. Their decline, however, seems to have been as much to do with the rise of political ideologies (both Marxism and Fascism) among urban Neapolitans. According to Behan (1996), the Fascist system incorporated many ex-*camorristi*. As an organisation, the Camorra did not re-emerge until after the Second World War. When it did, it was largely due to US efforts to harness Italian crime groups in the post-war control of Sicily and parts of mainland Italy. Although Ianni and Ianni (1972) claim that the 'real' Camorra did not re-emerge after the defeat of Fascism, commentators such as Jamieson

(1995) and Behan (1996) suggest otherwise. Behan illustrates the rise of the Camorra, both in terms of its activities in the illicit drug trade and its involvement in political corruption.

According to Ianni and Ianni (1972: 23), the Camorra has structures similar to those of the Sicilian Mafia. In Naples, there were twelve 'centres' or geographical areas that the *camorristi* controlled. Each centre was broken down into *paranze* (a local word for 'boat'). At the head of each 'boat' was a *capo parenze*, supported by a treasurer who looked after financial affairs. Unlike the Mafia, which traditionally relied mainly upon kinship or godparental ties between its members, the Camorra recruited from young criminals who the leaders initiated into the movement as apprentices. Behan (1996: 184) emphasises the 'horizontal' structure of the Camorra, with individual gangs operating more or less independently. The Anti-Mafia Commission also emphasised the number of Camorra groups (over one hundred), the tendency for substitution of leaders and the rapid processes of disintegration and reconstitution.

The role of the Camorra in promoting social order (albeit at a cost) was similar to that of the Mafia, at least in its earlier forms. Behan writes:

> The *Camorra* is actually much more of a 'parallel state' than an organisation committed to destroying or taking over government power... *Camorra* control becomes a widely known fact, conditioning both the local population and the political structure. When this position of power is reached, all manner of criminal activities can flourish, privately sanctioned by local political leaders.
>
> (1996: 112)

For Behan (1996: 194), the Camorra remains a 'more efficient instrument for social control than the official representatives of law and order'. As such, only measures that ensure social justice are likely to eradicate organised crime of this kind. Law enforcement alone is not likely to do so. For further discussion of the nature and growth of the Camorra, see Behan (2002).

As was the case in Sicily and Naples, Calabria was home from the eighteenth century to a criminal secret society that (like the Mafia) specialised in selling and bartering protection and influence. The local dialect referred to this society as the *'ndrangheta* but also by the name of Onorata Società (The Honourable Society). It reached its peak as a social force in the mid-nineteenth century. According to Ianni and

Ianni (1972: 21), who have compared it with the Sicilian Mafia, there is a close similarity between the two societies. Both had kinship-like social organisation and gave central importance to the 'man who has won respect'. However, the nature of Calabrian stubbornness seems to have meant that the 'ndrangheta were less adaptable than the Mafia and the nature of the mountain terrain in which they operated was very different from conditions in Palermo or Naples. Although when writing in the 1970s the Iannis were convinced that the 'ndrangheta was in decline, more recent analysis by Jamieson (1995: 152) continues to place it among the three major crime groups in Italy.

The relationship between the Mafia and the Italian state has changed in the past three decades. The Anti-Mafia Commission was in operation from 1963 until 1976, when other measures superseded it. In 1987, a large 'maxi-trial' in Palermo resulted in the conviction of over 400 mafiosi. Action by the Italian state to combat the Mafia led to considerable violence. Jamieson (2000) has noted that the campaign by the Mafia against the government began in Sicily in 1992 and continued with bombings in Rome, Florence and Milan. In May 1992, the killing of the magistrate Giovanni Falcone by bomb attack provoked wide public outcry. Even so, only two months later, a second blast killed special anti-Mafia prosecutor Paolo Borsellino and his police escort. The government sent in military troops to illustrate their determination not to concede to the Mafia.

Thereafter, the government introduced a number of measures intended as a serious effort to control the Mafia. These included special search powers for police and the power to use electronic surveillance and telephone tapping. They also introduced measures for the seizure of Mafia assets and an American-style programme for the protection of witnesses. They established special authorities to carry out criminal prosecutions in the provinces. At the national level, they introduced a specialist police unit to carry out investigations, the Direzione Investigativa Antimafia.

The police have arrested and prosecuted a large number of mafiosi because of these measures. The number of Mafia-related murders decreased and a number of repentant mafiosi gave evidence against their former leaders and colleagues. For a detailed account of these operations, see Jamieson (2000). The conviction in 2002 of the former prime minister Giulio Andreotti illustrates that the authorities are serious about combating the Mafia and its supporters at the highest level.

However, Jamieson (2000) also points out that social measures are as important as law enforcement in efforts to combat the Mafia:

Continuing law enforcement efforts are necessary, but policies should focus as much on the anti-*Mafia* of prevention as the anti-*Mafia* of repression: tolerance of a 50 per cent unemployment rate among young people in traditionally *Mafia* dominated regions is a sign of unforgivable neglect.

(2000: 234)

Above all is the need to reverse decades of belief in the population that the Mafia has any kind of legitimate role in replacing the state in the provision of protection. Ultimately, this requires the relegitimisation of public power and institutions and the recognition that the state is not a hostile force but a guardian of the collective good.

Chinese organised crime

Extensive Chinese immigration into the USA during the mid-nineteenth to early twentieth centuries encouraged the development of Chinese communities in many American cities. San Francisco was predominant in developing a large Chinese community. According to Asbury (1933: 2004a), by 1889 the Chinese population of San Francisco had grown to around 45,000. Often subjected to attack by other immigrant groups, the Chinese concentrated in specific areas for mutual protection and commerce. The underworld that developed in the Chinese quarter was never an integral part of the Barbary Coast area of San Francisco, but remained a separate entity (Asbury 2004a: 165). The main activities associated with Chinese criminal groups (Tongs) during the late nineteenth century included gambling, opium dens and prostitution. Asbury cites the Hop Sing and Suey Sing groups as the first to appear, near the Californian goldfields. Thereafter, Tong groups became an important influence on the development of Chinese organised crime in San Francisco and other parts of California (Asbury 2004a: 184–97). Tong groups became influential wherever a Chinatown developed in the American cities, particularly in New York. The pattern of development of Chinese criminal gangs in the USA and elsewhere is therefore parasitical on existing (largely law-abiding) communities (US President's Commission on Organized Crime 1984). According to Lyman and Potter (2004: 341), Tongs, who are Chinese criminal street gangs not based on traditional 'secret societies' as are the Triads, continue to operate in ethnically defined, tightly organised Chinese communities in many cities. Similar developments are evident in Canada.

The growth of organised crime of Chinese origin has also been evident in Europe since the early 1970s. Before then, although there was a limited amount of Chinese immigration into Europe, the existence of Chinese organised crime groups was virtually unknown. However, during the 1970s the activities of a number of rival Triad gangs increasingly became a focus of attention for the police in the Netherlands and the UK. Although involved mainly in drug trafficking and the control of Chinese gaming establishments, these groups followed a pattern of growth similar to that described by Ianni (1974) in relation to ethnic succession. Both the Netherlands and the UK had long histories of association with Chinese communities in the Far East, stemming from their time as colonial powers. Substantial Chinese communities had developed in many of the major cities of both countries.

The growth of the activities of these more traditionally organised Triad groups provides an important example of the extent of Chinese organised crime. Triads, which have links to similar groups in Hong Kong, Macao and Taiwan, have a worldwide membership that may exceed 100,000 (Lyman and Potter 2004: 342–5). Bresler (1980) identifies the activities of a number of Chinese Triad groups operating in Europe and traces their origins back to Hong Kong, Malaysia and Singapore. In particular, he notes their activities in heroin trafficking with sources in the so-called 'Golden Triangle' in South-East Asia. There is little doubt that by the mid-1970s Triad organisations had deeply embedded themselves in organised crime in a number of jurisdictions, including the Netherlands, the UK, Canada and the USA.

Who are the Triads? The earliest Triads had their origins in the Fujian province of China. They came into being as a martial secret society, apparently dedicated to resistance to the Manchu (Ch'ing) dynasty. As a martial society, they practised Kung Fu as a form of self-defence. Bresler (1980) points out that their activities had always had a darker side in the provision of 'protection' by adventurers who became members of Triad groups. Eventually, the power of the Triads metamorphosed into corruption and, finally, into widespread criminality. Triads such as the Green Pang controlled Shanghai in the 1930s and were prominent in the bloody defeat of communist trade unions during the reign of Chiang Kai Shek. Later, during the communist takeover of China, they fled to Hong Kong. Other Triad groups also sought refuge in Hong Kong. These included the Sun Yee On and Fuk Yee Hing from Shanghai. Later, the 14K Triad from Canton and others joined them.

When the wave of Chinese migration to the West started in the late 1960s, the concentration of Triad groups in Hong Kong provided a springboard for expansion. According to Bresler:

> Within the ranks of these legitimate and entirely honourable immigrants was, inevitably, a hard-core Triad criminal element: protection men, illegal gamblers, prostitute operators, loan-sharkers, racketeers, blackmailers – and drug traffickers.
>
> (1980: 39)

Not surprisingly, they continued their activities in their new countries. However, their activities were not only domestic, they were international. The globalisation of commerce and communications made their task easier.

Although the Triads have simplified the ritual for entry in recent years, initiation is still required. Like other crime groups that have traditional origins as secret societies, Triads are hierarchical. At the top is the '489' or *Shan Chu* (Hill Chief). Next in the hierarchy is the '438' or *Heung Chu* (Incense Master – responsible for ceremonial duties). The '415' (White Paper Fan) is responsible for administration and finance. The '426' (Red Pole) is an expert in martial arts and the '432' (Straw Sandal) is the unit's messenger, responsible for liaison with other branches. The ordinary members of the group are '49s' (Bresler 1980: 37–8). These numbers are of considerable significance for gang members and for Chinese communities more generally. According to Bresler, all these numbers have a specific meaning:

> It will be noticed that they all begin with 4 and this refers to the ancient Chinese belief that the world was surrounded by four seas, thus indicating the universal nature of the *Triad* movement. 489 and 438 are said to have been selected because the Chinese characters for 21 (the sum of 4+8+9) and for 3 and 8, when written together, form the Chinese characters for 'Hung', the early Ming Emperor in whose name the whole *Triad* organization began in the first place. 426 is constructed as 4x15+4, which equals 64. This refers to the 64 diagrams of Chinese script invented by a legendary emperor named Fu Teh which is said to be the basis from which all Chinese script has evolved. 432 becomes 4x32+4, giving us 132, which is the actual number of persons (128 monks and 4 others) supposed to have lived in the original Triad monastery near Foochow. Finally, 49

derives from 4x9 which equals 36. This refers to the number of oaths sworn by all new Triad members.

(1980: 38)

Although all Triad groups follow these principles, they remain largely independent. The independence of Triad groups from their Hong Kong roots means, for example, that the Dragon Head group in the UK does not necessarily give allegiance to the Hong Kong group of the same name. In this sense, the Triads remain fragmented, operating in an ad hoc manner, without centralised leadership (Booth 1999).

Criminologists have made extensive studies of their operations. According to Finckenauer (2001), the organisational structure of Chinese organised crime in the USA is complex. There are a great variety of Chinese criminal organisations, including street gangs, secret societies, Triads, Tongs and Taiwanese crime groups. Some are strictly US based, whereas others are involved in international organised crime. However, there is no ground for believing that there is a well-organised 'Chinese Mafia'. According to Chin:

My findings … do not support the notion that a chain of command exists among these various crime groups or that they co-ordinate with one another routinely in international crimes such as heroin trafficking, money laundering, and the smuggling of aliens.

(Chin 1996b: 123, quoted in Finckenauer 2001)

Finckenauer (2001) identifies a number of Tong-related gangs in New York (the Fuk Ching) and San Francisco (the Wo Hop To and the Wah Ching). According to Finckenauer, Tong-affiliated gangs like the Fuk Ching have a hierarchical structure, with an *ah kung* (grandfather) or *shuk foo* (uncle) at the head. The top gang position is *dai dai lo* (big, big brother), with *dai lo* (big brother) and *yee lo/saam lo* (clique leaders) below them. In the rank and file are the *ma jai*, or little horses. Violence is common in enforcing discipline and against other organised crime groups.

According to Chin (1996b), the international activities of groups such as the Fuk Ching include drug trafficking, kidnapping and the smuggling of immigrants into North America. On the domestic scene, their main activities in New York's Chinatown include extortion and gambling in the particular areas in which they are dominant. More recently, these groups have been able to diversify their efforts into legitimate businesses, such as restaurants, fish markets and video stores. The West Coast gangs have penetrated the entertainment industry. The Chinese communities in New York and on the West Coast are well aware of the activities of Chinese organised crime. However, with the exception of their smuggling of illegal immigrants, the public at large is relatively unaware of their activities.

Despite the action taken against them by police in Hong Kong, the UK, Netherlands, the USA and elsewhere, Chinese organised crime groups have been constantly active, especially in drug trafficking and in illegal human smuggling by so-called 'snakehead' gangs. As Chapter 4 has suggested, there are examples of collaboration between the Sicilian Mafia and Chinese organised crime in the supply of heroin from South-East Asia for the US market. For a more extensive analysis of Triad gangs in the context of illicit enterprise, readers should refer to Chu (2000). Chin *et al.* (1998: 148) provides a useful analytical table setting out the activities of the various factions in Chinese organised crime (see Table 5.1).

The diversity of Chinese organised crime provides a good example of how criminal groups may present evidence of a degree of organisation without high levels of central control. In this sense, they are following the pattern debated in Chapter 1, a more fragmented and complex form of organisation than that predicated upon rational (or even traditional) models. Recent research by Zhang and Chin (2003) shows the declining significance of the Triads' entrenched culture and organisation. Organised Chinese criminal groups are increasingly following the Mafia in developing their own independent structures. The fact that they are now widely dispersed through many jurisdictions means that they are highly resistant to control and law enforcement measures that are designed to deal with more tightly defined traditional organisations.

Japanese organised crime

The Yakuza (also known as the Boryokudan – 'the violent ones') are the main international organised crime group emanating from Japan. There are also large motorcycle gangs (*bosozku*) operating in the country although their activities are primarily domestic. Hill (2003: 36–64) describes the origin of the Yakuza in the *tekiya* (itinerant pedlars) and the illegal *bakuto* gambling gangs of the seventeenth century. According to Hill, some of the leaders operated as labour brokers, supplying construction workers for the large public works

Table 5.1 The role and function of various Chinese crime groups in heroin trafficking and human smuggling

	Heroin trafficking	Human smuggling
Hong Kong-based triad societies	Trafficking heroin from the Golden Triangle to Hong Kong via China or Thailand and exporting to Australia and Europe	Smuggling Chinese to Hong Kong
Taiwan-based crime groups	Trafficking heroin from the Golden Triangle to Taiwan via Thailand or China	Providing ships and passports to US and China-based snakeheads or acting as transit point snakeheads, also involved in smuggling Chinese to Taiwan
China-based crime groups	Working together with Hong Kong and Taiwan-based crime groups in trafficking heroin from the Golden Triangle to China and exporting to Hong Kong or Taiwan	Acting as little snakeheads for foreign-based big snakeheads
US-based Tongs	Some Tong members, working together with heroin traffickers, triad members or gang leaders involved in importing heroin into the US	Some Tong members, especially members of Fujianese organisations, are involved in smuggling Chinese to the US
US-based gangs	Some gang leaders, working together with heroin traffickers, triad members or Tong members, involved in importing heroin into the US	Mainly helping the big snakeheads collecting the smuggling fee
Heroin traffickers	Mostly Chinese entrepreneurs in Hong Kong, Taiwan, China, Southeast Asia, Australia and Europe.	
Snakeheads or human smugglers	Some snakeheads are former heroin traffickers. Mostly US or Thailand-based Fujianese with friends and relatives in China and major transit points, involved in smuggling Chinese to the USA, Japan and Europe.	

Source: Z-L. Chin, S. Zhang and R.T. Kelly (1998) 'Transnational Chinese Organized Crime Activities', in P. Williams and D. Vlassis (eds) *Combating Transnational Crime: Concepts, Activities and Responses*, Special Issue of *Transnational Organized Crime*, 4/3–4: 127–54.

programmes that the Shogun lords had initiated. By the nineteenth century, the Yakuza had gained strongholds within the larger Japanese cities by organising bands of construction workers. The hostels for itinerants that the gambling bosses also ran attracted gambling customers, labourers and potential gang members. Labour broking, and the deduction of a percentage of the labourer's wages, is a continuing feature of the Yakuza (Hill 2003: 37).

The connection between the Yakuza and the samurai warrior class is complex and, for outsiders, somewhat difficult to evaluate. According to Hill, many of the samurai formed gangs when they were no longer required after the stabilisation of Japan in the seventeenth century. The modern Yakuza claim to be the descendents of the *machi yokko* gangs who derived from samurai origins. Characteristic of these gangs was the profession of reactionary political views, exaggerated attire, elaborate rituals and defiant self-exclusion (Hill 2003: 38). Hill also observes that by the late nineteenth century these groups were not operating primarily as gamblers but were also exercising protection over the prostitution, entertainment and construction industries. In this sense, according to Hill, the Yakuza were behaving in ways that some analysts associate with the Sicilian Mafia and similar organisations (2003: 40).

The organisation prospered after the Second World War, aided by the expanding black market in the immediate post-war period, especially in foodstuffs and drugs. The growth of market opportunities, especially in the growing entertainment industry, in bars, restaurants and prostitution, enabled an expansion of Yakuza operations. The use of brutal methods for enforcement was commonplace. They also began to penetrate legitimate businesses. Factional warfare was the outcome, although by the 1960s Yoshio Kodama, the Yakuza 'godfather', had united the main factions under his leadership (Kaplan and Dubro 1986: 93–9). Gang membership seems to have peaked during the early 1960s, with around 180,000 members distributed across 5,000 gangs. According to Lyman and Potter (1997: 281), by the late 1990s the numbers had reduced to an estimated 110,000 members belonging to some 2,500 gangs of Yakuza. If correct, despite the reductions since the high point of the 1960s, the Yakuza forms one of the largest organised crime groups in the world.

The structure of the modern Yakuza syndicates comprises a large number of *ikka* or (fictive) families (Hill 2003: 64–5). The hierarchy is that of the Japanese household and the key relationship that of father–child or master–apprentice. The *kaicho* is the boss or father of the organisation, with absolute authority. The *wakoto* is the deputy or captain, with the rank-and-file membership consisting of *wakai shu* (soldiers). According to Hill, the formal hierarchy is similar to that which exists in legitimate corporations, or in the military. It is similar to the formal rank structures of the American Cosa Nostra and Chinese Triads (Hill 2003: 66).

Three major groups appear to be in contention for control: the Yamaguchi Gumi, Sumiyoshi-Kai and the Inagawa-Kai. The latter are the two largest Tokyo-based groups. Each has an estimated membership of 8–15,000 (Lyman and Potter 2004: 346–7). Groups are self-regulating, with norms of behaviour that protect the security of the gang, including unquestioning obedience. Punishments include beatings, expulsion, finger amputation and death. The films *The Yakuza* (1975) and *Black Rain* (1989) depicted finger amputation, which expresses sincerity to erase past misdeeds. It is perhaps the best-known aspect of Japanese Yakuza culture in the West, although Hill remarks that there is clearly an upper limit to the number of times that a penitent can credibly and physically express such sincerity! However, the empirical evidence does not sustain their portrayal as 'evil empires' with an iron code of discipline. Despite the rules, the temptation to maximise self-interest at the expense of the boss or the group is strong (Hill 2003: 73–5).

Major activities of Yakuza groups include protection, drug trafficking, gambling, labour brokering, management of prostitution, loan-sharking, debt collecting and drawing money from fake social clubs. According to Hill, protection is implicit in all Yakuza activities. Specifically, it encompasses a range of activities, including such things as reducing threats to business operations from bad customers, suppliers, employees and predators, demanding 'bodyguard fees' and providing goods and equipment from gang-controlled businesses. Drug trafficking includes supplying amphetamines, which are the drugs of choice in Japan. Gangs are mainly involved in the latter in terms of importing drugs into Japan, rather than exporting. The management of gambling (which is illegal in Japan) extends from small operators through to luxury gambling trips and illegal bookmaking. The labour brokers who supply workers for the construction industry are mainly Yakuza members. The Yakuza also monopolise the management of so-called 'date clubs' and street and foreign prostitutes (Hill 2003: 92–136).

Yakuza groups have also been heavily involved in political corruption and financial scandals in Japan. This includes infiltrating the legitimate economy and asset stripping. During the 1980s, the two most powerful and well-funded politicians in Japan were making direct use of them (Hill 2003: 177–84). The Yakuza have also been involved in importing firearms to Japan from the USA. Lyman and Potter (2004: 347) have noted that during the past two decades, the Yakuza have infiltrated legitimate business in the USA as a means through which they can hide their illegal capital. In particular, they have invested in the West Coast and in Hawaii.

Although in recent years there have been efforts in Japan to control the Yakuza, it is too soon to say whether this will be a long-term success. They do not appear to have the wider international impact of Chinese crime gangs, but law enforcement agencies continue to regard them as a serious threat. Readers interested in further study of the Yakuza are encouraged to read Hill (2003), which sets out a detailed and exemplary analysis, and Kaplan and Dubro (2003), which expands and replaces their earlier (1986) study.

Chapter 6

Land of opportunity: organised crime in the USA

Organised crime in the USA has been the subject both of popular speculation and of academic study. It has attracted the attention of social commentators and journalists for many years. Since the 1960s, it has increasingly attracted the attention of criminologists, many of whom have been sceptical about official accounts of its nature. Chapter 1 compared a number of theoretical models that are relevant to the development of organised crime in major American cities. This chapter extends the review to include a more detailed assessment of the evidence relating to the development of organised crime in the USA. It compares its many manifestations, from gang activity to corporate crime. It makes further reference to Cressey's model (1969: 1972), especially in relation to its influence on US policies in dealing with the phenomenon of organised crime.

The review of organised crime in the USA has four stages. First, it assesses the growth of organised crime since the late nineteenth century, including the rise of gangs and gang culture. It discusses the arguments relating to the so-called alien conspiracy thesis, which imputed organised criminal tendencies to the groups of Irish, Jewish and Italian-American origin who emigrated to the USA in large numbers the nineteenth and early twentieth centuries. Secondly, it examines the rise of syndicated crime in the major American cities and the protection rackets and illegal markets with which it is associated. It discusses the importance of the prohibition era in fuelling the growth of such groups. This includes an assessment of evidence relating to the rise and fall of the so-called Cosa Nostra or Mafia 'families' and other groupings. Thirdly, the chapter reviews the pluralisation of organised crime in the USA since the 1960s. This includes the growth of motorcycle gangs, prison gangs and other, non-traditional forms of organised crime. It examines the role of ethnic groups of Hispanic, Afro-American and Asian origin, referring to what Ianni (1974) has called the 'ethnic succession thesis'. It examines present-day organised crime and sets out a critique of US federal domestic and international policy since 1967, including the impact that this has had on investigation. Finally, it examines the ambivalence between official policies aimed at tackling organised crime and the extent to which it has become embedded in American culture, especially its representations in cinema, theatre, literature and music. It concludes that the public obsession about gangsters and organised crime more generally is encouraged by the entertainment industry and is an important part of America's cultural heritage.

Early origins: the 'alien conspiracy' theory

According to Woodiwiss (2001: 6), from the earliest days of the settlement of the country by a white population, some form of organised crime has always been evident in American society. From the beginning, legal and criminal justice systems in the USA were set up in ways that showed a great deal of latitude to organised crime. The enactment of prohibitions and the use of regulatory systems that did not consider business violations to be crimes, only served to increase this tendency. Woodiwiss argues that commercial crime imported from Europe, including counterfeiting, banking and investment fraud, had an influence on crime in America's formative years. Transhipment of convicts from the English, Scottish and Irish courts during the period before Independence provided an unwelcome influence. The slave trade itself also provided a background of racketeering that disfigured the process of white settlement of the country (Woodiwiss 2001: 22–33).

The rise of gangs in American cities was evident from the mid-nineteenth century. According to Woodiwiss (2001: 61), as the cities grew, they experienced the development of a gang culture like that then characterising many European cities. From the 1830s, such gangs were active in city politics and in the illegal economy. Their activities included the control of prostitution and demands for protection money. Although the ending of the American Civil War promised a new order in business and politics, according to Woodiwiss:

> In practice, the United States continued to make the same compromises with local and regional elites, as other great powers had made during their processes of state building. Successful criminal activity adapted to the new American order rather than challenged it.
>
> (2001: 67)

While the growth of gangs is an evident fact, the claim that Irish and Italian immigrants imported highly organised forms of crime during the late nineteenth and early twentieth centuries has less credibility. This claim, which Lyman and Potter (2004: 65–6) refer to as the 'alien conspiracy theory', seeks to place the blame on outsiders for the prevalence of organised crime in American society. For example, the involvement of Irish immigrants in a series of murders in the anthracite mining country of north-eastern Pennsylvania in the 1870s led to the widely-held belief that a criminal gang known as the 'Molly Maguires' had perpetrated them. In fact, the belief that organised crime was specifically an Irish import diminished as soon as the courts convicted those responsible.

More seriously, the idea that organised crime was an Italian import began to take root after a series of incidents in New Orleans at the end of the nineteenth century. Italian immigrants were the largest group to arrive in New Orleans during that period and such large numbers caused considerable resentment among the existing residents. According to Woodiwiss, people first commonly used the word 'Mafia' when anti-Italian feeling was at its height following the killing of David Hennessey, the New Orleans police chief, in 1890 (Woodiwiss 2001: 97–9). Hennessey had been particularly vigorous in his investigation of killings that were the outcome of a conflict between rival Italian extortion gangs and this may have led to his death. A less charitable interpretation is that he had favoured one faction over another.

Although circumstantial evidence indicated that Italians had shot him, the court did not convict any of them of the killing. In the uprising that followed his death, the mob killed a number of Italians, including some that the enquiry into the Hennessey shooting had never implicated. Thereafter, however, the population widely believed that a gang of Sicilians with allegiance to a secret society had committed the Hennessey murder. Despite the distorting nature of the murder, there is credible evidence that real *mafiosi* were included in the Italian immigrant population, but their number was small and there is no clear evidence that they ever founded a Mafia crime dynasty.

Studies of the growth of gangs in several American cities by the historian Herbert Asbury also show up the weakness of the alien conspiracy theory. Asbury first published his studies of gangs in New York, Chicago, San Francisco and New Orleans between the 1920s and 1940s. Interest in Asbury, stemming from the arch-gangsterphile film version of *Gangs of New York* by Martin Scorsese, has led to the recent revival of his work (Asbury 2002, 2003, 2004a, 2004b). For Asbury, who studied the hundred-year period of gang activity up to the 1940s, gangs were loosely organised groups that exhibited considerable diversity in their membership. His studies of gangs show a more complex, less highly structured pattern of relationships than many of the accounts that followed them, including those emanating from official sources.

Asbury's study of the gangs of New York sets out a picture of a war of 'each against all' of the kind feared by the English philosopher Thomas Hobbes (1588–1679). Life in these gangs was, for many participants, certainly brutish and short. Although gangs contributed to both social and to economic survival, many gang members paid a high price. Gangs with picaresque names such as the Dead Rabbits, the Bowery Boys, Eastmans and the Five Pointers were brawling thieves and robbers. Others such as the Gophers, Hudson Dusters and Gas Housers were more akin to an armed rabble than to gangs, as Asbury conceived them. Their activities spanned around a hundred years of the history of the city, concentrated around the tenements of the Five Points and Bowery areas. Much of the gang activity of the late nineteenth and early twentieth centuries was concerned with gaining or maintaining territory, often using mob brutality. According to Asbury, some of these gangs in their earlier forms could muster as many as a thousand members. They were loosely organised, in the sense that their leaders could effectively marshal and direct them but their memberships were not static. They consisted of a wide variety of people, although the Irish were probably in the majority. In contrast to the longer existence of these groups, the police quickly dispatched smaller youth gangs. However, Asbury concedes that small, more professional groups, consisting of gunman and burglars, had more durability.

Interestingly, Asbury was convinced that the era of the gangs in New York that he had described had ended during the later 1920s. Of the possibility of continued conflicts between the gangs that the citizens of New York feared, Asbury says:

> But the conflict never materializes, and it is quite unlikely that it will ever come again, for there are now no gangs in New York, and no gangsters in the sense that the word has come into common use. In his day the gangster flourished under the protection and manipulation of the crooked politician to who he was an invaluable ally at election time, but his day has simply passed. Improved social, economic and educational conditions have lessened the number of recruits, and organized gangs have been clubbed out of existence by the police, who have always been prompt to inaugurate repressive campaigns when permitted to do so by their political masters.
>
> (Asbury 2002: xiii–xiv)

This judgement may now seem premature, given the continuing activities of a wide variety of criminal groups. Asbury was rightly pointing to an important watershed indicating a change in the meaning of the word 'gangster'. However, the departure of the kinds of warring gangs that he had described was only the beginning of another kind of gangsterdom: the one initiated by the era of prohibition.

The history of the gangs whose criminality was based in the gambling dens and whorehouses of the Barbary Coast area of San Francisco attracted Asbury's attention during the 1930s (Asbury 2004a). He also explored the history of the gangs of New Orleans during this period (Asbury 2004b). In addition to gangs of Irish, French and Italian origin, he points to the arrival of Sicilian elements, whom he suggests became dominant in Italian-American crime in the region and formed an organised co-partnership to commit crime in the city. This partnership, known as the Stoppagherra Society, was allegedly organised by four men from Palermo, driven from Sicily by the authorities in 1869. This gang kept the Italian-American community in New Orleans in fear for over twenty years and carried out a number of killings. According to Asbury, it was action by police chiefs David Hennesey and his brother Mike against the leaders of this gang that led eventually to their assassination (see above).

In 1940, Asbury set out an informal history of the Chicago underworld (Asbury 2003). Exploring the history of gangs in the city both before and after the Great Fire of 1871, he describes the growth of gangs there, concluding with the activities of Johnny Torrio and Al Capone, whom Asbury regarded as 'the biggest of the big shots'. He describes the divisions of territory in the city by the gangs and their exploits in bootlegging during the prohibition era. According to

Asbury, the Chicago gangs did not involve only Italian-Americans; nor does he suggest that Italian-Americans totally 'controlled' organised crime gangs throughout the USA in the period up to 1940. Overall, Asbury's work presents a diverse and fragmented picture of the activities of crime groups over a long period, a rich picture of the illegal activities of a wide variety of people that is far from the vision suggested by the alien conspiracy theory. His work has many parallels to that of the Chicago School, whose studies of gang life were discussed in Chapter 2.

Unfortunately, the fragmented forms of gang that Asbury depicted were not sufficient to refute the alien conspiracy myth. On the contrary, during the 1950s two New York journalists (Lait and Mortimer) led the way in popularising the myth in the publication of *Chicago Confidential* (1950). They followed this by *New York Confidential* and by *USA Confidential* shortly thereafter. These authors claimed that racketeering was in the hands of 'immigrant hordes', although they failed to produce evidence of the Mafia as a coherent, centralised, nationwide conspiracy (Woodiwiss 2001: 102–4). Nevertheless, other literature and government sources continued to give credence to the alien conspiracy theory thereafter. It had long been a convenient peg upon which to hang the activities of criminal groups. It had a certain convenience, both for the Federal authorities and for those intent on defending public perceptions of American culture.

As will be evident, however, while it is certainly true that there were real crime groups, committing real offences, they did not stand outside the social fabric of the American cities. Daniel Bell is right, in this sense, to suggest that crime is part of the American way of life, providing a 'queer ladder of mobility' for its participants (Bell 1960). Most cities already had some form of organised crime before the large-scale influx of Italian-Americans in the late nineteenth and early twentieth centuries. Their activities have continued in a variety of ways. The key questions are (as intimated in Chapter 1) what was the real nature of these groups and how did they operate? It is to these questions that the debate will now turn in discussing the further development of syndicated criminal gangs in the USA during the period from prohibition onwards.

Syndicated crime: illegal markets and racketeering

The penetration by organised crime of US commerce, industry and politics has an extensive history. Theft, bribery and the control of prostitution and gambling were often central to gang activity of the kind that Asbury described, but other forms of enterprise crime have also been prevalent. The control of labour unions and the growth of corporate racketeering have provided important vehicles to enable organised crime to operate. Activities such as loan-sharking, control of 'sweatshop' labour, racketeering connected with the waterfront and (later) with airfreight, and infiltration of the waste disposal industry have provided opportunities for a wide variety of criminal groups. Activities of this kind are nothing new. Organised criminal groups since the end of the nineteenth century have always been ready to respond to the growth of new markets and to the development of new technologies.

The prohibition of the sale of alcohol in the USA in the 1920s enabled gangsters to gain unprecedented influence over the social, political and economic fabric of the country. The prohibition era was a significant watershed whereby organised crime syndicates were able to establish a firm grip on an important market. The Federal government introduced prohibition of the manufacture, distribution and sale of alcohol by the Eighteenth Amendment to the Constitution in 1919. The Volstead Act followed nine months later, providing the mechanism for enforcement. Bootlegging (illegal trafficking in alcoholic liquor) and 'speakeasies' (illicit drinking clubs) were soon in operation, in a widespread disregard of the ban. The scale of the dissent is evident in the fact that, at the height of prohibition, Chicago alone had over 10,000 speakeasies in operation (Lyman and Potter 1997: 103–4).

In effect, prohibition transferred the once legitimate income of brewers, distillers and barkeepers to anyone willing to break the law. The scale of the enterprise ensured that only organised crime could deliver it effectively. Many entrepreneurial criminals took advantage of the prohibition era and the massive demand for alcohol that it produced. Gangs soon established an elaborate system for importing, producing and transporting goods that were beyond the legal limit. This is a classic example of the tenets of Smith's enterprise model, which Chapter 3 discussed in detail (Smith 1975). The servicing of an illicit industry on this scale took a great deal of organising, although this does not mean that only formal-rational types of organisation could deliver the goods. There were many examples of criminal gangs and formerly legitimate businesses striking up working alliances between themselves. Partnerships were the order of the day. According to Woodiwiss:

Some pre-Volstead brewing and distilling interests formed alliances with criminals to organize successful robberies of existing stocks and then began to develop long term arrangements. One major Chicago brewer, Joseph Stenson, made an estimated $12 million out of such an arrangement…[with] John Torrio, formerly of New York, who had been involved in various Chicago prostitution and gambling activities since 1909.

(2001: 186)

Perhaps the most notorious of the prohibition era gangsters was Al Capone. Capone survived a number of attempts on his life by rival gangsters. However, although Astbury claims that he and his associates had an interest in over 70 per cent of rackets in the city, Capone did not, strictly speaking, 'run' Chicago or the Chicago rackets (Woodiwiss 2001: 196–7). As Haller (1990) has shown, the illegal enterprises that Torrio, Capone and their associates ran between 1925 and 1930 were in the form of partnerships. Capone and Torrio were senior partners in a cluster of illicit enterprises, but the relationships in the group were not those generally associated with the bureaucratic form of organisation. These were enterprises of small scale. Gangsters like Capone were criminal entrepreneurs, not skilled bureaucrats. They were hustlers and dealers, accustomed to personal negotiations and taking risks:

In short, the various enterprises of the so called 'Capone gang' were not controlled bureaucratically. Each, instead, was a separate enterprise of small or relatively small scale. Most had managers who were also partners. Coordination was possible because the senior partners, with an interest in each of the enterprises, exerted influence across a range of activities.

(Haller 1990: 221)

For Woodiwiss (2001), Haller's analysis helps to explain why Capone's removal as a criminal force (on tax evasion charges) made no difference to the extent of illegal enterprise in the city.

In addition to the partnership between legitimate interests and organised criminal groups, there was also a high level of collusion between police, local officials and bootleggers. The courts convicted of corruption many agents of the Federal Prohibition Bureau. Opponents of prohibition mounted a massive campaign, which aimed to repeal the legislation against alcohol. It 1933, ratification of the Twenty-first Amendment effectively ended the prohibition era.

As Smith suggests, the inevitable result of creating a new service industry of the kind that prohibition produced is that the servants quickly realised that they could be the masters. They obtained their training in business administration through prohibition and soon took control of the rackets from their more legitimate associates. Racketeering broadened into a system of exploitation for the criminal class (Smith 1975: 70). Everywhere, the prohibition era provided a springboard for organised crime such that even after its repeal America felt its effects in other areas of criminality. According to Lyman and Potter:

> Prohibition required a concentration of power in criminal activity at two levels; within individual cities and states and on a national scale. After 1933, the new organizational structure was carried over into other forms of enterprise, such as gambling and labour racketeering.
>
> (1997: 105)

Although it is right to be sceptical about the extent to which highly formalised criminal organisations facilitated its development, there can be little doubt that syndicated criminal activity continued to develop post-prohibition in many American cities. The development of the Chicago, New York and Philadelphia mobs after prohibition provides little evidence of co-ordinated, bureaucratic organisation. Nevertheless, organised crime in Chicago continued comparatively unabated, despite Capone's removal. Sam Giancana, who had worked for Capone in the 1940s, took over gambling rackets there. The FBI regarded him as the head of the Chicago group known as 'The Outfit' until mob rivals shot him dead in 1975 (Lyman and Potter 2004: 108–10). Philadelphia had organised criminal groups of Irish, Jewish and Italian descent. They were active in gambling, loan-sharking and disposing of stolen property. Predominant among these until 1980 was the 'family' headed by Angelo Bruno. Again, however, although this family played an important role in crime it had no co-ordinating role (Lyman and Potter 2004: 134–5). No ethnic group dominated organised crime in Philadelphia.

According to Lyman and Potter (2004: 110), the New York mob probably represents the best-known example of the emergence of Italian-American organised crime in a single city. Gangsters such as Vito Genovese, Joe Adonis, Frank Costello, Charles 'Lucky' Luciano and Joseph Columbo became legends as heads of criminal syndicates in New York. Benjamin 'Bugsy' Seigel and Meyer Lansky, who were deeply involved with the Hollywood film industry, dominated the gaming business, extending their influence to Las Vegas and throughout the USA (see Lyman and Potter 2004: 125–30).

Later, John Gotti became the prototype for a new breed of Italian-American criminals, having taken over the Gambino syndicate from Paul Castellano. Gambino had selected Castellano to take over the syndicate's operations after his death. Police believe Gotti organised the fatal shooting of Castellano in order to become the most powerful gang-leader in New York. Nicknamed 'The Teflon Don' because he was difficult to convict of substantial offences, he was undoubtedly a major figure in the New York criminal underworld during the 1980s. The authorities finally secured the conviction of Gotti in 1992 for murder and racketeering. The court sentenced him to life imprisonment. He died in prison in 2002 (Lyman and Potter 2004: 130–2). However, criminologists remain doubtful about his role as the head of the Mafia in that city or nationally. This scepticism has not generally been the characteristic response of law enforcement or of Federal policy on organised crime.

Efforts in the USA to tackle organised crime have a long history. The Department of Justice founded the Bureau of Investigation in 1908, mainly to deal with organised prostitution. In 1935, this became the Federal Bureau of Investigation, with a specific remit to deal with Federal offences across America. This includes organised crime. It first chief, J. Edgar Hoover, pursued this goal relentlessly, although it was not until 1963 that he chose to go along with the Mafia conspiracy theory. However, despite Hoover's earlier reluctance, there have been a number of presidential committees of enquiry that supported the thesis that the Mafia is at the centre of organised crime in the USA.

In 1950, the US Senate set up a Special Committee to Investigate Organized Crime in Interstate Commerce under the chairmanship of Senator Estes Kefauver. The Committee called over 600 witnesses, many of whom asserted their right to silence under the Fifth Amendment. The Committee claimed that an international criminal conspiracy known as the Mafia originating in Sicily was responsible for organised crime in the USA. In its third interim report, the Committee claimed that:

> there is a sinister criminal organization known as the *Mafia* operating throughout the country with ties in other nations in the opinion of the committee. The *Mafia* is the direct descendent of a criminal organization of the same name originating in the island of Sicily … the *Mafia* is a loose knit organization … the

binder which ties together the two major criminal syndicates as well as numerous other criminal groups throughout the country.

(Kefauver 1951, quoted in Smith 1975: 121–2)

However, there was never any direct or indirect evidence to support the '*Mafia* model' (Lyman and Potter 1997: 27). Again, according to Daniel Bell, whose article 'Crime as an American Way of Life' first appeared in 1953:

Neither the Senate Crime Committee in its testimony nor Kefauver in his book presented any real evidence that the *Mafia* exists as a functioning organisation. One finds police officials asserting before the Kefauver committee their belief in the *Mafia*: the Narcotics Bureau thinks that a worldwide dope ring allegedly run by Luciano is part of the *Mafia*, but the only other 'evidence' presented – aside from the incredulous responses both of Senator Kefauver and Rudolph Halley when nearly all of the Italian gangsters asserted that they didn't know about the *Mafia* – is that certain crime bears 'the earmarks of the *Mafia*'.

(Bell 1960: 126, quoted in Lyman and Potter 1997: 27)

In fact, the only information to support the Mafia thesis came from law enforcement officials. In effect, the Committee gave in to the temptation to believe that organised crime in America must have come from an alien conspiracy, something with which Bell and other sceptical liberal sociologists could not agree without evidence. Although the Committee was successful in exposing a number of major criminals such as Lansky and Costello, they did not find the Mafia.

In 1957, local police raided the home of Joe Barbera in Apalachin, New York, where a meeting had been assembled, allegedly to endorse Vito Genovese as the new 'boss of bosses' for the mob and to decide whether to go into drug trafficking on a large scale. The so-called 'Apalachin Summit' formed an important part of the Mafia legend and provided considerable embarrassment for the FBI, who had until then consistently denied its existence. Thereafter, Hoover began a campaign to build up the FBI as the nation's main opponent to the Mafia (Lyman and Potter 1997: 28–30). The difficulty of interpreting the meeting at Apalachin remains. Although there was plenty of expert opinion to confirm that this was indeed a meeting of the top Mafia commission, as Lyman and Potter remark (1997: 30), the list bore no relationship to the supposed distribution of Mafia families. However, as a convention of Italian garment manufacturers, it made excellent sense!

Joseph Valachi gave evidence, in 1957, before the McClellan Committee, which had been set up to review the relationship between drugs trafficking and organised crime. Valachi provided information that tended to confirm the Mafia legend, claiming to have participated in over thirty murders in the thirty years during which he has been a *mafioso* working for the Gambino family. Valachi introduced the term *La Cosa Nostra* and referred to 'The Commission', the mob's supreme council. He named nearly 300 people as members of the *La Cosa Nostra*, although he denied the use of the term 'Mafia' during his testimony (Maas 1968). There have been a number of convincing critiques of Valachi's claims, notably by Albini (1971) and Smith (1975). These commentators have pointed out that his testimony was uncorroborated and contained a number of inconsistencies and contradictions, throwing serious doubt upon the claims. Nevertheless, he remained a major source for the Mafia legend and, as such, was an influence on official thinking on organised crime in the USA for a decade.

Although not originally intended to do so, in 1967 President Johnson's Commission on Law Enforcement and Administration of Justice again reviewed organised crime. Its task-force report again endorsed the Mafia legend. It said that the core of organised crime consisted of twenty-four groups operating criminal cartels across the nation. Their membership was exclusively of men of Italian descent. The work of Cressey, who was an adviser to the Commission, heavily influenced the task-force report. Cressey's paper entitled 'The Functions and Structure of Criminal Syndicates' supported Valachi's organisational concepts and accepted the Cosa Nostra claim (Cressey 1967). He later further elaborated this in his *Theft of the Nation* (Cressey 1969).

Cressey's perspective informed official thinking on organised crime for a decade or more. For Cressey, organised crime and the Mafia or Cosa Nostra are synonymous. However, he conceded that its presence in the USA may not have been the result of direct transportation but rather the response of hoodlum immigrants to a new cultural setting. What was not at issue for Cressey was the bureaucratic and rational structure of the Cosa Nostra, where each level in the hierarchy has a well-defined role. This thinking lay behind the adoption in 1970 of the Racketeer Influenced and Corrupt Organisations (RICO) Statute, which provided measures to enable the prosecution of gang members for conspiracy and for the management of a criminal organisation.

In 1983, the President's Commission on Organized Crime endorsed the stand the Kefauver and McClellan committees had taken. The Commission, which President Reagan set up, sat for three years under the chairmanship of Judge Irving R. Kaufman. Its terms of reference were to investigate the power and activities of 'traditional organised crime' and 'emerging crime groups'.

In their evidence to the Commission, law enforcement officers continued to insist that traditional organised crime was identical with the activities of the Cosa Nostra. However, they also stressed the activities of other groups in the field, including motorcycle gangs, prison gangs and other emerging 'foreign-based' organisations. The most profitable criminal activity identified was drug trafficking: something in which all groups were involved to a greater or lesser extent. Even some of its members regarded the work of the Commission as a missed opportunity to tackle organised crime; but its recommendations were a serious attempt to produce policies to deal with the problem. These included efforts to suppress illicit drug markets, extended measures to seize criminal assets, and the use of more wiretaps, informants and undercover operations.

Critics have suggested that the Kaufman Commission's only real purpose was to maintain public support for the existing government policies on organised crime. The American people had been encouraged to see organised crime as the product of separate major organisations, rather than the output of fluid networks of smaller ones. For Woodiwiss (2001: 310–11), the Kaufman Commission represented a 'dumbing-down' of the discourse on organised crime within the USA itself. It allowed the government to avoid confronting the faults in US laws and institutions, leaving tougher and more unworkable policing as the only option.

The 'ethnic succession thesis' and the new pluralism

Despite the fact that the findings of the Kefauver and McClellan Committees had focused on Italian-American involvement in organised crime, by the early 1970s it was clear that other ethnic groups were also involved. Building on his earlier work on crime groups of Italian origin, Ianni (1974) carried out research into the activities of black and Hispanic ethnic groups. In work that echoed some of the claims of Thrasher (1927), Zorbaugh (1929) and members of the Chicago School, Ianni described the systematic takeover of whole areas of criminal activity by black and Puerto Rican networks. According to Ianni (1974), the only way in which ghetto dwellers in the American cities could escape from their underclass status was by the interdependent routes of crime and politics. In his words:

> the aspiring ethnic, blocked from legitimate access to wealth and power, is permitted to produce and provide those illicit goods and services that society publicly condemns but privately demands – gambling, stolen goods, illegal alcohol, sex and drugs – but not without paying tribute to the political establishment.
>
> (1974: 107–8)

These ethnic groups developed their abilities and involvement in organised crime through their experience of street gangs and prison culture. They were also closely integrated into local ethnic communities. As such, organised crime is a functional part of the American social system. For Ianni (1974), it is inevitable that there will be an ethnic succession in organised crime under such circumstances. As it became for the Italian-American immigrants in the earlier part of the twentieth century, so it becomes for succeeding ethnic groups. Ethnic succession persists and transcends the involvement of any particular group. It is a function of social and economic life, falling on a continuum that has the legitimate business world at the other end.

Of course, it is possible to level the accusation that Ianni's thesis is simply the 'alien conspiracy thesis' updated to reflect urban life in the late twentieth century. Members of ethnic groups simply replace the alien immigrants of the earlier theory. However, according to Ianni, to say that certain groups are prevalent in the activity is not to say that organised crime is ethnically bound. It is possible to find the roots of organised crime correlated with deprived urban social conditions, particularly in the ghetto. The development of such groups where there is a lack of effective social order and economic opportunity promotes a growing sense of militancy, some of which manifests itself in a type of criminal solidarity. Organised crime in these groups is therefore a product of their poverty and powerlessness, not of black or Hispanic cultures per se (Ianni 1974: 325–6).

In addition to the growing involvement of contemporary black and Hispanic gangs, other groups were also increasingly active. Much of the criminological evidence that the 1983–5 President's Commission on Organized Crime accepted pointed towards the fragmentation of organised crime and the growth of non-traditional forms alongside the pre-existing Irish, Italian and Jewish gangs. Asian crime gangs, youth gangs, prison gangs and motorcycle gangs were all in evidence by the early 1970s. These groups have continued to proliferate.

The growth of the activities of Asian crime groups in the USA has been evident over many years (see Chapter 5). During the 1980s, Chinese gangs had the reputation of being the largest importers of heroin into the USA. Currently, they are also active in the smuggling of people and in protection rackets. In an extensive discussion of the growth of Chinatown gangs, Chin (1996b) suggests that although many members of Chinese gangs in the USA are foreign-born, American-born Chinese are also increasingly becoming involved. In Chinese gangs, such as the Green Dragons and the Fuk Ching, many of the members are adolescents. However, they often have close affiliation to adult Triad and Tong gangs. According to Chin, Chinese gangs establish their own territory but have no distinct divisions of labour. Those senior to them mainly assign lower level members to their tasks. Both the Triads and Tongs provide mentors for youths to nurture their criminal careers, but the youth gangs are generally separate from the adult groups. The structure of the Triad gangs was discussed in Chapter 5. However, like other organised crime groups, they do not comprise a criminal cartel. Chin argues that his extensive research shows that in the USA there is no 'Chinese Mafia' with a cohesive chain of command.

Chapter 2 examined the structure and goals of youth and street gangs. According to Lyman and Potter (2004: 271), youth gang activity in the USA expanded during the 1970s and 1980, mainly due to the growing market in illicit drugs. A National Institute of Justice Survey in 1991 identified 3,876 gangs comprising over 200,000 members across 79 of the largest cities in the USA. Members range in age from 8 to 25 years of age. Such gangs are often characterised by their use of firearms, including automatic weapons, and are violent and predatory. Drug dealing is often the predominant activity. Large black gangs, such as the Los Angeles-based Crips, have many thousands of members organised into 'sets', each of which may have between 30 and 100 members. Brantley and Di Rosa (1994) claim that the Crips were organising these sets into a nationwide super gang with a chief-executive style leadership. Their main rivals (the Bloods) are a smaller gang but with similar aims. Authorities estimated the combined membership for both gangs in Los Angeles at over 80,000. Hispanic gangs, such as Los Angeles' Inca Boys and the NSM (North Side Mafia) are also significant, following the patterns set by the

Crips and the Bloods. Whether such gangs are part of 'organised crime' remains a matter of debate. Although some of the smaller and less violent 'sets' might not qualify, the activities of many appear to do so. Their use of firearms, the extent of their activities and the degree to which they subscribe to a common culture using violent methods that ensure solidarity indicates that organising forces are at work (Lyman and Potter 2004: 271–81).

Outlaw motorcycle gangs have provided an important element in organised crime in the USA since the 1960s. Lyman and Potter (2004: 282–94) provide a useful assessment of the extent of such gangs, their activities and the degree of their organisation. It is clearly not right to subsume all of the 800 motorcycle gangs operating in the USA under the rubric of 'organised crime'. However, the authorities regard the major gangs such as the Hell's Angels, the Outlaws, the Pagans and the Bandidos as engaged in organised crime activities. These gangs have clear structures. They are organised into 'chapters', with national officers, road captains, sergeants-at-arms and a hierarchy of members. The gangs operate as enforcers and manufacturers of illegal drugs. They have been involved in virtually every type of criminal activity, including prostitution, gun-running, theft, extortion and murder. Sometimes they have operated in collusion with other organised crime groups, including on one occasion, the Gambino family. They routinely make use of sophisticated communications and surveillance technology and firearms. In his analysis of the activities of outlaw motorcycle groups, Wolf (1991) points to the subculture of machismo that exists within the groups. The gangs exclude women from formal participation but in fact they play an important social role. Women fall into one of three main categories: 'broads', who drift in and out of the subculture; 'mamas', who maintain socio-sexual relations and sometimes an economic role; and 'ol' ladies', who have more permanent relations as wives or girlfriends. The role of women seems to be mainly to provide a means of defining the masculinity of male members of the organisation. The law enforcement agencies have prosecuted members of all of the outlaw motorcycle gangs for organised crime-related offences at various times (Lyman and Potter 2004: 287–94).

In contrast to the gang-related activity by black, Hispanic, Asian and outlaw motorcycle gangs, much organised crime in the USA falls into the 'enterprise crime' category that Chapter 3 discussed in some detail. Woodiwiss (2001) sets out a critical account of the industrial and corporate racketeering that took place from the 1950s onwards. Exceptionally high levels of growth in the economy during this period provided new opportunities for both gangsters and businessmen to indulge in racketeering on a massive scale. Prominent among those who took advantage of this post-war prosperity were those who sought to profit from illegal pay-offs and kickbacks associated with labour racketeering in transport and on the waterfronts of America. Control of the Teamsters Union by gangsters such as Jimmy Hoffa ensured that they could plunder pension funds with impunity and operate kickback schemes with little challenge. Concerted attacks on Hoffa and other union leaders by Robert Kennedy during the late 1960s began to counter this threat. The demise of union power during the Reagan presidency of the 1980s severely reduced union membership. As a result, according to Woodiwiss, gangsters are now rarely needed as union busters (Woodiwiss 2001: 312–25).

The extent of corporate racketeering in this period is also remarkable. Price-fixing in supposedly fair public tenders costs US consumers millions of dollars. Woodiwiss quotes the claim by Box (1983) that the proceeds of these scandals amounted to more money than was stolen in all the country's robberies, burglaries and larcenies during the years when price-fixing occurred (Woodiwiss 2001: 326). Most prominent among the corporate scandals during the 1980s are those that involved savings and loan institutions. The savings and loan (S&L or 'thrifts') network took deposits and offered mortgages to potential property owners and investors. In the period before the Reagan presidency, these schemes were highly regulated. They suffered severely in the inflation of the 1970s. The deregulation introduced by the Reagan regime in the 1980s released them from the financial limitations that hitherto had made them unprofitable. Together with the new Federal guarantees that protected them, deregulation of S&L schemes presented a unique opportunity for greedy and corrupt businessmen. Long-shot investments, speculative real estate loans and 'cash for dirt' transactions were examples of the extreme risk-taking that accompanied many S&L schemes. 'Looting', collective embezzlement and illegal loans lined the pockets of those who ran them. According to Punch:

> The deviance inspired by this new opportunity structure was rich and creative. It inspired a new cynical vocabulary of terms such as 'land flips', 'dead cows', 'dead horses', 'daisy chains' and 'cash for trash'…Some quipped that S&L stood for 'squander and liquidate'.
>
> (1996: 16)

Some schemes did not begin with the intention of becoming deviant. Corrupt businessmen formed others with the sole intention of milking the thrifts for all they were worth (Punch 1996: 18). It is not possible to confirm with total accuracy the extent of the fraud perpetrated during the S&L scandals. According to Woodiwiss, estimates suggest that it would cost $200 billion to bail out insolvent thrifts and the total bill would be around $500 billion by 2021. Against this huge bill, the average prison term for convicted S&L fraudsters was around two years (Woodiwiss 2001: 329). Do the actions of these involved in these scandals amount to organised crime? Although the fraud was not ostensibly perpetrated by gangsters, those responsible for the crimes associated with the S&L scandals could not have committed them without a considerable amount of organising. In some cases, especially where fraud was clearly deliberate from the outset, there is little difficulty in answering that question in the affirmative.

Environmental crime and the disposal of dangerous waste are scandals of major proportions in the USA. Although not within the US homeland, the Bhopal tragedy that killed up to 5,000 people in India in 1984 was a result of extreme negligence by an American corporation. The dumping of large amounts of toxic chemical waste near Niagara Falls between 1947 and 1952 is an example of corporate crime that corrupt business has repeated in other parts of the USA. Woodiwiss provides an extensive account of these events and their consequences (Woodiwiss 2001: 334–6). Organisations that care for little else than their profits are often guilty of negligence or reckless conduct. Executives of corporations operating with recklessness that affects the safety of communities are in no different position from the individual who acts with recklessness towards another individual. They are equally culpable. Where there is evidence of the operation of an organising group, it may well be right to include such actions and omissions within the rubric of organised crime. The question of whether these activities amount to 'organised crime' should also be judged against the criteria which we examined in Chapter 1.

Many of the cases cited above relate to organised crime committed within the USA itself. Although this may span several of the states of the Union, it is usually not international in character. Often its effects are localised, relating to limited numbers of corporate or individual victims. The USA is often the end-user of illicit products, such as drugs, or the recipient of illegal immigrants, or the domicile of victims of fraud committed by groups from outside its jurisdiction. In other cases, especially in relation to the effects of corporate crime, it has cultural, social, political and economic influences beyond the borders of the USA. For example, the influence of American organised crime in Canada is evident. Readers with an interest in the development of organised crime in that country should see Beare (1996). There are also many examples of contact between US organised crime networks and those in other parts of the world, for example, in the connections between outside drug producers and traffickers and distributors within the USA.

It is important not to make the mistake (as happened in the case of Italian-American organised crime from the very start) of assuming that there are direct organisational links with an ethnic homeland, but there are undoubtedly connections. For example, Asian organised crime appears to have a true diaspora, with linkages in the USA and many other countries. The globalisation of commerce and communications has also made it inevitable that there will be linkages across many jurisdictions. What is of perpetual interest for students of US organised crime, however, is the extent of its adaptability and the relationship that it has with local, national and international politics. It seems unlikely that it will cease to generate such interest in the near future.

Goodfellas: gangsterism and the cult of celebrity

The extent to which organised crime has penetrated the very fabric of American life is an important question. The American fascination for crime has a long history, especially in the cinema. In this respect, it probably mirrors aspects of US culture more generally. Bell (1960) argued that, for the American, the heroic virtues were to be found in the duel with morality:

> The American was 'the hunter, cowboy, frontiersman, the soldier, the naval hero' – and in the crowded slums, the gangster. He was a man with a gun, acquiring by personal merit what was denied him by complex orderings of stratified society. And the duel with the law was the morality play par excellence; the gangster, with whom ride our own illicit desires, and the prosecutor, representing final judgement and the force of law.
>
> (Bell 1960: 117)

The gangster has therefore played an important but paradoxical role as an icon celebrating freedom of action in the face of a wide range of circumstances: ranging from the necessity of acting in the face of social and economic deprivation to the moral ambiguities of illicit wealth. Although most Americans do not become actual gangsters, they can at least have a vicarious share of the supposed heroism that the entertainment industry provides.

Representations of gangsterdom in American cinema are extensive. Early examples include *Little Caesar* (1931) starring Edward G. Robinson, *The Public Enemy* (1931), starring James Cagney and Jean Harlow, and *Angels with Dirty Faces* (1938), starring James Cagney, Pat O'Brien and Humphrey Bogart. These films represented the gangster as an extraordinary individual often in violent conflict with competitors, with the law and with society itself. James Cagney in *White Heat* (1949) depicted the gangster at his most psychopathic. *The Enforcer* (1951), which starred Humphrey Bogart, received the privilege of a prologue from Senator Estes Kefauver, extolling the importance of bringing top criminals to justice.

Many of the films made during this period depicted violence and syndicated crime in terms of flawed individuals, driven by greed and by the need for power. However, only a few of the characters in the genre during the period from the 1930s to the 1950s were portrayed as all bad, a fact possibly influenced by the involvement of real gangsters in the Hollywood film industry. This was the heyday of the gangster film, although it represented a way of life that was far from what most audiences had personally experienced. The depiction of behaviour apparently devoid of moral scruple on screen seemed to heighten public fascination with the genre. Gangster life, like that of the gunslinger in the iconography of the Old West, represented a heroic struggle against malevolent forces to which people could relate.

More recently, films such as the *Godfather* series (1972, 1974, 1990), *Once Upon a Time in America* (1984) and *Goodfellas* (1990), have attempted to portray gangster life in America's crime families, presenting a more humanistic, nuanced and morally ambivalent account of the impact of organised crime on individuals, their families and associates. *Film noir* offerings such as *Chinatown* (1974) and the more recent *L.A. Confidential* (1997) depict organised crime per se, rather than subsuming it under the mantle of gangsterdom. These films have tended to contrast the individualistic freedom of action represented by the gangster role with the more all-enveloping, pervasive nature of organised crime in the American cities.

In contrast, films such as Quentin Tarantino's *Reservoir Dogs* (1992) and *Pulp Fiction* (1994) tend to illustrate gratuitous rather than strategic or tactical gang violence. Of course, one can always argue that such films provide moral lessons. In the case of *Reservoir*

Dogs, some commentators argue that the several attempts by the psychopathic gangsters in the film to define their 'profession' may help the audience 'deconstruct the criminal subculture as a parody of "legitimate capitalism"' (Fox and McDonagh 2003: 630). That violence and the gangster genre will continue to intrigue the public is not in doubt. For example, the film version of *The Gangs of New York* (2002), loosely based upon Herbert Asbury's writings on New York gangs first published in 1927, provides a highly stylised, violent illustration of early American city gang life in period costume.

At the lighter end of the show business spectrum, musicals such as *Guys and Dolls* (1955) cloak gangsterdom with the pseudo-respectability of light comedy. Leonard Bernstein's *West Side Story* (1961) romanticises the lives of street gangs, in a modern version of Shakespeare's *Romeo and Juliet*. The children's musical film *Bugsy Malone* (1976) encourages new generations to celebrate the gangster idiom, without the need for a moment's serious thought. More recently, gangster chic was alive and well in the 2002 cinema remake of Bob Fosse's stylish stage musical *Chicago*. There is little doubt that these shows fall into the category of 'light entertainment'. It is less than clear, however, why gang life should provide such a popular vehicle for such productions.

The extent to which some parts of the entertainment industry have first-hand experience of gangsterdom is worth examining. There is certainly clear evidence of a real relationship between gang life and show business. Munn (1993) sets out a detailed review of the connection between Hollywood, as the centre of the US film industry, and major figures in the world of organised crime. He produces evidence showing that in its heyday this relationship was a two-way street. Not only did gang leaders such as Charles 'Lucky' Luciano and Al Capone compete to control aspects of the Hollywood film industry during the 1930s, but celebrities from within the industry such as actors Virginia Hill, Jean Harlow and George Raft were also happy to have deeper, romantic or financial involvements with top gangsters. Luciano's involvement in Hollywood began with supplying drugs to celebrities and developed into wider financial depredations. His henchman in this enterprise, the notorious Benny 'Bugsy' Seigel, ran the film extras union during the 1930s, drawing protection money from the studios amounting to millions of dollars a year (Munn 1993: 136). The film *Bugsy* (1991) starring Warren Beatty as Seigel and Annette Bening as Virginia Hill provides a somewhat unconvincing portrait of Seigel's involvement in Hollywood during this period.

According to Munn, the film actor George Raft was heavily involved with organised crime over many years and was a long time friend of 'Bugsy' Seigel. Munn says: 'George Raft was the one major movie star who was a gangster both on and off the screen' (Munn 1993: 9). Sam Giancana, who took over the Chicago syndicates in the 1950s, sponsored a number of Hollywood stars, including Marilyn Monroe (Munn 1993: 228–9). Giancana, who was also associated with John F. Kennedy, survived until 1975, when a member of his own organisation shot him dead (Lyman and Potter 2004: 108–9). Reports by journalists and from official sources also provide evidence of connections between the singer Frank Sinatra, politicians and members of syndicated crime in the USA (Lyman and Potter 2004: 452, 463).

There is evidence that some high profile gangsters regarded their real-life activities as a form of show business in themselves. Leading figures in organised crime in the USA, such as Al Capone and John Gotti, certainly manipulated the cult of celebrity. While this was no doubt for the purpose of self-aggrandisement, it may also have had the more practical aim of encouraging public support which might someday be useful in evading legal responsibilities.

In popular music, the development of so-called 'gangsta rap' in the 1990s showed that the gangster theme was also fascinating to young people. The extent to which some musicians and singers were actually involved in crime alongside the music is also evident. The death of music and film idol Tupac ('2pac') Amaru Shakar in Las Vegas in September 1996 in a Crips versus Bloods drive-by shooting remains controversial. Subsequently, Tupac has become an icon to the many that admire his lifestyle and music. The white rap artist Eminem has also given apparent support in his music to gang culture and the use of firearms. The conviction in 2002 of a member of the British band So Solid Crew for gun-related crime shows that some musicians do not merely confine their activities to the music itself.

There is a real danger, however, in being dismissive about gangsta rap or providing a superficial analysis of a complex phenomenon. In her exemplary study of the genre, Quinn (2005) argues that gangsta rap is deeply rooted in the political and social disenfranchisement that black youth could not express because of the decline in the culture of black protest during the 1970s and thereafter:

> Gangsta captures in vigorous terms the values of an increasingly non-politicized generation, which has seen political protests lose

much of their resonance. Its mode of critique is to dramatize how and why young, disenfranchised people fall short in their civic engagement and protest strategies.

(Quinn 2005: 15)

Quinn emphasises the importance of the responses of black youth to such exclusion in the development of gangsta rap. These include the expansion of gang membership through recruitment of black and Latino youth, the effects of the penal system in producing solidarity; and their negative reaction to law enforcement and to mainstream social institutions. The development of the music is in symbiosis with these real-world responses. Gang members 'were already narrativizing their own past and planned exploits, drawing on a mixture of personal experience, local tales and mainstream pop culture.' (Quinn 2005: 55). Rappers such as Snoop Dogg performed at gang meetings. Rap themes included such things as territorial identity, covert action, gun imagery and subcultural tastes and practices (Quinn 2005: 59). Quinn also identifies the changes in gangsta rap, from the earlier more expressive culture towards a more overt commercialism in later examples. Quinn's deconstruction of the gangsta rap genre is a highly detailed account of a phenomenon that assesses its role in the development of American culture, its effects on youth and its relationship to crime. She shows the extent to which a powerful medium can influence both those who are deeply involved in its messages and the public sphere more widely.

In contrast to the influence of film and music, the growth of gangster chic in fashion is perhaps a phenomenon of which even a profound sceptic should not make too much fuss. Preferences for T-shirts with apparent endorsements of criminal allegiances, dark suits, black shirts, white ties and dark glasses, and other stereotypical gangster-related forms of dress do not necessarily imply that gang culture is taking over society. The gangster chic phenomenon in fashion may be part of a lifestyle rebellion by some groups. It may be an ephemeral style promoted by fashion houses or simply a passing fad. However, as critics of modernity such as Roland Barthes argue, clothes are carriers of information. They are systems of signs and indicators of allegiance and belief (Barthes 1983). Alongside the public fascination with the gangster genre in cinema, stage, literature and music, gangster chic in fashion is a phenomenon that should claim critical attention.

The fascination with gangsterdom and organised crime is not confined to the USA. It is difficult to be sure, however, whether this is due to the pervasive influence of the American entertainment industry or whether the same attachments to the iconic image of the gangster exist elsewhere in the world. The similarities are evident in books, cinema, the theatre, music and fashion from the 1930s onwards. In Britain, Graham Greene's *Brighton Rock* (1938) illustrated the impact of gangster life and violence on a provincial seaside town and its racetrack. Although it makes an important moral statement about the life and times of local bad boys, one is entitled to suspect that the lives of gang members were more exciting to the reading public than the moral lessons that Greene provided. In France, Jean Genet both took part in crime and promoted crime as lifestyle by means of books and plays. In Britain, recent excursions into gangster literature include Jake Arnott's *The Long Firm* (1999), *He Kills Coppers* (2001) and *True Crime* (2003). Even a minimal amount of observation of high street and airport booksellers will reveal the extent to which the public in Britain and elsewhere is now addicted to gangster and crime fiction.

British cinema represents the gangster image somewhat differently from the American cinema, although there are links between them (Chibnall and Murphy 1999). MGM UK's *Get Carter* (1971) provided a moral tale with an outcome that looked like just desserts for the main protagonist. Others have sought to present quasi-documentary accounts of the lives of contemporary gangsters. Films in this genre such as *The Krays* (1990) have provided welcome outlets for actors who like to be dressed to kill. More recently, hard-man films, such as *Lock, Stock and Two Smoking Barrels* (1998) and *Essex Boys* (2000) have added to the British contribution to this genre, although reviews have sometimes been less than complimentary.

The connections between gangland and show business are almost as evident in Britain as they are in the USA. The Kray brothers (see Chapter 8) made many contacts in the world of show business and politics, including Lord Boothby and the ubiquitous George Raft. In fact, the Home Office took Raft's involvement in organised crime and gambling and syndicated crime so seriously that, in 1967, Home Secretary Roy Jenkins declared him *persona non grata* in the UK. This action prevented Raft, who was to become the front man for the Colony Club in London's West End, an establishment allegedly controlled by Meyer Lansky, from further involvement in gambling ventures within the UK. The Home Office also banned Lansky, along with a number of others reputed to have connections with organised crime (Munn 1993: 249–57). Society photographer David Bailey photographed the Krays with many show business celebrities during the 1960s. Other show business people were also associated with organised crime in a variety of ways. For example, the popular actress Barbara Windsor was married to a gangster (Ronnie Knight) who was involved in serious crime. More recently, British actor Jamie Foreman, son of Kray gang associate Freddie Foreman, has specialised in playing art-imitates-life parts in film and TV roles, including *Gangster No. 1* (2000) and *Family* (2003).

The list seems endless. On both sides of the Atlantic, the entertainment industry continues to add gangster genre titles to supplement seemingly never-ending examples of its alter ego, the cop drama. Television schedules are awash with fictional and documentary examples. Only the funeral of the Princess of Wales, with 19.29 million viewers, stopped the television programme *Heartbeat* being the most watched programme of 1997 with 18.35 million viewers (Mawby 2003: 218). Of course, one might maintain that such works are simply good entertainment or moral tales, over which one should not draw curmudgeonly and unwarranted conclusions. Perhaps the entertainment industry has good reasons to promote this material in terms of return on investment and audience ratings. However, this does not explain the seemingly insatiable appetite of the public in the USA, Britain and elsewhere for gangster-related material across the entertainment spectrum.

In summary, what conclusions may a neutral observer draw from the fact that gangster life fascinates the public, the media and the entertainment industry almost to the point of obsession? Clearly, most members of the public and people working in the entertainment industry have no personal involvement in gang activity. Rather, the evidence points either to a kind of moral ambivalence about violence or to a vicarious addiction to risk and danger that is more exciting than mundane day-to-day existence. Public ambivalence is evident in the difference in attitudes between the reality of gang life and its consequences and its appearances in gangster genre works in the field of entertainment. On one hand, there is real fear of gangs within some communities. This includes fear of violent crime, such as drive-by shootings. On the other hand, the high degree of fascination among the public at large for gang life provides evidence of a degree of celebration of the gangster genre and its associated violence. It is difficult to believe that public interest in gangsters is simply for the purpose of mindless entertainment. The very existence of gangsters and former gangsters as celebrities illustrates the extent to which an observer should take this phenomenon seriously. As Bell (1960) rightly claimed, organised crime is part of an American way of life. Having said that, the reason why gangster chic and gang-life images are formative of public attitudes in the USA and elsewhere remains an under-researched area.

Chapter 7

New waves and the *pax mafiosa* thesis

The new types of criminal group who have challenged the prominence of syndicated crime in the US are not the only developments worthy of note in recent decades. Although they remain a significant influence, organised crime has moved beyond the era of domination by the earlier Mafia-style gangsters to a more pluralised panorama of sometimes competing and sometimes collaborating groups. This is true across the world. For example, organised crime in Europe is no longer (if it were ever such) the sole province of traditional groups like the Mafia or localised family gangs. A more widely constituted mixture of indigenous gangs, fraudsters and criminal groups from immigrant communities provide a range of illicit enterprises, covering virtually all of the activities discussed in Chapters 3 and 4. Although the word 'transnational' may be problematic, such groups are certainly active internationally. Organised crime in Russia and the post-Soviet states has also expanded rapidly following the political changes of the late 1980s. It is now a subject attracting the attention of an increasing number of analysts. The growth of organised crime in the developing world has been in parallel to these new waves of organised crime in the USA, Europe, the post-Soviet states and elsewhere.

This chapter reviews the development of these new waves and their implications. First, it reviews non-traditional forms of organised crime that have been on the increase in Europe, with a diversity of groups operating in the EU states, including Germany, the Netherlands, Britain and elsewhere. Secondly, it discusses the development of organised crime in Russia and the post-Soviet states of Eastern and Central Europe, identifying some of the key factors that have contributed to its development in this region. Thirdly, it examines the internationalisation of organised crime groups across the world, including the growth of organised crime in the developing world, setting out the debate relating to the criminogenic asymmetries that encourage this trend. The chapter concludes with a discussion of the so-called *pax mafiosa* and 'merger' theses in the work of Sterling (1994), Jamieson (1995) and Robinson (2002). These analysts have concluded that developments in organised crime provide evidence of a worldwide conspiracy between criminal groups that are ever more likely to collaborate in committing serious crime. What may appear to be pluralisation, they argue, is in fact evidence of a merger, of the development of converging international networks that are tightening their grip on commerce and business and increasingly affecting social and political stability. Here, the chapter examines in more detail the collaboration between the Mafia, Asian crime groups, Colombian drug cartels and others.

Non-traditional organised crime in Europe

The growth of organised crime in Western Europe in recent years has been significant. In comparing organised crime in the USA and Western Europe during the 1980s, Fijnaut suggested Europe differed from the USA because the activities of European criminal groups appeared primarily to follow traditional criminal operations, such as prostitution and gambling (Fijnaut 1990). At that time, organised crime had not systematically penetrated industry, government, the police and the legal system to the same extent as in the USA. Later studies, however, recognised that organised crime in Europe had begun to affect legitimate sectors of the economy, the liberal professions and the banking system. Gangs regularly used corruption, intimidation, violence and disinformation to achieve their aims (Fijnaut *et al.* 1998).

Van der Heijden (1996, 1998) confirms the continued involvement in the EU states of the main criminal groups of southern Italian origin and identifies a number of other groupings that have become prominent in European international organised crime. The Dutch, who have extensive involvement in the transportation industry, not surprisingly play a major role in smuggling drugs and illegal immigrants. Turkish, Pakistani, Chinese and other Asian groups are involved in drug trafficking. In many EU states, indigenous and immigrant groups maintain international contacts with drug trafficking networks, including those in the producing countries.

Organised crime in Britain shows many of these characteristics. There has long been evidence of 'family' origins in some groups which mimics that of Italian-American Cosa Nostra style gangs. Indeed, there is some evidence to suggest that one of the New York 'families' considered the notorious Kray gang, which was active during the 1960s, as a possible 'London connection' (Pearson 1973: 175–6). However, the scale has always been somewhat smaller and in general the activities of indigenous organised crime groups in the UK have been associated with robbery, fraud and the illicit drug trade. Chapter 8 discusses the growth of organised crime in Britain in more detail.

There are considerable temptations in assuming that organised crime in Europe is concerned only with gang activity of the kind represented by the Sicilian Mafia, Asian Triads, indigenous gangs and so on. In recent years, commentators have been encouraging a wider interpretation of international organised crime, which includes white-collar crime, money laundering and international fraud. A degree of scepticism about extensive amalgamation of European criminal groups is well justified, although some increase in cohesion is evident. Van Duyne, who expresses doubts about the merger thesis and about the possibility of a pending Mafia takeover, accepts that some groups are collaborating. According to Van Duyne, organised crime in Europe:

> was (and mainly still is) a matter of networks of separate crime enterprises some of which under favourable circumstances have grown into 'trading communities'.
>
> (1996: 109)

Key issues in relation to these trading communities include various types of cross-border crime, especially the illicit drug trade, discussed in Chapter 4 at some length. Organised cross-border fraud, including that against the EU itself, and large-scale investment and other types of corporate fraud and white-collar crime complete a complex picture. This growing (if still limited) collaboration between some criminal groups implies that a law enforcement approach confined to national jurisdictions is outdated and parochial. It does no justice to the nature of internationally operating crime enterprises (Van Duyne 1996: 111).

For further analysis of developments of organised crime in Europe, readers could usefully refer to Van der Heijden (1996, 1998) and Savona (1999, 2000) for analysis of trends in money laundering in Europe and beyond. Levi (1998) analyses the pattern of these developments. Chapter 9 examines the policies that Europe, the UN and the international community have taken to combat organised crime.

Glasnost Mafiyas? Post-Soviet organised crime

Perhaps one of the most notable trends in recent years is the growth of organised crime emanating from Russia and the post-Soviet states following the end of the Cold War. It is important to recognise that the growth of post-Soviet organised crime is not entirely due to discontinuities in social and political control between the old and the new regimes. In part at least, contemporary organised crime in Russia and elsewhere in the former 'Eastern Bloc' bears the legacy of certain kinds of organised criminality that already existed during the Soviet period. However, its more recent forms have proved to be particularly virulent, with many gangs extending their operations into the western democracies and the developing world. The full trajectory of post-Soviet organised crime is not yet clear. Analysts need to consider both best and worst case scenarios in seeking to understand the path that Russian organised crime might follow in the next two or three decades (Williams 1997). Nor is it yet entirely clear how organised crime will develop in states that were formerly under Soviet control. The growth of organised crime in the newly democratised Baltic Sea states and the states of Eastern and Central Europe is evident, although again it is difficult to predict how it will develop.

In considering Russian organised crime it is necessary from the outset to enter a cautionary note. Although there is a broad consensus that it poses a substantial threat to political and economic development in Russia and other states, a number of controversies remain. Some of these relate to ideological questions. For example, are analysts correct to regard Russian organised crime as an unavoidable outcome of the collapse of authoritarian government? Is it an example of what may happen anywhere when a state allows an unregulated free-market economy to operate? It is important to bear these questions in mind when analysing what appears, on the surface at least, to be a problem relating primarily to crime control.

According to Finckenauer and Voronin (2001: 4–5), Russian organised crime has its roots in Russian history, in particular in the seventy years of Soviet power, which only ended with the political changes of the late 1980s and early 1990s. During the Soviet period, an extensive professional criminal class came into being. Drawing upon their shared experiences as prisoners in the Russian prison system, a perverse system of rules, behaviour and values bound them together into a 'thieves' world'. An elite of criminals (*vory v zakone*), who lived according to a 'thieves' law', were their leaders. Russian organised crime grew out of this movement and out of the *nomenklatura* (the government organisation and its high-level officials). Individual *apparatchiks* developed relationships of mutual benefit with the 'thieves' world' – of benefit both to the officials themselves and to the criminals with whom they were associated.

The first Russian organised crime groups appeared at the end of the 1960s. The state apparatus not only allowed criminal activity, it encouraged, facilitated and protected it. There were three levels of activity:

- Top level activity by high level party and state officials who abused their power, across a range of markets

- Underground or shadow economy participants who exploited connections with enterprises of the state command economy for illicit gain

- Professional criminals who ran the various illegal activities such as drugs, gambling, extortion and so on.

(Finckenauer and Voronin 2001: 4–6)

The growth of private enterprise, especially the privatisation of state property, greatly accelerated the growth of organised crime. However, as Shelley (1997) rightly argues, ordinary Russian citizens seem only to have exchanged one form of authority for another.

Finckenauer and Voronin (2001: 7) maintain that this process is as much political and economic as it is criminological. Russian organised crime groups make extensive use of government apparatus to protect and promote their criminal enterprises. Most businesses in Russia, whether legal or not, must operate with the protection of a *krysha* ('roof'). Police or security officials, employed by the 'business' outside their official capacities, provide this protection. In other cases, officials are 'silent partners' in the criminal enterprises they protect.

In addition to these political and economic factors, Russian organised crime has features in common with that in other parts of the world:

- Systematic use of violence, including both the threat and the use of force;
- Hierarchical structure;
- Limited or exclusive membership;
- Specialization in types of crime and a division of labour;
- Military style discipline, with strict rules and regulations for the organization as a whole;
- Possession of high-tech equipment, including military weapons.

(Finckenauer and Voronin (2001: 6)

Analysts regard the extent of contemporary organised crime in Russia as substantial but accept that it is difficult to quantify its extent with any accuracy. According to Dunn (1997: 63), the Russian Ministry of the Interior estimates of organised gangs in Russia grew from 785 in 1990 to more than 8,000 by mid-1996. Around 120,000 people are active members of these gangs, although as many as 3 million people may be involved in different capacities. Russian organised crime controls an estimated 50,000 companies and accounts for up to 40 per cent of Russia's GNP. In this sense, it is inseparable from the Russian economy.

There are an estimated 150 gangs operating in Moscow alone. Six wield real power, including three Chechen gangs. Other major gangs operate from St Petersburg, Yekaterinburg and Vladivostok. The structure of Russian organised crime is generally hierarchical but there is little reliance on family ties in most of the gangs. In general, gangs are either of ethnic or geographic origin (Dunn 1997: 65–72). The activities of many groups are truly international in character. The Russian Ministry of the Interior estimates that around 110 Russian crime groups operate in forty-four countries, including most of the EU states. In 1994, the FBI identified groups operating in New York, Chicago and six other major American cities. Their activities ranged from the control of prostitution and pornography to extortion, car theft, drug trafficking, counterfeiting and trade in arms. Money laundering is extensive, promoting 'capital flight' from Russia itself, as well as enabling the conversion of 'dirty money' from criminal activities in Russia and elsewhere.

Russian émigré groups have been involved in billion-dollar gasoline and diesel fuel tax frauds in the USA. However, Block (1996) is sceptical about whether the criminal role of Russian émigrés in these frauds is part of a Russian '*mafiya*'. Rather, analysts should see it for what it is: 'enterprise crime':

> Analysis centred on enterprises, whether the enterprise is international drugs smuggling or money laundering for tax evasion or beating quotas on the importation of automobiles, removes the activity from the overheated world of criminal exotica in which organized crimes are typically explained by some form or other of 'mafiology'.
>
> (Block 1996: 157)

Although the press frequently refers to Russian organised crime groups as '*Mafiyas*' or '*Mafias*', the similarity between them and those operating in Italy or in the USA is questionable. Media representations tend to reaffirm orthodox interpretations of Russian organised crime as a Mafia, but their patterns of behaviour do not support this thesis. Varese (2001) and Hill (2003) have also suggested that there are similarities to the Sicilian Mafia to the extent that Russian organised crime is often concerned with the provision of protection services in the new market economy. While it is true that protection is a major activity, it is not the only factor. Most Russian crime groups are prepared to diversify their activities into such things as drug trafficking, prostitution, human smuggling or any other activity that is likely to be profitable. Rawlinson (1997, 1998) points to the danger of drawing too many parallels between them and using the term 'Mafia' in this way.

Williams (1997) has analysed Russian organised crime by drawing a contrast between two different assessments. The first postulates a worst-case scenario, summarising the views of the most sceptical thinkers about Russian organised crime. According to this scenario, it is and will remain predatory, universal and extremely violent. It is highly structured and authoritarian (notably because of its ex-KGB, MVD and strong ethnic groupings). It exhibits comparative excellence in the sense that it is more ruthless, more skilful and more successful than organisations such as the Italian Mafia, the Chinese Triads or the Colombian cartels. It has an alarming potential to deal in the worst commodities relating to terrorism, for example, nuclear materials. It has links with the Colombian cartels and other organisations, although the emergence of a *pax mafiosa* threatening global security and stability remains debatable (see below). The worst-case scenario also emphasises the political consequences of Russian organised crime: it is a threat to democracy. The collusive relationship between the Russian state and organised crime could indicate that it might even become the world's first criminal superpower (Williams 1997: 3–11).

The best-case scenario denies that Russian organised crime poses a threat to national or international security. On the contrary, it fulfils positive functions in Russian economic and social life. For example, if the state cannot enforce contracts or recover debts because of a legal deficit, people will look to organised crime to do so. It represents the ultimate form of capitalism: one that is unregulated by law or morality. On this judgement, criminal organisations are the most progressive since they are the main supporters and beneficiaries of the privatisation process. They are the equivalent of the 'robber baron' entrepreneurs of the nineteenth century who played an important part in the industrialisation of the USA. As social and political reform proceeds, so organised crime will become normalised, in the sense that commerce will assimilate it into normal business processes. There will be a gradual transition from illicit to licit business (Williams 1997: 5–7).

Williams rightly emphasises that both approaches have serious shortcomings. The worst-case thinkers, he argues, are too mesmerised by the threat from Russian organised crime to assess it critically, while the best-case analysts are too enamoured of a free-market economy to accept its limitations. Who is right will probably depend on whether the early generations of capitalists want to legitimise their businesses and accept more regulation. In short, will there be a gradual 'cleansing process'? In contrast, in the worst-case model, organised crime will increasingly be the dominant force in Russian society. In these conditions, corruption becomes the all-pervasive phenomenon, 'leading ultimately to a collusive relationship between the Russian State and Russian organised crime' (Williams 1997: 26). Only the judgement of history will confirm one or other of these outcomes.

The growth of organised crime in the so-called 'transitional' states of Eastern and Central Europe has contributed to the new wave of problems that are confronting the international community. Organised crime in the Czech Republic, Hungary, Poland and the Baltic Sea states has caused concern in Europe, not least because most of these states became part of the EU in 2004. However, organised crime in these states is not only of Russian origin. Indigenous groups have emerged in the wake of the political changes of the 1990s and have formed international alliances. As such, they have become part of the pattern of European organised crime, collaborating with existing networks in Europe and beyond.

Hungary provides a useful case study to illustrate the problems of organised crime in the newly democratised states of Eastern and Central Europe. Billings (1997) provides a chronology of events in Hungary from October 1980 to March 1998. See also Wright (1997) for an earlier version of the following points. In Hungary, the change from a one-party state to democracy was comparatively rapid. During 1989, political changes took place through which the former regime was replaced by a system of parliamentary democracy. The new regime held free elections and a new constitution guaranteed fundamental human rights. Privatisation accompanied the decline of central state control. Large state companies were sold off and the new regime encouraged the ownership of private property. Since 1989, there have been further reforms and increasing entrepreneurial activity in the business sector.

Organised crime in Hungary developed in three phases. In the 1970s, the police successfully acted against several organised crime groups based on kinship. Their organisation and methods resembled those of the Sicilian Mafia in its earlier format. By the early 1980s, however, organised crime groups not based upon family allegiances began to appear, mainly involved in property crime. This continued until 1984–5, when their leaders seriously started to convert the proceeds of crime into legal enterprises. The state permitted a degree of privatisation during this period and many who had become rich from crime bought into legitimate businesses, including restaurants and night clubs. Because they had bought into prominent positions in the leisure industry, some were also able to advance their criminal activities through the control of prostitution and gambling.

The change of regime in 1989–90 brought about the third phase of this development. The further privatisation of property meant that those who had acquired substantial financial resources could more easily put their money into business and could operate more openly in the economic domain. Their influence extended into public law, politics and international relations. The fertile conditions provided by the opening of borders to foreign visitors and refugees, and the problems of unemployment and inflation, also served to fuel the growth of organised crime.

By the mid-1990s, the range of activity of criminal gangs in Hungary had become extensive. The development of power struggles between rival gangs in Hungary was no surprise to external observers. Gangs in Budapest struggled for control of a wide range of rackets from the control of prostitution to gaming and drugs. In November 1996, the killing of Josef Prisztas, following seven hand-grenade explosions outside nightclubs, served to raise public awareness and fear of organised criminal gangs in the capital. Prisztas was a well-known figure in the criminal underworld and police are said to believe that his killing was linked to the grenade attacks as the city's ten main gang leaders stepped up their so-called 'turf wars' over the control of sex and gambling.

Because of their ready availability, gangs used military grenades in many of these attacks. Twenty-six incidents of this kind took place in Hungary during 1996 alone. Although these incidents appear to be internecine, their effect upon the public imagination and fear of crime was extensive. In Budapest in 1998 a car bomb exploded in the city's busiest shopping district killing four people, including a police informant and his lawyer and injuring twenty-five bystanders. This was one of around 150 gangland-style attacks during this period and the police linked it to the growing presence of Russian organised crime in Hungary.

Along with other jurisdictions in Eastern and Central Europe, Hungary has become an important junction for international organised crime. Although other cities are also centres for gang activity, the ideal location of Budapest as a base for criminal gangs has helped to consolidate the development of international organised crime in Hungary. Most of the so-called *Mafiyas* of Eastern Europe (Russian, Ukrainian, Serbian and Bulgarian) have branches there. However, there is also evidence that organised crime exists in other cities. For example, during the mid-1990s, Hungarians called Szeged '*Mafiya* City' because of its prevalence there.

The activities of organised criminal groups cover most of those with which the West has long been familiar. Money laundering, gangland conflicts over the control of prostitution and gambling, drug trafficking, trade in stolen motor vehicles, trading in arms and radioactive substances, various forms of economic crime and corruption have all been evident. Hungary still has an extensive cash economy and as such is particularly vulnerable to money laundering. Events in the former Yugoslavia have clearly exacerbated the problems of organised crime in Hungary, which has provided a ready market for stolen vehicles, arms and counterfeit currency. The Hungarian market has reportedly received investments from profits gained from the extensive operation of organised crime in the Ukraine.

One major influence on the expansion of organised crime in Hungary has been the collapse of the power structures of the old regime. This has weakened state control, especially by those institutions that formerly exercised strong direct controls over crime. The authorities (especially the police) are only slowly acquiring the degree of strength and legitimacy that the new environment requires. The government can only solve these difficulties through a wide range of ameliorative measures, including changes in law and measures to improve the professionalism of the police.

The Hungarian government has put into place a number of measures to deal with organised crime. In 1995, Istvan Nikolitis, the Minister for the Secret Services, set up a special task force to combat the so-called 'mafiyas' and to prevent international criminals gaining a foothold in the country's political establishment. Their main brief included investigating large transfers of money. The government also instituted an organised crime department to work under the direct supervision of the national Director of Crime. This department had little success, due to the general low level of resources and experience. The Hungarian national police disbanded this unit in 1999 after it failed to make a single major arrest.

Hungary has also received assistance from other governments in dealing with the problems of international organised crime. Police in Britain, France, Germany, Holland and other EU states have provided organisational and technical support. There is operational co-operation with the Austrian, Belgian, British, Dutch, German (Bundeskriminalamt) and Italian police, both bilaterally and through the EU. There are also regular contacts at the strategic level on issues such as drugs and vehicle crime. In 1989, Hungary signed the Vienna Convention on Drugs and Psychotropic Substances. The Hungarian government has also built up working contacts with the Ukrainian and Russian authorities.

However, the USA has become the predominant partner in providing support, training and advice on organised crime. The FBI has provided advice on witness protection, plea bargaining and the use of undercover agents. There is regular contact between the Hungarian police and the regional offices of the FBI and the US Drug Enforcement Administration (DEA) in Vienna. In 1994, the Hungarian National Police and the FBI signed a co-operation agreement to combat organised crime. This agreement included a framework for information-sharing to help the police track and prosecute members of international criminal networks in Eastern and Central Europe. In a speech to senior Hungarian police officers, FBI director Louis

Freeh said that there was evidence that Russian and other criminal organisations were forming links with Sicilian, Colombian and Asian criminal networks. Activities cited included drug trafficking, public corruption and international trade in nuclear materials. He urged the use of more electronic surveillance methods to infiltrate organised crime. The development of the international police academy in Budapest, financed with the help of $3 million in aid from the USA, illustrates the extent of American commitment to the prevention of the growth of organised crime in this region.

Early in 2000, at the 'request' of the Hungarian government, the FBI set up an office in Budapest with agents working as full-time investigators with authority to carry firearms. Although Hungarian officers work alongside the FBI, in fact the Hungarian government has conceded a considerable amount of sovereignty to a foreign state that is outside the EU. This may be a model for similar US 'outreach' activities in the Baltic States, South Africa and elsewhere. In 2000, targets of the Budapest FBI office included Seymon Mogilevich, a Russian who has operated out of Budapest for a decade. His crime interests include forced prostitution, gun-running and trade in illegal nuclear materials. US investigators have linked him to a vast money-laundering scheme at the Bank of New York. Other targets include the Moscow Solntsevskaya gang, allegedly headed by Sergei Mikailov, who the FBI believes is using Budapest as a base.

The effectiveness of judicial co-operation alone has clearly not convinced either the Hungarian or the US governments. The reason for US operational involvement seems reasonably clear. It is a reflection of wider US foreign policy. It is better to defend US interests on the Danube than on the Delaware. On the other hand, the Hungarian authorities have taken the need for real support very seriously. In a speech in Hungary's National Assembly just four hours after the bomb blast in central Budapest that killed four people, the prime minister designate Victor Orban pledged tough new measures to deal with organised crime and disorder. In seeking US support, the Hungarians have probably made the right choice. On the evidence, they would have to wait a considerable time for any EU measures to become effective, despite the requirement which the EU places upon new entrants to accept both Schengen and Europol.

In summary, the processes of democratisation and privatisation since the demise of communism in 1989 have clearly accelerated the growth of organised crime in Russia and in the former Soviet states. The hiatus between the demise of state power and the development of a true civil society has been the fertile ground upon which organised crime has flourished. It is worth remembering, however, that in Hungary, Poland, the Czech Republic and some of the Baltic Sea states, the process of accession to the EU has ensured the development of regulatory structures and agencies for the control of international organised crime. In other states, especially in the Balkans, governments and the international community have much more to do.

Globalisation and the internationalisation of organised crime

Globalisation of commerce and communications has produced new victims of organised crime and new perpetrators. Although criminals from developing states have preyed upon the West, developing states have also become victims of international organised crime, both directly and indirectly. Passas (1998: 22–3) argues that some analysts do not fully understand the significance of the process of globalisation for international organised crime. Most analyses, he suggests, focus on the type of cross-border misconduct (such as drug trafficking, people trafficking, money laundering or white-collar crime) without understanding the underlying nature of the problem. He maintains that it is possible to trace the causes of corporate crime and other illegal enterprise to 'criminogenic asymmetries'. These he defines as:

> structural disjunctions, mismatches and inequalities in the spheres of politics, culture, the economy and the law. Asymmetries are criminogenic in that (1) they generate or strengthen the demand for illegal goods and services; (2) they generate incentives for particular actors to participate in illegal transactions; and (3) they reduce the ability of authorities to control illegal activities.
>
> (Passas 1998: 22–3)

The globalisation of commerce and communication exacerbates these asymmetries. It undermines the sovereignty of nation states, which are thereby less able to regulate cross-border business transactions. Globalisation reinforces inequalities of power and wealth both within nation states and between them. Typically, these inequalities are most visible between the states of the West/North in the developed world, and those of the South, among the developing countries. Economic crime therefore becomes even more of a possibility for organised crime groups across this divide. The fragmentation of enterprises and transactions over more than one country produces many opportunities for illicit activity (Passas 1998). Unless the international community recognises the need to develop holistic approaches to international organised crime based on asymmetries of the kind Passas describes, it is unlikely that the problem will be contained. This especially applies to drug trafficking and people trafficking, some of the debates discussed in Chapter 4. For insightful perspectives on these problems, see also Ryan and Rush (1998) and Viano (1999).

Organised crime groups will operate in any jurisdiction where they are able to make a profit. This applies not only to the major groups we have already examined but also to groups from other jurisdictions who have found new ways in which to make money. The activities of organised crime groups whose origins are in the developing countries are also becoming evident. In Africa, for example, organised crime groups from Benin, Ghana, Nigeria, Sierra Leone and South Africa have been increasingly evident (Lyman and Potter 2004: 363–6). Although space does not permit an exhaustive review on a region-by-region basis, the development of international organised crime in Nigeria provides a good example of this phenomenon.

Nigeria is only one of a number of states in the developing world where globalisation has enabled organised crime to develop beyond its own territory. Ebbe (1999) has identified the internal factors that have led to the growth of organised crime in Nigeria. Organised crime and the legitimate economy of the country are closely integrated. Nigerian criminal gangs operate from a territory that is notorious for its corruption. In recent years, they have expanded their operations to include a variety of financial frauds, particularly credit card fraud, cheque fraud, bank fraud and drug trafficking (Lyman and Potter 2004: 366–71).

According to Ebbe (1999), there are three types of organised crime groups in Nigeria. The first consists of secret societies that operated long before 1960. The second consists of traditional crime groups that came into being after colonial rule. The third are the so-called '419 syndicates' that emerged in the late 1970s and that now operate throughout the world. 'Advanced fee' or '419' frauds are so-called because they relate to that part of the Nigerian penal code that addresses such offences. In these frauds Nigerian nationals, purporting to be government or banking officials, make contact with individuals or businesses in developed countries. They tell them that they are seeking a reputable foreign company or individual for the deposit of an overpayment of many millions of dollars on a procurement contract. The 'scam' letter promises the transfer of large sums of money from these contracts.

If there are favourable responses to the letter, the perpetrator then makes excuses as to why they cannot immediately send the money. The perpetrator then requests the payment of 'advanced fees' to cover the processing of funds, unforeseen taxes, licensing fees and so on. The perpetrator also asks the recipient to provide personal and financial details, such as bank account numbers. Fake government and banking documents support each stage of the fraud. Thereafter, the victims discover that they have lost large sums of money in providing these advanced fees. There are many variants to these frauds, mainly targeting gullible investors in the developed world. Agencies such as the US Treasury have set up operations to target '419' fraud gangs because of the extent to which the perpetrators target US citizens.

How did organised crime of this kind develop in Nigeria? Ebbe (1999) argues that a symbiotic relationship between criminals and the government is the basis of these developments. Because totalitarian regimes lack the checks and balances that are characteristic of democracies, they become predatory states. Predatory states help to foster the nexus between politicians and criminals. Ebbe argues that Nigeria has been a predatory state since 1966, except for a brief period of democratic reform in the early 1980s. The dividing line between politicians and criminals is often hard to discover. The existence of inter-ethnic conflict does not help to resolve this problem. Ebbe argues that there are considerable difficulties in combating these groups. Weak law enforcement, corruption and the existence until 1999 of military government have not enabled Nigeria to tackle it effectively on its home ground. Whether the present civilian government can control organised crime in the longer term is uncertain, although it is now making increased efforts to tackle corruption.

Claims about criminogenic asymmetries between North and South may help to explain certain types of crime such as fraud and drug trafficking. However, certain aspects of international organised crime between the developed and developing world seem less explicable by economic, cultural and political difference than by the existence of global, profit-oriented co-operation. Some commentators have suggested that the extent of co-operation between crime groups is increasing. Sterling claims that a kind of conspiracy (a *pax mafiosa*) has developed in recent years (Sterling 1994). Her thesis is based upon the idea that co-operation between the main crime groups serves their interests better than conflict. According to Sterling, a new global network of organised crime, a worldwide 'Mafia international' has emerged since the fall of communism. In this network, the Sicilian Mafia, the American Cosa Nostra, Russian organised crime gangs, Colombian drug cartels, Japanese *Yakuza* and Chinese Triads are working together. Evidence for this thesis includes what she describes as summit meetings between the leaders of national organised crime groups held in Prague in 1992.

Jamieson (1995) also argues that major 'traditional' organised crime groups have spread throughout Europe and the rest of the world. The Mafia, Camorra and *'ndrangheta* have all undergone important changes in recent years. The need to keep pace with competition from Asian and Colombian crime groups in an international context of expanding criminal/business opportunities has led to a shift away from their primary role of localised protection. The Mafia diaspora, however, has been a two-way process. It has required co-operation both from non-Mafia elements outside Italy and from 'family' who have taken up residence in other parts of the world, including the USA, Australia, Canada and parts of Europe. Other factors, such as more effective law enforcement and the fall from grace of the collusive political classes in Italy itself, have also had their effect. According to Jamieson:

> The overall effect of these changes could be described as the syndication of Italian organised crime, a form of *pax mafiosa* directed at maximising profit and minimizing conflict.
>
> (Jamieson 1995: 152)

Jamieson gives examples of incursions by groups of southern Italian origin into Switzerland, many of the Germany *Länder*, Belgium, Cyprus, Greece, Albania, Spain, Portugal, the Netherlands and the UK. Their connections are expanding into Eastern and Central Europe in joint ventures with post-Soviet organised crime groups.

Similarly, drawing on empirical evidence of such collaboration, Robinson (2002) claims that there has been a virtual 'merger' between many of these groups. Robinson traces the connections between crime groups and suggests that development in digital communications and international markets have facilitated this process. The growth of international 'cybercrime' is perhaps the most important contemporary example.

This view of international organised crime, therefore, depicts a high degree of integration. There is certainly some evidence to support this view. The collaborating groups involved include indigenous criminal groups, Mafia networks and Asian gangs who have extended their operations to include many European jurisdictions. However, although there is evidence of a degree of collaboration in Sterling (1994), Jamieson (1995) and Robinson (2002), as Chapter 1 shows, other evidence emphasising the dynamic 'networked' nature of organised crime groups provides a counterbalance to these arguments. Here again, we have to take care not to over-rationalise the organisational structures of these groups. Although they may be proliferating and may co-operate in some arenas, this does not mean that an international organisational structure enables them to do so. Given the extent to which these groups continue to work independently in many cases, we are entitled to remain sceptical as to whether the *pax mafiosa* or 'merger' theses represents the reality of international organised crime at the turn of the century.

Chapter 8

Home firms: the British experience

This chapter examines the evidence for the existence of organised crime in Britain. The first part of the chapter sets out a historical review of the activities and growth of criminal groups in Britain in the period from the seventeenth until the beginning of the twentieth centuries. The second part examines the development of criminal gangs in the period until the late 1960s, contrasting the advent and operation of different types of gang. Some commentators might regard this era as the heyday of 'Britain's gangland', featuring the activities of gangsters from the very specific type of underworld that existed during the inter-war and immediate post-Second World War periods. The third part of the chapter reviews aspects of the contemporary scene in Britain, examining the transition from the earlier forms of gang life in the UK to a more fragmented, more diversified panorama of criminal groups. This part of the chapter draws contrasts between the gangs that were part of Britain's gangland in its heyday and more recent criminal gangs, comparing their degree of organisation, their activities and their modes of operation. It reviews the ever-increasing predominance of their involvement in drug trafficking. It also examines the relationship between organised crime and new communities in the UK, referring in particular to the question of whether some aspects of organised crime in Britain are an example of Ianni's 'ethnic succession thesis' (Ianni 1974).

British gangs: a historical perspective

There is little doubt that bands of thieves and marauders have existed in Britain since the earliest times. 'Social' crimes, such as poaching and illegal distilling, frequently involved group activity. Around the coasts, gangs of wreckers and smugglers made extensive use of the sea for trafficking in illicit goods and plunder from distressed vessels (Emsley 1996: 4). The extent to which such groups were 'organised' is controversial, although some vestigial structure must have been necessary through which they planned and carried out their operations.

In general, crime in Georgian England showed a gradual increase with surges due to the Napoleonic wars (Emsley 1996: 21–49). Lack of resources saw many disadvantaged individuals living on the proceeds of crime during this time. The period was distinctly ambiguous, however, due to the official acceptance of a symbiotic relationship between crime and commercialism. Paradoxically, the courts routinely rewarded thief-takers for the capture of criminals and recovery of property despite those thief-takers being themselves extensively involved in criminality. The most notorious of the thief-takers was Jonathan Wild (1682–1725). Under the cover of his thief-taking activities, he built a considerable business in receiving stolen goods. According to Daniel Defoe, who was an avid chronicler of the time, Wild had reached the peak of his power in 1724, employing around 7,000 thieves and even owning a ship for the export of stolen goods.

Commentators such as Klockars (1974) have no doubt about the degree of organisation that Wild required in running his criminal empire. It also required a considerable degree of organisation for Wild to retain his place as the 'thief-taker general'. According to Klockars (1974), Wild continued thief-taking activity throughout his career. By 1720, he had destroyed most of the major gangs in London. His parallel criminal activities eventually led to his downfall. The warrant of detainer that eventually set out some of his crimes said that he had 'divided the town and country into so many districts, and appointed gangs for each, who regularly accounted to him for their robberies'. The court found Wild guilty of crimes relating to receiving stolen goods and sentenced him to death. His hanging took place at Tyburn in 1725 (Klockars 1974: 1–24).

In addition to the gangs in the capital and its surrounds with which Wild was mainly concerned, highwaymen and robbers existed throughout the country during this period. It is mistaken, however, to see highwaymen such as Dick Turpin as romantic individualists. Interestingly, in his detailed review of the subject, Hallsworth chronicles Turpin as an early 'street criminal' who worked with others in robbing travellers (2005: 27–8). In the early years of his criminality in the 1730s, Turpin was a member of the Essex Gang led by Samuel Gregory, who was active in attacking country houses in Essex and robbing their occupants. The use of firearms was commonplace, both for intimidation and for settling scores between gangs (Sharpe 2004: 106–28). After the arrest and prosecution of members of the Gregory gang, Turpin turned to highway robbery, the criminal activity for which he became notorious. He did not always operate alone, however. Despite the unwarranted myths that sprang up around his activities, in reality Turpin was a ruthless criminal, who treated his victims with violence and total disregard for their safety. Eventually, the courts tried him for a number of crimes. His hanging took place at Knavesmire, York in 1739 (Sharpe 2004: 2–7).

Sharpe also points to the activities of a number of other gangs of highwaymen and footpads who operated in concert at that time. According to Sharpe, such gangs exhibited a degree of organisation. They were:

> normally fairly small, and like one suspects criminal gangs of all periods, were fairly loose associations, with members splitting off and forming subgroups with peripheral contacts being called in as occasion demanded ... But in the early eighteenth century, contemporary fears of organised crime had already awarded a central importance to the criminal gang.
>
> (Sharpe 2004: 104)

It is certainly the case that by 1750 the number of gangs involved in robbery had reached serious proportions, especially in and around London. In that year, the growth of robberies in the capital prompted Henry Fielding to set out his *Enquiry into the Causes of the Late Increase of Robbers* and to recommend a system of policing for their apprehension. The proliferation of gangs of ship pilferers on the Thames in the late eighteenth century led to the formation of the River Police, who preceded the formation of London's Metropolitan Police by several decades. Robert Peel and other reformers also cited the rise in crime and public disorder as the primary reason for the introduction of the New Police to the Metropolis in 1829. The extent to which it is possible to attribute the growth of crime to the activities of highly organised criminal groups, however, is highly dubious. The grouping of criminals in these enterprises seems to have been largely adventitious and temporary.

The policing reforms that Peel instituted, however, did not fully solve the problem of gang crime. According to Emsley (1996), the continued existence of gangs in Victorian England, in cities, towns and rural areas, is clear. He points to the example of the several gangs that lived and worked in Horncastle, Lincolnshire in the 1840s as examples of Victorian gangs. He cites a similar example in the Redman Gang of Houghton Conquest in Bedfordshire. Merthyr Tydfil's 'China' area also produced criminal groups (Emsley 1996: 108–10). In addition to these localised groups, Emsley points to gangs of travelling pickpockets and burglars whom analysts might today regard as 'professional' criminals. Many of these had regular links with well-known receivers of stolen goods. These gangs often combined to commit offences but their membership was not rigid, nor were they long-lived. Other groups of individuals, who acquired names like the Wolds Rangers of East Riding or The Rodneys of South Staffordshire were probably no more than vagrants or wandering labourers (Emsley 1996: 172–3). Morton (1992) cites the existence of gangs such as the Dover Road Gang and the Green Gate Gang as providing difficulties for the police in north-east London in the early 1880s. Again, however, whether it is right to regard these groups as examples of 'organised crime' is a matter for debate.

In addition to robbery and house burglary, economic crime was certainly evident in the eighteenth and nineteenth centuries. Such crime clearly needed a considerable amount of organisation to make it lucrative and to conceal its purposes. According to Emsley (1996: 6–7), although historians have not yet explored this in sufficient detail, considerable sums were embezzled and fraudulently appropriated during the Hanoverian and Victorian periods. Frauds relating to the new railway companies were endemic (Locker 2004). Other forms of corporate crime included those where criminals swindled investors through fraudulent building societies and investment schemes. The extent to which the groups that routinely perpetrated this type of crime exhibited permanence and structure is not clear. As indicated in Chapter 3, academics are now examining this area of crime more thoroughly. The overlap between the more gang-oriented perception of organised crime and white-collar crime is becoming more evident (Ruggiero 1996; Levi 2003: 444–6).

Official action did not permanently affect the incidence of gang activity in Britain during the late nineteenth century. On the contrary, by the turn of the century in London, many gangs were in evidence, including those who had come into the country as immigrants. In 1902, the police arrested the members of two rival Russian gangs, the Bessarabians and Odessians, who had preyed upon local communities for protection money. These gangs, who had been in violent conflict for some years, disbanded because of a combination of police action and natural attrition. Many members went to the USA where they joined forces with local crime groups or, in one case, joined the police force! (Morton 1992: 2–5; Wensley 1931: 111–13).

Frederick Porter Wensley, who rose to command the Criminal Investigation Department (CID) at New Scotland Yard during the inter-war period, made the point that 'not all gangs were from Chicago', indicating that local influences, especially in London, were sufficient to encourage gang activity. Citing the example of the Russian gangs and indigenous gangs, particularly those from the East End of London, he claimed that one of the chief difficulties in dealing with gangs is to distinguish between those engaging in simple hooliganism and those who specialise in organised theft. The dividing line, he suggested, is very fine (Wensley 1931: 104–13). Wensley, who was the most important figure in the development of detective work in London during the 1920s, was instrumental in setting up the Metropolitan Police Flying Squad, whose remit was specifically to combat criminal gangs who worked across local policing boundaries (Wensley 1931: 39, 196; Frost 1948: 12–17). In fact, the more 'organised' gangs of this type appeared to represent a shift from the often somewhat ad hoc groups that had existed during the nineteenth century. The basis of these new forms of gang life was a new type of 'underworld', one based upon shared social backgrounds, often reinforced by family ties. It was a shift towards what we might justifiably regard as the heyday of British gangland.

The heyday of Britain's gangland

Morton (1992) provides a useful account of the activities of gangs in London and elsewhere in Britain during the twentieth century. Of particular note are the activities of the Sabini brothers, who ran a mixed alliance of criminals of Italian and Jewish origin. The Sabini family included Charles (known as Darby), Harryboy, Joseph, Fred and George. According to Morton, they were evident leaders of London's underworld from the 1920s. They based their activities mainly upon racecourse protection, often in collusion with corrupt police officers. Morton rightly points out that not all gangs were

London-based, nor did the Sabinis invent racecourse protection. He credits this to Glasgow gangs who preyed on Paisley and other racecourses in the late nineteenth century. Similar gangs existed in other major cities such as Birmingham, Manchester, Liverpool and Sheffield. The infamous Sheffield 'gang wars' between the Mooney and the Garvins gangs were sparked by struggles for the control of gambling at racecourses (Sillitoe 1955; Bean 1981). Morton (1994) sets out the activities of many of the most prominent gangs of this period.

In and around London, gangs in conflict with the Sabinis included that run by Billy Kimber known as The Brummagem Boys. Kimber's gang concentrated mainly on protection activity in the Midlands and the north of England. Whether this amounted to anything approaching 'organised' crime on the scale experienced in the USA during this period is doubtful. According to Pearson (1973), Darby Sabini was the nearest Britain got to an 'organising' gangster in this period. The internment of the Sabinis as enemy aliens, following the outbreak of the Second World War, certainly destroyed their empire. Darby Sabini died in Hove, Sussex in 1950, rich, contented and to a degree respected (Pearson 1973: 30; Morton 1992: 13–32).

The vacuum provided by the demise of the Sabinis and the extensive opportunities provided by the 'back market' during the Second World War, facilitated the rise of other gangs in London thereafter. Again, Morton (1992) and Morton and Parker (2004) provide detailed and credible accounts of these developments. Prominent among the rival gangs were those led by Billy Hill, Albert Dimes and Jack Comer, also known as Jack Spot. Billy Hill was a Londoner, having been born in 1911 in Seven Dials near Leicester Square. Dimes was of Italian origin, whereas Spot had Polish immigrant parentage. Spot, who had become something of a hero due to leading a Jewish group against Moseley's Blackshirts in the 1930s, was primarily involved in protection of illegal drinking clubs and in racecourse protection in London and the North of England. This period was characterised by internecine warfare between Hill, Dimes and Spot, with the latter fighting a knife battle in Soho in 1955. During this period, a number of gangs, including those of the Richardsons, the Krays and the Nash brothers, also began to come to prominence (Morton 1992: 33–94).

Clearly, it is possible to say much more about the detailed history of these events, although lack of space precludes this. Interested readers should read beyond this current text to form a more detailed assessment of gang crime during this period. The work of Morton

(1992, 1994, 2002) and Morton and Parker (2004) is worth study. Again, however, it is necessary to raise the question of the extent to which these gangs were 'organised' in terms of their structures and objectives. On the limited amount of evidence set out here, it is not possible to claim with any legitimacy that the gangs described were formal-rational organisations.

The 1960s provided what can be regarded as the zenith of the development of 'underworld' gangs in Britain. Of course, a number of gangs existed during this period on a temporary basis, forming specifically for the commission of a specific crime or series of crimes. The 1963 'Great Train Robbery' provides a good example of this, following a long-term trend that continues until today (Read and Morton 1992: 69–85). However, other gangs operating in the late 1950s and 1960s appeared to have a broader and more cohesive basis than many of those that had preceded them. They continued to adopt violent methods, but gangs in this new idiom were involved in a greater and more sophisticated variety of quasi-business enterprises than had hitherto been the case, with activities ranging from so-called long-firm frauds to drug trafficking and extortion.

The gangs discussed below provide useful case studies. While these primarily relate to London gangs, similar gangs existed in other major British cities as Morton (1994) has shown. Although there are a number of overlaps, the distinction between temporary criminal gangs, which form for a limited time and for specific purposes, and those that have a broader set of goals and more permanence is an important one.

The names of the participating families provide the key to much of the gang activity in London during the 1960s, both north and south of the Thames. Over the years, these families built webs of allegiances, although feuds and violence stretched and tore these linkages, sometimes fatally. Frankie Fraser, who in recent years has run excursions into London's gangland for crime-curious tourists, was notorious for his involvement in a wide range of violent and other crime (Fraser 1994). Fraser was closely associated with the Richardson brothers, Charles and Edward, who for a number of years in the 1960s ran a large criminal operation centred on long-firm frauds. Although they had a lucrative scrap metal business with five yards in and around south London, they were always closely associated with criminal groups, not least because their business dealt (at least in part) in stolen metal.

Charlie Richardson, who apparently regarded himself primarily as a businessman, was leader of the group. According to Morton

(1992: 103–4), however, he was also keen to assert himself as the predominant force in the south London underworld. After a brief altercation about territory with the Kray brothers, this became a reality during the 1960s. In his autobiography Richardson pleaded that this was just a matter of business:

> To outsiders it might have looked like a gang, but gangs are what kids have – or big kids in American films. I was a businessman who had to protect his interests.
>
> (Richardson 1992: 126, quoted in Morton 1992: 104)

However, despite the fact that the Richardson brothers became wealthy from criminal enterprises such as stolen scrap metal, long-firm frauds (see below) and protection, they achieved their power largely through violence. They meted out violence to rivals or to associates who did not follow their wishes in running 'the business'.

In fact, long-firm frauds (colloquially known as 'LFs') had been running since the 1920s. Their basis was obtaining goods on increasing credit until the company went into liquidation. The gang sold most of the goods that they fraudulently obtained through the London street markets. According to Morton (1992: 107), in the 1960s a properly run LF could expect to realise a profit of between £100K to £150K. The Richardsons also benefited from a major swindle at the National Car Park at Heathrow Airport and from gaming machines.

Although violence was endemic to their power, a combination of violence and betrayal eventually brought them down. The fight at Mr Smith's Club in Catford in March 1966 culminated in the shooting of Eddie Richardson, Frankie Fraser and others. This event served to break the Richardson hold on the south London underworld. The police arrested Eddie Richardson and Frankie Fraser, among other participants. They charged Fraser with the murder of Richard (Dicky) Hart, a Kray associate who was one of their opponents in the Mr Smith's Club fracas. However, the trial only convicted Fraser of affray because the prosecution could not prove that he fired the fatal shot.

While all this was taking place the police were conducting a secret enquiry into the activities of the Richardson gang, making use of former gang associates as witnesses. They arrested Charlie Richardson in July 1966 and charged him with offences including conspiracy and long-firm frauds. The investigation revealed international crime links, including connections in South Africa. The trial also revealed evidence of the torture that the gang had meted out to their opponents and to reluctant associates. The judge (Mr Justice Lawton) sentenced Charlie Richardson to 25 years' imprisonment, and Eddie Richardson and Frankie Fraser to ten years each, with terms of imprisonment for other members of the gang.

The demise of the Richardson gang showed that the police would not tolerate the attempt to create a criminal hegemony in south London; certainly not one covering such a wide range of criminal activities and accompanied by extreme violence. Despite its 'business' ethos, it is difficult to see the activities of the Richardson gang simply in terms of 'enterprise crime'. Readers who wish to examine the history of the Richardson brothers in more detail should refer to Cater and Tullett (1990: 59–84) and Morton (1992: 95–129).

Whereas the Richardson power base was south London, the Kray brothers dominated a large part of the crime scene in the East End of London during the 1960s, spreading their activities into the West End clubland and beyond. They became increasingly active in protection rackets and in long-firm fraud. The twins (Ronnie and Reggie Kray) were undoubtedly the main driving force, and with their elder brother Charlie and a number of long-term henchmen they made a formidable combination in carrying out a wide range of criminal activities.

Born into a world of East End petty criminality, the Kray brothers built a reputation for violence that matched and later possibly exceeded that of the Richardsons. Although the Richardsons tended to keep a lower profile, the Krays were ostentatious, almost caricaturing the gangster image. Their activities included 'protecting' clubs in north and east London and in the West End. They also took protection money from Peter Rachman, notorious for renting out slum properties and terrorising his tenants.

Their ownership of a number of clubs attracted celebrities from show business, sport and politics. For reasons that are difficult to assess in retrospect, these people seemed to regard it as desirable to associate themselves with the Krays in this way. Always to be seen with their 'minders' and immaculately dressed, the Kray twins' self-conception was clearly that of gangsters on the American model. They entitled their organisation The Firm, apparently reflecting a degree of structure and cohesion. Ronnie Kray's nickname, 'The Colonel', was an indication of personal aggrandisement but also of pretensions to a leadership style that aped that of a military hierarchy.

Although the courts had convicted the Krays for assault and other offences earlier in their criminal careers, it was not until 1964 that the police subjected them to a comprehensive investigation. On this occasion, however, although the police laid serious charges relating to demanding money with menaces and other offences, the court acquitted them. Thereafter, they appeared increasingly to regard themselves as beyond the reach of justice (Morton 1992: 150–1; Pearson 1973: 169–72).

During the mid-1960s, friction between the Richardson and the Kray gangs came to a head. During a meeting between the two sides at which there was animosity over 'business' rivalry, George Cornell (a Richardson associate) insulted Ronnie Kray. A further confrontation between Ronnie Kray and Frankie Fraser in a West End club compounded the animosity. The story of the dispute between the factions is set out in detail in Pearson (1973: 181–4) and Morton (1992: 153–6).

The shooting of Dicky Hart (a Kray associate) at Mr Smith's Club helped to drive the situation over the brink. On 9 March 1966, the day after the shooting at Mr Smith's Club in South London, Ronnie Kray walked into the Blind Beggar public house in the East End and shot George Cornell dead at point-blank range with a Luger pistol. Cornell, who had survived unscathed the fracas at Mr Smith's Club the day before, was an obvious target. In his autobiography, Ronnie Kray said:

> Richard Hart had to be avenged. No one could kill a member of the Kray gang and expect to get away with it…Less than twenty-four hours after the Catford killing and here he was, drinking at a pub that was officially on our patch. It was as if he wanted to be shot.
>
> (Kray and Kray 1988: 72)

Although Ronnie Kray (or his amanuensis) wrote this some years after the event, it undoubtedly sums up the ethos of mutual animosity, rivalry and 'turf war' that characterises gang activity. The escalation of violence is no different from that discussed in relation to the work of Decker and Van Winkle (1996).

Police and criminals in London and beyond were well aware that Ronnie Kray had shot George Cornell. However, despite the fact that witnesses were present at the shooting, none was prepared to identify Ronnie Kray as the killer. The police placed him in an identification parade but the witnesses did not pick him out. Thereafter, he appears to have regarded himself as even further from the reach of justice. Meanwhile, the activities of the Kray twins and The Firm became even more bizarre.

In December 1966, three members of the Kray gang went to Dartmoor and assisted Frank Mitchell to escape from a prison working party. Mitchell, referred to in the press as the 'Mad Axeman' from one of his crimes, was in Dartmoor prison serving a long sentence. Physically very strong but mentally deficient, Mitchell was allowed a considerable number of privileges by the prison authorities. This made his escape relatively easy. The Krays kept Mitchell in a small flat in the Barking Road in the East End and provided him with female companionship. Members of the gang wrote letters on his behalf to the Home Secretary asking him to specify his release date but the authorities first required Mitchell to surrender. As he was not prepared to do so, the Krays discontinued the letter writing.

In fact, as Morton (1992: 159) rightly suggests, Mitchell had only exchanged one prison cell for another. He was besotted with the female companion that the Krays had provided and gradually became more difficult to handle, maintaining that the police would never capture him alive. On Christmas Eve 1966, members of the Kray gang told Mitchell that they were moving him to another location and took him to a waiting van. According to Albert Donogue, who later gave evidence against the Krays, Freddie Foreman and Alfie Gerard shot him in the van. Despite extensive searches, the police never found his body.

Jack McVitie, a north London criminal and 'hard man', had worked for the Krays. This included distributing illicit drugs and carrying out other odd jobs, such as spying on the Krays' rivals the Nash brothers. McVitie was also a freelance robber and as such was asked to contribute to the Kray funds but refused. When they gave him money to kill their former financial adviser Leslie Payne, he pocketed the advance fee and boasted that he had cheated the twins out of the money. In autumn 1967, McVitie disappeared. In fact, the Lambrianou brothers had taken him to an address in Stoke Newington in North London where Reggie Kray and other gang members confronted him.

At first, Reggie Kray tried to shoot McVitie but the gun did not fire. He then stabbed him in the face and stomach. Charlie Kray and Freddie Foreman, who although from south London was a long- time friend of the twins, disposed of the body. As with Mitchell, the police never found McVitie's body. Although Reggie later admitted that he killed McVitie, he expressed no remorse (Kray and Kray 1988). Readers can obtain a more detailed account of the killings of Cornell, Mitchell and McVitie in Pearson (1973: 188–221) and Morton (1992: 131–67). The latter is a particularly useful source of information on the Krays and other gangs.

In the period from March 1967 to May 1968, the police mounted a secret operation against the Kray gang. As in the case of the enquiry into the Richardson gang, specially selected officers carried out this investigation. The investigating team slowly gathered information on long-firm frauds, assaults and other incidents but without obtaining clear evidence to substantiate charges that were more serious. The breakthrough for the squad came when the Krays gave their associate Alan Bruce Cooper a subcontract to kill George Caruana, a West End strip-club owner. The police arrested Paul Elvey, nominated by Cooper to carry out the execution, just before he boarded an aircraft in Glasgow with explosives intended to blow up Caruana. Cooper, who had been involved with the Krays in their expansion into international crime, agreed to co-operate with the police.

In May 1968, the police arrested the Kray brothers along with members of The Firm and other associates during dawn raids. Although the police charged them initially only with conspiracy to murder Caruana and with fraud offences, members of the Kray gang began to protect their own interests and provide evidence against the brothers. Witnesses from the Blind Beggar shooting also became confident enough to identify Ronnie Kray as the assailant. Participant accounts of the investigation are in Cater and Tullett (1990) and Read and Morton (1992).

The trial of the Kray brothers for the Cornell and McVitie murders and other offences took place in summer 1969. Ronnie and Reggie received life sentences. Charlie Kray and Freddie Foreman received ten years each for their part in clearing up after the McVitie murder. The court later found the twins and Freddie Foreman not guilty of the Mitchell murder. Apart from release to attend funerals or for medical attention, the twins remained in prison for the rest of their lives. Ronnie died in Broadmoor in 1995, aged 61. Charlie Kray, after release from his sentence for involvement in the McVitie murder and other offences, later received a conviction for serious drug trafficking offences. He died in prison in April 2000 aged 73. Reggie Kray also died in 2000, after losing his battle against cancer.

The activities of the Kray brother have spawned a large number of books, both from the Krays themselves and from their associates. The 'official' Kray website at http://www.thekrays.co.uk provides interesting reading, although much of the content is sycophantic. The written and electronic sources on this subject range from unwarranted apologias to useful insights into the life and times of London's leading gang members. Serious students in this field need to take critical care in distinguishing between the two.

Were the Richardson and Kray gangs involved in something recognisable as 'organised' crime? The answer to this depends on the definition of organised crime that is applied. If the definition demands evidence of formal-rational organisation, then these gangs were not organised in this strict sense. On a lesser test of organisation than that of Weberian bureaucracy, however, there is certainly evidence of rudimentary strategy, of a structured hierarchy and of specific roles assumed by gang members. Certainly in their heyday, although their core teams were comparatively small, both the Richardsons and the Krays controlled a large number of associates on a day-to-day basis. However, emotion rather than calculation often drove their goals. Cunning rather than systematic rational thinking was their normal mode of decision-making. If it is right to regard them as in any sense 'organised', they were such only in terms of a loosely-coupled oligarchy, characterised by charismatic leadership and underpinned by sentiment and violence. Although pre-modern and pre-bureaucratic in form, it is still valid to apply the term 'organised' to such structures.

The demise of the Richardson and Kray gangs in the late 1960s left a power vacuum that the police expected any one of a number of London criminal groups to fill. The Nash brothers, who had uneasy relationships with both the Richardsons and the Krays over the years, had well-established roots in north London. During the 1960s, they were deeply involved in the protection of clubs in the West End and were likely candidates. However, they suffered severe curtailment of their power following the conviction of James Nash for assault in a fracas during which he shot club manager Selwyn Cooney, fatally, and Billy Ambrose. Although the court acquitted him of the murder, the jury found him guilty of serious assault. The judge sentenced him to five years' imprisonment. The Nash group remained active during the 1960s and beyond. Despite their activities, the extent to which they filled the place vacated by the 'Kray firm' remains controversial.

Other families and groups, however, were also active, although none was keen to follow the example of the Krays in promoting their own demise through exposure and publicity. The police successfully prosecuted both the Dixon and the Tibbs family crime groups during the early 1970s, although the criminal fraternity did not regard them as being in the same league as the Kray or Richardson gangs. However, one might argue with some justification that these prosecutions marked the end of an era. Before this time it was still possible to identify clear links with the 'underworld' represented by the Sabinis,

Jack Spot and Billy Hill. In general, however, the period from the 1970s onwards was not characterised by underworld relationships of the kind that were evident in that earlier era.

No doubt criminal groups continued to settle old scores and there were a considerable number of shootings of criminal rivals and informers (Morton 1992, 1994). Hobbs (1995) however, rightly remains sceptical about the cohesive nature and continuance of the underworld that these events represent. He says of the British crime scene:

> What is normally referred to as the underworld relates to a specific section of the West End of London, at a specific time, late 1930s to early 1970s. It also relates to a specific set of economic conditions surrounding gaming and drinking clubs. This was the context within which criminals from well-established enclaves in north, south, east and west London, along with a sprinkling of Italians and Maltese, formed a particularly vivid mosaic of business and pleasure.
>
> (Hobbs 1995: 111)

This perceptive insight explains, to some extent, the disintegration of earlier modes of gang crime since the 1970s. It is possible to make similar points about the era within which the Glasgow razor gangs operated, or those in Sheffield, Manchester, Liverpool and Birmingham. No group could fill the vacuum that the demise of the Krays and others had left because the social conditions under which their influence had flourished had declined. In its place came new social conditions that generated other modes of group criminality and other forms of 'organised' crime.

For critical discussion of the extent to which police corruption and investigator attitudes had a bearing on the activities of some criminal groups in London during this period, see Morton (1993), Cox *et al*. (1977) and Hobbs (1988).

Contemporary aspects of organised crime in Britain

According to Hobbs (1995), contemporary professional criminals now roam a territory of the mundane that we cannot distinguish from that which ordinary members of the public occupy. The activities of contemporary organised crime groups differ from those of preceding eras. Global drug markets, international fraud and other forms of enterprise crime make the old forms redundant. Although contemporary British organised crime groups maintain their local character, they are more likely than were their predecessors to take advantage of opportunities emanating from Europe, the USA and elsewhere. The fact that many groups are now involved in drug trafficking means that they are automatic participants in global markets. This factor alone distinguishes them from the British organised crime groups that existed before the 1960s. Again, Hobbs provides telling insights. Professional crime:

> has moved from an occupational foundation of neighbourhood-oriented extortion and individualistic craft-based larcenies towards an entrepreneurial trading culture driven by highly localized interpretations of global markets.
>
> (Hobbs 1995: 115)

In a later paper, however, Hobbs rightly claims that the criminal 'family firm' is far from obsolete. It continues to provide:

> some measure of dependability and consistency in a socio-economic realm marked by fragmentation and uncertainty …Permutation of old established brands, first generation felons, legitimate businesses in the process of criminal mutation, and a multitude of venture capitalists, their peers and subordinates in confederations at various stages of formation and disintegration, abound. Further, it is this multiplicity of interlocking entre-preneurial networks of firms and individuals that, when imposed upon multi-national terrain, constitutes the rich and alluring zone that is so called 'transnational organized crime'.
>
> (Hobbs 2001: 556–7)

If this is accurate, it is right to understand contemporary organised crime in Britain (as elsewhere) in terms of a new, fuzzier logic of activities and relationships in fragmented and contradictory social networks. There is evidence of both 'family' and 'non-family' firms in Britain, and mixtures of both. As Chapters 3 and 4 show, drug and people trafficking and other forms of enterprise crime are predominant activities.

The fact that contemporary organised crime in Britain is of a very different nature from that which preceded it is not simply because it is no longer the preserve of particular families. Morton rightly suggests that crime in London is not and never has been a purely family-controlled affair (Morton 1994: 49). The robbery in November 1983 where a gang stole £26 million in gold bullion from the Brinks-Mat warehouse at Heathrow is a classic example. This was a case where collusion with one of the security guards and threats of extreme violence from the robbers led to a highly concentrated police enquiry. Frank Cater, who was in charge of the police unit that investigated the case, provides a detailed account of the robbery and its investigation (Cater and Tullett 1990: 232–53). Tony Black, a security guard who was involved with the sister of one of the robbery team and was involved in setting up the robbery, confessed to the police. Subsequently the police arrested Brian Robinson, Michael McEvoy and Tony White for the robbery. Thereafter they arrested others, including the notorious Kenneth Noye and Tommy Adams, for handling some of the proceeds. In December 1984 the court convicted Robinson, McEvoy and Black for their parts in the robbery. The jury acquitted White but the judge sentenced Robinson and McEvoy to twenty-five years' imprisonment and Black to six. Noye received fourteen years but the jury acquitted Adams. This case is notable for the fact that it brought together a number of prominent criminals, who were free to operate without reference to a dominant criminal group or 'crime family'.

In other cases, however, family-based groups continued to be active. The Adams family, also known as the 'The A team', were allegedly one of the most powerful crime groups to emerge in London in the 1980s and 1990s. According to Morton (2002: 67–74), they had built up a multi-million pound empire based upon gun and drug running from Eastern Europe and Israel to Britain and Ireland. In 1985, the court acquitted Tommy Adams (a leading light of the A-team) of handling some of the proceeds of the Brinks-Mat robbery. The police also suspected members of the family of being involved in a number of shootings. The courts convicted some members of the team of drug-dealing. There is no evidence, however, that they sought to dominate the underworld in the way that their predecessors had done. Their primary goal was wealth. In September 2000, the *News of the World* newspaper survey of Britain's wealthiest criminals listed Tommy Adams as second behind Curtis 'Cocky' Warren, a leading Liverpool criminal who had been deeply involved in drugs-dealing over a long period.

Warren, whose criminal career began as a member of Liverpool's street gangs, is perhaps the paradigm example of a new breed of transnational organised criminals. He made extensive use of his local criminal connections but his activities were global. His direct connections with major Colombian, Turkish, Moroccan and European producers and traffickers were at the highest levels. His network consisted of 'joeys' or 'gophers' who would deal with his requirements. He was prepared to deal with corrupt police and other officials, both in the UK and elsewhere. For specific operations, a cellular structure of companies, connections and associates provided layered protection to enable him to complete major drug deals. Barnes *et al.* (2000: 206–8) cite an example of a major cannabis smuggling operation from Morocco through Spain in 1995. The structure included a front company, an overseas fixer, a regular driver and several odd-job men to complete the operation. Warren was able to operate until 1996, when the Dutch authorities arrested him with others of his gang for importing a large amount of cocaine into Holland. The operation, which involved co-operation between the Dutch and British customs and police, recovered 400 kilos of 90 per cent pure cocaine in a container imported by ship into Rotterdam. Searches of premises in the Netherlands revealed 1,500 kilos of cannabis resin, 60 kilos of heroin, 50 kilos of ecstasy, 960 CS gas canisters, several hand grenades and ammunition, three firearms, false passports and around £370,000 worth of guilders. The authorities estimated the total haul at around £125 million (Barnes *et al.* 2000: 256–60). In June 1997 Warren appeared before a court in Holland for major drug offences. The court president accepted that he was the head of a criminal organisation involved in the large-scale importation and exportation of cocaine, ecstasy and cannabis. He sentenced him to twelve years' imprisonment (Barnes *et al.* 2000: 277). Again, Warren and his associates were able to operate independently, without reference to any criminal elite who were in control of a wider underworld.

Although the Adams family and Curtis Warren perhaps represent the higher echelons of British organised crime, indigenous crime groups are not responsible for everything that falls under its rubric. Chapter 6 discussed Ianni's 'ethnic succession thesis', which suggests that aspiring members of ethnic groups who are blocked from legitimate access to wealth and power respond by producing and providing illicit goods and services that society publicly condemns but privately demands. These include gambling, stolen goods, illegal alcohol, sex and drugs (Ianni 1974: 107–8). Although Ianni applied this to the growth of black and Hispanic gangs in the USA, the growth of ethnic criminal groups in the UK and elsewhere in Europe should encourage an examination of whether Ianni's thesis is valid here.

There is a considerable amount of evidence to suggest the existence of ethnically-based criminal gangs in the UK. Morton (2002: 78–85) discusses the activities of Turkish gangs and 'Yardie' groups of Afro-Caribbean origin in London and the violence and gun crime associated with their activities. Although people are now more likely to refer to the so-called 'Yardies' as 'crews' or 'posses', the existence of ethnically-based gangs whose origins are in the Caribbean is clear. With their origins in the political struggles in Jamaica in the 1980s, where they were blamed for around 500 murders, many came to London and took up the running of illegal drinking and gaming houses. Prominent in the Brixton, Notting Hill and Harlesden areas of London, they extended their activities to international drug dealing, whilst maintaining their links with counterparts in Jamaica. According to Morton (2002) there are still a number of Jamaican gunmen working in the Yardie milieu, although the majority of 'hitmen' among the so-called Yardies are now British-born black criminals (Morton 2002: 80).

The shootings in Birmingham in January 2003 of Letitia Shakespeare and Charlene Ellis were the result of a dispute between opposing local gangs, the Johnson Crew and the Burger Bar Boys. This tragic shooting produced a public outcry from the local Afro-Caribbean community, but at first little in the way of hard evidence. Subsequently, the courts convicted four men aged between 19 and 24 for their murders, including Charlene's half-brother. Although this particular crime assumed national importance, it is symptomatic of the wide-ranging increase in youth gun crime in London, Manchester, Birmingham, Nottingham and other UK cities in recent years.

The Metropolitan Police Operation Trident, which was first set up in 1998 to combat black-on-black gun crime in Brent and Lambeth, has seen success both in arresting armed youths and in helping to curtail the importation of drugs by groups from the Caribbean (Morton 2002: 75–85). Similar specialist operations have been set up in other UK cities including Operation Ventara (Birmingham), Operation Goodwood (Manchester), Operation Stealth (Nottingham), Operation Safeguard (Leeds), and Operation Atrium (Bristol). The fact that gun crime continues to rise in some areas clouds the extent to which these operations have been successful. In Nottingham, for example, in 2005 the Chief Constable appealed for more resources, including detectives from other police forces, to enable his force properly to investigate a spate of shootings in that city. The tendency in the press is to assume that much of this mayhem is the work of highly organised groups. Evidence for this, however, is thin. Despite the 'Yardie' origins that are the basis of these fears, conflicts between rival small-area networks seem more likely to be the norm. Overall, however, this is an under-researched area.

Other ethnic groups from China and from the Indian subcontinent have been active in organised crime in Britain for some years, especially in relation to drug trafficking. Albanian and Romanian gangs are active in the sex industry and trafficking in women. Turkish gangs are involved in drug importation. It is possible that criminal groups from Eastern and Central Europe will become increasingly active in Britain, in the wake of the expansion in 2004 of the EU under the Treaty of Nice (2001). More openness in the borders of the EU will facilitate the mobility of criminal groups of all kinds, both ethnically based and indigenous.

The UK government has also recognised the problem of organised crime in relation to ethnic and other gangs involved in people smuggling. According to the National Criminal Intelligence Service (NCIS), the impact of international organised immigration crime is immense. The UN estimates that its global profits exceed $12 billion. Would-be immigrants can pay up to £20,000 to come to the UK. Organised immigration crime bears all the hallmarks of organised crime (see Chapter 4).

Much of the operational activity by the British authorities relating this subject is not in the public domain, especially where it touches on potential terrorist activity. However, readers will find a limited amount of information on the UK Home Office website and elsewhere. Project Reflex is a major operation which co-ordinates the activities of the National Crime Squad (NCS), NCIS, police forces, immigration authorities and other UK agencies in this respect. The government initiated Project Reflex in May 2000. Progress is discussed in the 2003 Home Office Departmental Report, available on the Home Office website at: http://www.homeoffice.gov.uk/docs2/annrep2003sec3b. html.

At a conference on the subject in London in November 2003, organised by the Association of Chief Police Officers (ACPO) and the Reflex multi-agency task force, then Home Office Minister Beverly Hughes announced the provision of £60 million for law enforcement work to disrupt people traffickers and to seize their profits. She also announced plans to strengthen the law to provide higher penalties for immigration crime. Project Maxim, which is the contribution of London's Metropolitan Police Service to Reflex, has met with success, identifying and arresting a number of gang members for offences ranging from fraud to conspiracy.

Clearly, there are a number of dangers associated with the argument set out in Ianni (1974) suggesting the existence of ethnic succession in the development of organised crime. In relation to organised crime in the USA, Woodiwiss (2001) has drawn attention to the tendency to demonise particular ethnic and cultural groups in the public mind. This reinforces the belief that organised crime is part of an alien conspiracy, rather than an integral part of American culture. In this way, the US public has demonised Irish, Italian, Jewish, black and Hispanic groups at various times. From the earliest times, racism and xenophobia have thus set the limits to the understanding of organised crime (Woodiwiss 2001: 8).

In Britain, there have been a number of wide-ranging critiques of policing in relation to ethnic minority communities and crime. Hall *et al.* (1978) provide a radical critique of the way in which the authorities in Britain responded to 'mugging' in the 1970s. According to them, the police and the press amplified the issue, converting it into a moral panic and producing a crisis where none really existed. Bowling *et al.* (2003) provide a comprehensive review of the literature on policing ethnic minority communities, including a critique of the issues relating to police targeting and criminalisation of minority ethnic groups, the use of excessive force and the discriminatory use of stop-and-search powers. According to Bowling *et al.*, the drift to a 'law and order society' and paramilitary-style police action undermines voluntary compliance with the rule of law but fails to reduce violence in the community. It also fails to produce the conditions for achieving social justice (Bowling *et al.* 2003: 549).

At first sight, the critiques of Hall *et al.* (1978), Woodiwiss (2001) and Bowling *et al.* (2003) seem to be in conflict with the arguments of commentators such as Morton (2002) and others who appear to identify a linkage between organised crime and some ethnic groups. Clearly, this is dangerous ground in a number of respects. First, even in cases where ethnic youth or street gangs are involved it is wise to remember that the degree of organisation might be limited, with gang activity being more likely to follow that observed in the US gang studies. This is certainly the case for many of the British-born youth gangs, crews and posses who are embroiled in the drug trade. It is certainly unwise to assume that gun crime and turf wars of this type are examples of large-scale clashes between opposing cartels.

Secondly, even in cases where larger ethnic crime groups are involved, there is a clear need to distinguish between the legitimate activities of the new ethnic minority communities and the fact that some examples of organised crime (and indeed of terrorism) may have their origins in ethnic groups. This is as important for the communities themselves as it is for the police and criminal justice agencies. Although community solidarity is important, the propensity for some cultures routinely to support those of similar background without reference to the circumstances may be highly damaging in the longer term. The Chinese concept of *guanxi* for example, means that community members may call upon the support of others, without reference to the prevailing social mores elsewhere. Similar social rules exist in other cultures, spilling over into both legitimate business and organised crime. Fear is also undoubtedly a factor. For these reasons, police often find it difficult to penetrate the so-called 'wall of silence' that surrounds the gang activity that is embedded in these communities.

Ideally, in liberal democracies where the rule of law prevails, the fact that ethnic gangs are involved in organised crime should be irrelevant. This is the stance taken by Project Reflex. Although the people being smuggled into various states are themselves from particular ethnic backgrounds, the focus of enforcement and multi-agency work is on the actual activities of organised groups, not upon their ethnicity. In this sense, the need is to respond to the activities of criminal gangs of all kinds. The authorities should certainly try to achieve this without demonising or discriminating against ethnic communities that have already settled in Britain permanently, or who are in the process of doing so. Indeed, for the police, much of the intelligence through which they can investigate the activities of criminal gangs comes from these communities. The issue of responding sensitively to such cultural or ethnic solidarity also needs to be understood in this context, ideally by involving the communities themselves in active partnerships as in the case of the gun crime scrutiny carried out in 2003 by the Metropolitan Police Authority (MPA).

Is it justified to regard the Ianni ethnic succession thesis as valid in contemporary Britain? Ianni is right to point (as other researchers into gang culture have pointed) to the propensity for minorities excluded from mainstream social and economic life to seek other, more lucrative ways of obtaining wealth and power. Ianni is wrong, however, to limit the argument to ethnic minorities, even though some may take this route. The succession is generational, social and economic, not necessarily ethnic. The answer lies in reducing exclusion, especially in reducing the blocking of social, political and economic opportunities for individuals, regardless of their origins.

In summary, it is evident that the existence of gangs in Britain since the eighteenth century provides a distinctive criminal legacy, the effects of which remain evident to this day. The singular underworld of the period from 1930–1970 that Hobbs (1995) describes was as much an attempt to obtain power and wealth for criminal gangs in their era as are the diverse underworlds of indigenous and ethnic gangs in this. Contra Hobbs, however, there is little evidence to suggest that both indigenous and ethnic gangs in Britain are part of the 'social mundanity' within which the majority of the population now exists. As the examples of the Adams family and Curtis Warren show, British organised crime has created new types of underworlds, albeit ones that have characteristics differing from its earlier singular form. When compared with their predecessors, the main differences are those that relate to their lines of control, to the diversity of their associations, and to the very different social, economic and political conditions in which they operate. They are criminal groups, however, in relation to which it remains valid to use the term 'organised crime'.

Chapter 9

Tackling organised crime: possibly together

In this chapter, we discuss the strategies that individual states and the international community have put in place to deal with the risks posed by organised crime and drug trafficking. First, we examine some of the problems that affect the possibility of gaining control over organised crime, including difficulties of measuring or estimating its extent. We discuss the use of regulatory strategies to deal with organised crime as a local and a global problem. Secondly, we discuss the work of law enforcement agencies in tackling organised crime. This includes issues that relate to investigation and law enforcement in national jurisdictions and in bilateral and multilateral action between states. It also includes a discussion of how the law enforcement agencies are improving investigation by making use of new technologies, and by better co-ordination and management of intelligence. Thirdly, we examine measures for international co-operation against organised crime groups, including the work of bodies such as the EU, the UN and the G7/8 group of nations in generating co-operation through international agreements. Finally, we review how the international community has sought to deal with the problem of drug trafficking.

Risk, control and regulatory strategies

The use of the term 'control' suggests that the international community can reduce and possibly eradicate the threats posed by organised crime and drug trafficking in the longer term. The idea of control was certainly a major part of the strategies of many states in relation to drug trafficking during the 1970s and 1980s. For example, belief in eradication of drug trafficking by taking concerted action at the supply end was a key characteristic of the 'war on drugs' model. However, the evidence indicates that the total eradication of organised crime may be little more than a pious hope. Crime groups have an uncanny durability. If the international community curtails their activities in one field, they simply arise in another.

In fact, the international community has not often been in agreement about the nature of organised crime and the steps that it needs to take to tackle it. There are considerable differences between practitioners, policy makers and criminologists in this respect. As we have shown in relation to the debate on organised crime in the USA in Chapters 1 and 6, we can no longer assume that large 'Mafia-style' organisations control it. We have examined the origins of the Mafia-centred myth in the work of Cressey (1969, 1972). We have identified its influence on a succession of US commissions on organised crime. Because it is part of US foreign policy, this has an influence beyond the USA itself. Woodiwiss (2001) argues that the USA has convinced the international community about the worldwide power of Mafia-style groups. He cites a conference held during 1994 as an example of how the USA has sought to influence the world to accept its beliefs (2001: 382). The conference, entitled Global Organized Crime: The New Empire of Evil, set out to show that global organised crime presents a greater challenge to security than anything the western democracies had to cope with during the Cold War. Speakers at the conference included FBI director Louis Freeh, CIA director R. James Woolsey, and Claire Sterling, who reiterated the *'pax mafiosa'* thesis (Sterling 1994 – see Chapter 7). Hobbs and Dunningham (1998) have noted the increased involvement of the 'cold war warriors' of the security services in this respect. According to Woodiwiss, this has led to a 'dumbing of the global discourse' on the subject. Because of US influence, the international community has now geared its strategies to a distorted understanding of organised crime (Woodiwiss 2001: 362–89). For further analysis of the differences between the criminologists, law enforcement officers and policy makers on the subject, readers should refer to Naylor (1997).

While states often talk in very general terms about 'controlling' organised crime and drug trafficking, a more exact use of the term presents a number of difficulties. Both theoretical and practical difficulties stem from the fact that 'organised crime' is a contested concept. Like the concepts of democracy and justice, it is (as a matter of principle) something that will always arouse endless disputes. We can only form judgements about its nature in the specific contexts in which we find it. If this is correct, it is important to formulate risk-management strategies that respond to the actual threats and challenges that it poses. What are the areas upon which these strategies should focus? Strategies to tackle organised crime need to take account of the social, economic and political domains within which it operates.

Firstly therefore, strategies should focus on taking action to deal with the risks that stem from the social domain, accurately identifying and dealing with the social context and key relationships which are important to the growth of particular criminal groups. In Chapter 1, we argued that we should understand its 'organisation' in terms of complex networks of social relationships. In some groups, familial ties are important, in others, ethnic or geographical origin is the crucial factor. States should therefore take account of the prevailing social conditions in formulating any policy or strategy to deal with the problem. This is particularly important in relation to street gangs from which major crime groups recruit their lower-level operatives. For example, as Jamieson (2000) rightly says in relation to Italian organised crime, it is mistaken to rely only on law enforcement measures, when local youth unemployment in the areas concerned is running at around 50 per cent. As will be evident when discussing international plans to combat organised crime, this is an area of weakness.

Secondly, because organised crime challenges the authority of the nation state, it is also important to adopt measures that correct its worst effects in the political domain. These include specific measures to prevent the corruption of public officials, judges and legislators. Political decision-making in this field is also about the allocation of resources to deal with the problem. In fact, the international community does not need to justify increased use of resources by resorting to the *pax mafiosa* thesis. The proliferation of organised crime groups already provides sufficient grounds to justify extensive action, whatever their organisational structure. Although we have pointed out weaknesses in dealing with the political impact of organised crime in states such as Russia and Nigeria, again this is an area where international intentions are comparatively strong. In particular, the international community recognises corruption as a key area for individual states to tackle.

Thirdly, it is important to adopt measures that deal with its impact in the economic domain. Some analysts suggest that we can hardly distinguish a free-market economy, totally unfettered by any legal or ethical constraints, from organised crime. However, even the most liberal of states need to adopt regulatory regimes to minimise the effects of fraud and other malpractices. Regulatory strategies and domestic legislation increasingly need to tackle the enterprise model of organised crime, recognising that illicit enterprise lies on a continuum that includes legitimate business activity. In fact, there is evidence that they are beginning to do so, in the adoption of anti-money laundering 'follow the money' measures (Naylor 2003). This is an area where international plans are explicit. Their implementation is comparatively strong. We examine this further below, both in relation to international measures and to the work of specialist agencies.

Strategies to tackle organised crime therefore need to take account of each and all of these domains: social, political and economic. Liddick (1999) rightly argues that we should continue to focus on the enterprise model of organised crime because it enables us better to understand the economic direction that organised crime has taken. However, he also emphasises the importance of social and political power, especially that reflected in the countless patron–client relationships that are evident in organised crime. In this sense, the enterprise model and the patron–client model that we discussed in Chapter 1 are not mutually exclusive. International bodies and law enforcement agencies need to take account of both models in considering how we should try to deal with organised crime.

In fact, there is already a trend away from pious rhetoric about potential eradication towards pragmatic measures aimed at managing the risks posed by organised crime across all of these domains. Wright (2002: 101–27) argues that 'policing' (in its widest sense) involves the management of risk, alongside criminal investigation and other law enforcement activity. Most importantly, the international community and individual states are now making serious efforts to measure and estimate the extent of the problem as part of an integrated approach to risk assessment in the field of organised crime. In addition to qualitative assessments of the threats posed by specific criminal groups, which all intelligence agencies carry out, quantitative evaluation of the extent of organised crime in each jurisdiction is an essential part of the management of risk. Burnham (2003) sets out the findings of a research project on behalf of the US National Institute of Justice (NIJ) on the possibility of quantifying the threat of international organised crime. He concludes that evaluative tools are available to enable this to happen, although he acknowledges the difficulties of compiling a cross-national database. Currently, countries compile such databases as they have by different methods. Consequently, data sets often are not comparable. The international community will need to resolve problems of co-ordination before it can make much progress (Burnham 2003: 65–77).

The European Union has encountered similar difficulties in making an overall assessment of the extent of organised crime and in developing credible systems for cross-national comparisons. The EU study on developing a statistical apparatus for measuring organised crime, assessing its risk and evaluating organised crime policies noted a number of difficulties and made recommendations for overcoming them (Savona *et al.* 2005). This study noted a lack of integration of police and other agency data that would be capable of providing a complete and reliable picture of organised crime. It recommended the adoption of means for the uniform interpretation of data across the EU, the use of an 'offender-based' rather than an 'offence-based' system and more integration and co-ordination among police and other public agencies and private data sources. Despite a number of remaining difficulties, this is a timely initiative in this important area of the management of organised crime risk. Effective evaluation will have a crucial role to play in a concerted EU-wide effort to tackle organised crime.

In relation to the evaluation of organised crime in the UK, Gregory (2003) provides an incisive analysis of the UK's Organised Crime Notification Scheme (OCNS) in the period from 1996 to 2002. He draws attention to the problems of defining suitable 'outcome measures' and to the difficulties of obtaining reliable and consistent data. Because of difficulties of definition of data fields and the implementation of suitable means for data collection, however, the extent to which the UK will be successful in developing effective intelligence products and in disrupting organised crime enterprises by measurable amounts continues to be problematic in the short to medium term. Despite these recent attempts to develop an empirical basis for risk-management strategies, only time will tell whether efforts to deal with organised crime in the social, political and economic domains have been successful.

Law enforcement: national and international co-operation

In addition to high-level measures that seek to regulate and to manage the risks that organised crime presents, investigation and law enforcement play important roles in bringing offenders to justice. Law enforcement acts against organised crime at several levels. At the first level, national law enforcement plays an important role in tackling domestic organised crime. By implication, it also helps to combat international organised crime. Many criminal groups graduate to the international level at some stage. In either case, traditional, reactive investigative methods are inadequate. Investigating organised crime by mean of 'proactive' intelligence-led strategies has long been the key to dealing with the problem. Proactive policing, making use of surveillance methods, informants, 'supergrasses' and 'sting' operations has characterised police efforts against organised crime in many jurisdictions for many years. For this reason, the agencies that investigate organised crime have adopted squad, task force or security service style deployments to deal with it (Wright 2002: 86–90). In the UK context, the security services have increasingly become involved in such operations, especially where terrorism is concerned.

The use of 'repentant' gang members to give evidence and witness protection programmes to protect them has characterised investigations against the Sicilian Mafia and similar groups. There are, however, dangers associated with these methods. Unfortunately, this kind of policing sometimes mirrors the very criminal activity that it seeks to confront (Dorn *et al.* 1992). Research has shown that there is a considerable amount of entrepreneurial 'trading' between detectives and criminal groups (Hobbs 1988). At worst, this can lead to corruption. Maguire and John (1995) have suggested that such methods have a high cost for the police organisation. This is true in terms of surveillance costs. It is also true in terms of both the economic and human costs of running informants, especially where officers may feel forced to lie to protect the lives of those who provide them with information (Dunningham and Norris 1999).

However, alongside these direct methods is a more technical route, which involves the use of specialised resources in an integrated intelligence system. Enforcement agencies increasingly make use of intelligence analysis to map the associations between actors, events and activities in a network. Such analysis enables them to chart and to evaluate the power and vulnerability of individuals within a crime group. Investigators make frequent use of specialised electronic resources as an aid to these methods. Although there is a tendency for all law enforcement agencies to guard their use of these techniques, they increasingly make use of them to support bilateral and multilateral co-operation. In Britain, a National Intelligence Model (NIM) supports enforcement and preventative action at the local, force and national/international levels.

At the second level, law enforcement relies on bilateral co-operation between states. Bilateral co-operation plays an important practical role in law enforcement operations. This is especially the case in terms of technical assistance and intelligence support for operations. For example, Germany has agreed to provide co-operation to combat organised crime to several states in Eastern and Central Europe. The Bundeskriminalamt (BKA) has sent liaison officers to numerous foreign embassies. Indeed, the police and customs authorities of many countries appoint liaison officers to foreign embassies or enforcement agencies. The USA has FBI agents as legal attachés at its embassies. In some cases, the level of co-operation provided will include direct operational support, as well as intelligence and help with resources. We have already discussed operational collaboration between the FBI and Hungarian national police in Chapter 7. We highlighted co-operation between the USA and the Colombian government (in collaboration between the DEA, US military and Colombian national police) in Chapter 4.

At the third level, multilateral co-operation in law enforcement in Europe and elsewhere has increased in the wake of the challenge of organised crime and terrorism. One reason for this is the increased mobility that has come with political integration and with political and economic migration. In 1985, following discussions throughout the EU, France, Germany, Belgium, Luxembourg and the Netherlands took a joint decision to create a territory without internal borders within the EU area. This became known as the Schengen area, taking its name from the town where the agreement was first signed. In 1997, the group expanded the number of participating countries to thirteen, following the Treaty of Amsterdam. Of the fifteen EU states, only Ireland and the UK opted out of the arrangements. The EU incorporated the Schengen *acquis* into its body of laws in 1999, making it part of the EU framework. New members of the EU are obliged to accept the Schengen *acquis*.

The Schengen agreement abolished the internal borders of participating states and adopted common rules for the free movement of persons within the Schengen area. The agreement also set out measures to improve co-ordination between the police, customs and the judicial authorities. It also set up an information system (SIS) to exchange information on individuals and on lost or stolen property. The EU approved a second generation SIS to cater for expected demand after enlargement in 2002–4. In March 1999, the UK asked to take part in some aspects of Schengen, namely police and legal co-operation in criminal matters, the fight against drugs and the SIS. A Council decision approved this request in May 2000.

Another important advance in EU multilateral law-enforcement co-operation in recent years has been the development of Europol. Staffed by police and customs officers, Europol started life in 1994 as the European Drugs Unit (EDU). Its purpose then was to co-ordinate the efforts of national European police forces in the fight against drug trafficking. In July 1999, its responsibilities widened, following ratification by EU member states of the Europol Convention. Although not without its critics, its full range of activities include investigating illegal trafficking in drugs, stolen vehicles and human beings. It investigates illegal immigration networks, sexual exploitation of women and children, pornography, forgery, smuggling of radioactive and nuclear materials, terrorism, money laundering and counterfeiting. The EU reinforced the role of Europol in December 2001 when the European Council approved the extension of its powers to all forms of international crime. The Council also agreed in 2002 to the principle of amending the Europol Convention so that Europol can participate in joint investigation teams and call on national authorities to conduct enquiries according to the Amsterdam Treaty.

Europol has been the subject of a certain amount of 'mission creep' since its foundation. The extent to which Europol will become the equivalent of the FBI, with all of the federal implications of the latter, is still a matter for debate. However, the trajectory of Europol has been firmly in the direction of taking increasing responsibility for the European management of intelligence on organised crime, drug trafficking and aspects of terrorism. In addition to intelligence analysis, it now provides expertise and technical support for investigations and operations in the member states. How the EU will reconcile the role of Europol with the active operational role of the FBI in states such as Hungary after their accession is highly questionable. For more information and debate on this subject, readers should refer to Fijnaut (1998) and Santiago (2000).

It is worth reminding ourselves of two important general points in respect of the limitations of law enforcement to deal with organised crime. First, whether it is operating at the national, bilateral or multilateral levels, the downside of law enforcement is the limit of the control that it can exercise. There are legal, jurisdictional and political limitations on its activities. We can contrast the restrictive regime faced by the investigative agencies with the flexibility of organised crime. Unlike organised crime, an agency operating under the rule of law has no extra-legal sanctions to deal with the competition.

Secondly, there are always problems of connecting top-level strategic measures of the kind set out above with the realities of law enforcement on the ground. As Van Duyne (1996) and Hobbs (2001) have noted, organised crime usually involves a great deal of localism. Stelfox (2003: 124) argues that it is visible to local police forces that are able to take action against it themselves or to draw it to the attention of national level law enforcement agencies. In Britain, the NCS and NCIS (and, from April 2006, the Serious Organised Crime Agency – SOCA) are able to adopt strategies that take account of local conditions, while maintaining links if necessary with agencies abroad. SOCA, created by the Serious Organised Crime and Police Act 2005, becomes operational in 2006. It merges NCS, NCIS and investigation teams of HM Customs and Excise to provide a co-ordinated national body to deal with organised crime. SOCA will have some 5,000 investigators and will have a substantial presence overseas. Again, only time will tell whether SOCA will be any more successful than the agencies that preceded it for tackling organised crime.

Of course, whether focused at national or local level, dangers are ever-present in this kind of policing. The conception of justice held by some law enforcement officers may not be the same as that expected by high-level policy. There is an ever-present danger of corruption and rule-bending of various kinds. The dislocation between the requirements of law and policy and the perceptions of law enforcement officers has long been the subject of studies by sociologists of policing (see, for example, Skolnick 1966; Bittner 1970). This means that the law enforcement authorities must ensure that their training is adequate and that they reward their officers properly for their work. Officers should also be highly motivated and morally prepared to tackle organised crime. If they are not, as experience in Australia and some other jurisdictions has shown, they become part of the problem, not the solution (Miller *et al.* 1997).

International conventions

Organised crime is both a national and an international problem. At the national level, it requires crime control policies that deal effectively with it by means of substantive legislation and law enforcement. Some jurisdictions regard the fact that organised crime groups are responsible for an offence as an aggravating factor. In others, there are restrictions on membership of criminal groups. For example, in Italy since 1982 there has been restriction on membership of Mafia-style groups. In the USA, the Racketeer Influenced and Corrupt Organizations Statute (RICO) makes it an offence to participate in the affairs of an enterprise through a pattern of racketeering activity (Williams and Savona 1996).

Currently, countries that apprehend offenders or extradite them from places where they have sought refuge take criminal proceedings against organised crime groups in their own jurisdictions. There is no international court to deal with them. However, the criminal justice systems of individual states cannot tackle organised crime acting alone. Fighting organised crime requires integrated action by the authorities of all states. International agreements are necessary to encourage and support such action. To achieve this, it has been necessary to change from the merely symbolic approach that characterised early attempts to deal with the problem to one that has more substance.

The role of the United Nations

In recent decades, the UN has developed a systematic approach to organised crime. In particular, it has sought to limit the opportunities for criminal activity by the development of clear goals and policies for prevention. It has also sought to reduce the vulnerability of legitimate industry to the depredations of organised crime (Williams and Savona 1996: 44–6).

The first involvement of the UN was in 1975 in Geneva, when the Fifth UN Congress on the Prevention of Crime and the Treatment of Offenders discussed matters relating to organised crime (Mueller 1998: 13; United Nations 1976). The Sixth Congress took place in Caracas in 1980 and extended the discussion to include crime and the abuse of power, and offences and offenders who were beyond the reach of the law. The Seventh Congress took place in Milan in 1985. It discussed developments in organised crime, including drug trafficking and corruption. The Milan Congress produced an action plan to respond to these challenges (Williams and Savona 1996: 108–18). Thereafter, the UN frequently debated the issue in the General Assembly and in the annual congresses on the Prevention of Crime and Treatment of Offenders.

In 1992, the UN established the Commission for Crime Prevention and Criminal Justice, which is a subsidiary body of the UN Economic and Social Council. The Commission has forty members and meets annually in Vienna. It formulates policies and recommends activities in the field of crime control. Its priority areas include action to combat organised crime, economic crime and money laundering.

In November 1994, the UN held a World Ministerial Conference in Naples. This conference was important, because it surfaced for the first time the idea for a global legal instrument against organised crime. The global action plan set out a detailed list of measures that individual states should take and made recommendations for co-operation between them. Despite the importance of this step, the scepticism of some of the developed countries was at the root of the anodyne language of the Naples Political Declaration and Global Action Plan, which was the main product of the event (Vlassis 1998: 356–62; United Nations 1995).

After further deliberations, however, the UN General Assembly adopted a resolution that set up an ad hoc committee to prepare a draft of a major convention against organised crime. The ad hoc group met on eleven occasions in Vienna between January 1999 and October 2000. The UN General Assembly adopted it at their millennium meeting in November 2000 and opened the Convention for signature in December 2000 at a conference that met in Palermo, Italy.

The 2000 UN Convention against Transnational Organized Crime has two main goals. The first is to eliminate the effects of differences between national legal systems, which have blocked mutual assistance in the past. The second is to set standards for domestic laws so that they can effectively combat organised crime. Under the Convention, governments commit themselves to:

1. Criminalizing offences committed by organised crime groups, including corruption and corporate or company offences;

2. Cracking-down on money laundering and the proceeds of crime;

3. Speeding up and widening the reach of extradition;

4. Protecting witnesses testifying against criminal groups;

5. Tightening co-operation to seek out and prosecute suspects;

6. Boosting prevention of organized crime at the national and international levels; and

7. Developing a series of protocols containing measures to combat specific acts of transnational organized crime.

(United Nations 2000a)

Protocols targeting specific types of crime supplement the crime fighting measures of the Convention. These include protocols to combat the smuggling of migrants, the trafficking and exploitation of women and children and the illicit manufacture and trade in firearms (United Nations 2000b).

After the adoption of the Convention, the UN encouraged as many states as possible to ratify it and to give effect to the measures it sets out. It is too early to provide an assessment of its effectiveness. However, it clearly provides the necessary political and legal framework for international action against organised crime. Readers can find a compilation of earlier UN documents in Bassouni and Vetere (1998).

Co-operation in Europe

European states have long sought to achieve effective legal and judicial co-operation. In April 1959, the European Convention on Mutual Assistance in Criminal Matters was opened for signature by member states of the Council of Europe. Under this Convention, states agree to afford the widest measure of co-operation in gathering evidence, and hearing witnesses, experts and prosecuted persons. The Convention sets out the formal rules under which such co-operation shall take place. In 1978 and 2001, the Council of Europe added protocols to the Convention to improve co-operation in specific fields. The 2001 protocol improves the ability of states to react to cross-border crime in the light of political, social and technological developments in Europe. This is relevant to efforts by the forty member states of the Council of Europe to tackle organised crime.

Member states of the EU have co-operated on justice and home affairs matters since the mid-1970s. The Maastricht Treaty (Treaty on European Union – TEU), which came into force in 1993, formally established the basis for co-operation. The Treaty of Amsterdam, which came into force in 1999, further consolidated these measures. The range of co-operation between EU states now includes police and customs co-operation and co-operation on criminal law. Fijnaut (1998) sets out a critical review of these developments.

The EU and European Commission encourage member states to improve their co-operation, to fulfil the goal of creating a European area of security and justice. The aim of the Commission is to close loopholes rather than duplicate international instruments or to build a comprehensive system of its own. To this end, it works closely with the UN and the Council of Europe. In the area of police co-operation, EU member states participate in Interpol but have developed Europol as an instrument to provide more intense co-operation in crime intelligence and operations.

The EU has initiated a series of measures aimed at tackling organised crime since the Treaty of Amsterdam. The Special Meeting of the European Council in Tampere in October 1999 formulated the strategy for incorporating preventive aspects into the international fight against organised crime. It also set objectives to secure an area of freedom, security and justice within the EU. Subsequently, the EU formulated an action plan on prevention and control of organised crime for the new millennium. This built upon the 1997 action plan (High Level Group on Organised Crime 1997). A 'scoreboard' system was set up to review progress on the measures (European Commission 2002). During this period, the EU was also actively involved in negotiations on the UN Convention against Transnational Organised Crime (United Nations 2000a). The EU signed the Convention and its three protocols in Palermo in December 2000.

To reinforce the fight against serious organised crime, the EU also agreed to set up Eurojust, a unit of national prosecutors, magistrates and police officers. Eurojust will act as a collective body at EU level but national delegates will also be able to act under their national laws. In March 2001, the EU created a pilot unit to test the idea. It was established in its final form in September 2003.

In May 2001, the European Commission launched the European Forum on Organised Crime Prevention. The Commission intends the forum to promote a balanced approach to organised crime. It involves external partners, the business community, researchers and civil society in general. Prevention is becoming increasingly important as a strategy for dealing with organised crime. Levi and Maguire (2004) note that although law enforcement rather than prevention has continued to dominate efforts to tackle organised crime, prevention through effective crime-reduction strategies is likely to play an increasing role in the field. They believe such prevention should contain two core elements:

1. the prevention or reduction of particular forms of serious crime (a focus on harmful *acts*); and

2. a reduction in the growth and development of organized criminal groups or formations, and in their involvement in the commission of those serious offences (a focus on harmful *actors*).

(Levi and Maguire 2004: 398)

Detailed and systematic analysis is a necessary precursor to interventions in both of these domains, although Levi and Maguire found surprisingly little evidence that the EU states were carrying out analysis of this kind. There was little attempt to analyse the structure of targeted groups, beyond immediate operational requirements. The infrastructure does not currently exist through which investigators can obtain a clear understanding of the various crime scenes, actors and their resources (Levi and Maguire 2004: 457). Although the authors point to a number of difficulties in this field, they have rightly identified an important area for development. Unless the international community takes serious notice of such research, it is unlikely that effective management of the longer-term threats that organised crime presents will be possible.

One area in which prevention has met with some success is in the field of money laundering. As we saw in Chapter 3, money laundering is the process by which criminal proceeds are 'cleaned', so that their illegal origins are hidden. The scale of the problem is enormous. The International Monetary Fund (IMF) has estimated that the aggregate size of money laundering may be somewhere between 2 per cent and 5 per cent of the world's gross domestic product. The EU has taken major steps against money laundering. In 1990, member states of the Council of Europe adopted the Convention on Laundering Search, Seizure and Confiscation of the Proceeds from Crime. The aim of the Convention is to facilitate international co-operation and mutual assistance in investigating crime and seizing criminal assets. Parties to the Convention undertake to criminalise the laundering of the proceeds of crime and to confiscate them. Many European states incorporated the Convention into their domestic laws and now take active steps to deal with the problem. In 1991, the EU Directive on Money Laundering gave effect to the Convention within EU states. During the late 1990s, many of the post-Soviet states signed and ratified the Convention. Levi and Osofsky (1995) set out a critique of the application of measures against money laundering in the UK.

A number of countries have created Financial Intelligence Units (FIUs) as specialised agencies to deal with the growing problem of money laundering within their jurisdictions. As of June 2002, sixty-nine countries had such groups. These units provide a focus for anti-money laundering programmes and information exchange within their own jurisdictions. In 1995, several of these units began to co-operate internationally on an informal basis. The group first met at the Egmont-Arenburg Palace in Brussels and adopted the name 'Egmont Group' thereafter. The group provides a forum for FIUs to systematise the exchange of financial intelligence and to improve communication between them.

There is little doubt that the EU is giving strategic priority to anti-money laundering activities. The first joint EU Council of Finance, Justice and Home Affairs Ministers in October 2000 provides evidence of the determination of the EU to tackle the problem. This meeting encouraged co-operation between FIUs of the member states. They also agreed to seek to amend the terms of the Europol Convention to extend the competence of Europol to money laundering in general, not just money laundering that is drugs related.

At the joint EU Council of Finance, Justice and Home Affairs Ministers held in October 2001, member states signed the above-mentioned protocol to the Convention on Mutual Assistance in Criminal Matters. The protocol represents an important improvement of the co-operation between member states in fighting economic and financial crime. The EU also reached agreement in October 2001 on updating the 1991 directive against money laundering. The new directive will broaden the scope of the original to cover not only drug trafficking but also other serious crimes. It also extends the directive to certain non-financial activities and professions, including lawyers.

The European Commission is a member of the Financial Action Task Force (see below) and participates fully in international bodies such as the Organisation for Economic Co-operation and Development (OECD) and the Council of Europe. The Council of Europe maintains a committee of experts on the evaluation of money-laundering measures. The Commission has also negotiated on behalf of the EU in respect of the relevant money-laundering provisions of the 2000 UN Convention on Transnational Organized Crime (United Nations 2000a).

It is worth noting, however, that there is still a certain amount of unease about the effectiveness of many of these measures. The Council of Europe Parliamentary Assembly made a number of recommendations in its paper entitled *Europe's Fight against Economic and Transnational Organised Crime: Progress or retreat?* They argued that despite the measures that the EU and other bodies had taken, economic crime has worsened and was likely to undermine Europe's political and economic foundations. They recommended a range of action, including updating the 1990 Convention and further work to fight corruption (Council of Europe 2001).

G7/8 and other bodies

Since 1975, heads of state or government of the major industrial democracies have met annually to discuss matters of political and economic importance. From 1977 onwards, membership of the so-called 'G7' has consisted of Canada, France, Germany, Italy, Japan, the UK and the USA. Starting with the 1994 Naples summit, the G7 and Russia met as the P8 ('Political 8'), following each G7 summit. Following the Birmingham summit of 1998, Russia became a full participant, forming the G8.

The political and economic impact of organised crime has encouraged world leaders to address the subject in their meetings. G8 has also developed a network of supporting ministerial fora, task forces and working groups. At the Halifax summit in 1995, the heads of government of the G8 countries recognised the global dangers of organised crime. They set up a group of senior experts to review and evaluate international agreements and to make recommendations. The group submitted its first report to the G8 leaders at the 1996 summit in Lyon, France. The Lyon Group drew up a list of forty recommendations, which the G8 countries and some other states have largely implemented. Their recommendations included guidelines on how countries can best work together. The Lyon Group has met at subsequent annual summits to discuss trends in organised crime, drug trafficking and associated matters. Recent work includes mutual legal assistance and extradition, firearms, 'high-tech' crime and international financial crime. For analysis of the involvement of G8 in measures to combat organised crime, readers should refer to Wrench (1997).

The Financial Action Task Force (FATF) carries out work on combating financial crime and money laundering. The G7 established this task force at the fifteenth economic summit held in Paris in June 1989. FATF is an independent body, although the OECD in Paris provides accommodation for its secretariat. It is not part of OECD. G7 gave the task force the responsibility of examining money-laundering techniques and trends and setting out means to tackle the problem. In 1990, it made forty recommendations that provide a blueprint for action against money laundering. These set out the principles of action that states should take including the following obligations:

- The criminalisation of the laundering of the proceeds of serious crimes (Recommendation 4) and the enactment of laws to seize and confiscate the proceeds of crime (Recommendation 7).

- Obligations for financial institutions to identify all clients, including any beneficial owners of property, and to keep appropriate records (Recommendations 10 to 12).

- A requirement for financial institutions to report suspicious transactions to the competent national authorities (Recommendation 15), and to implement a comprehensive range of internal control measures (Recommendation 19).

- Adequate systems for the control and supervision of financial institutions (Recommendations 26 to 29).

- The need to enter into international treaties or agreements and to pass national legislation which will allow countries to provide prompt and effective international co-operation at all levels (Recommendations 32 to 40).

Although not an international convention binding on states, many countries have made a political commitment by adopting the recommendations. FATF revised the recommendations during 1996 to take account of new threats. From 2003, FATF will work to promote co-operation with other regional and international initiatives in the field of money laundering. G8 have since agreed that it should continue its work.

The US media has criticised the FATF for its supposedly intrusive approach, which, it claims is against the rights of citizens to privacy (Rahn 2002). Criticism of operational activity by FATF is not well directed because it is primarily a policy-making body. However, it is certainly the case that there is only tenuous public oversight of this body. G8 are making little attempt to ensure its democratic accountability.

International measures for drugs control

Turning to the question of international measures for the drug control, the international community has long recognised the necessity to get agreement between nations on managing the problem of drug trafficking. The UN organisation has initiated much of this work. The main instruments are as follows:

1. The 1961 UN Single Convention on Narcotic Drugs (as amended in 1972). This aims to combat drug abuse by means of co-ordinated

action between states to limit possession, use and import/export of drugs. It also aims to combat drug trafficking by means of international co-operation.

2. The 1972 UN Convention on Psychotropic Substances. This extends the spectrum of drugs of abuse and introduces controls over a number of synthetic drugs, according to their abuse potential and to their therapeutic value.

3. The 1988 UN Convention against the Illicit Traffic in Narcotic Drugs and Psychotropic Substances (the 'Vienna Convention'). This provides comprehensive measures against drug trafficking. These include provisions against money laundering and the diversion of precursor chemicals for manufacture of synthetic drugs. It also provides for international co-operation for the extradition of traffickers, controlled deliveries and transfer of proceedings.

Subsequently the UN General Assembly, its Economic and Social Council and the Commission on Narcotic Drugs (CND) have passed a number of resolutions exhorting states to act against drug misuse. In particular, the subject was included at the so-called 'Millennium Summit' of the UN in September 2000. It has been the subject of yearly resolutions by the UN General Assembly since that date. The UN Office on Drugs and Crime (UNODC) provides a means for co-ordinating information on the activities of the UN Drugs Control Programme.

Europe has also been particularly active in seeking to consolidate action by states against drug misuse and trafficking. The Pompidou Group of European States was set up in 1971 to provide a forum for ministers, officials and professionals in the field to co-operate and exchange information. The Council of Europe incorporated it into its Social Cohesion Directorate in 1980. The Group collaborates with the UN, the EU and specialist organisations such as Interpol and the World Customs Union. It currently has thirty-four members, including the European Commission.

The EU participated in the Conference on the Illicit Traffic in Narcotic Drugs and Psychotropic Substances in 1988 and ratified the Vienna Convention in the same year. Thereafter, the EU put into place a number of measures to consolidate its anti-drugs activities. In 1989, it created the European Committee to Combat Drugs (CELAD), which created the first European Plan to Combat Drugs. The EU adopted this plan in 1990. The TEU came into force in 1993 and for the first time included drugs in an EU treaty. Also in 1993 the European Monitoring Centre for Drugs and Drug Addiction (EMCDDA) came into being. The Centre, which is located in Lisbon, is responsible for collecting and disseminating information on the drug situation in Europe.

The Treaty of Amsterdam, which came into force in May 1999, strengthened these measures. At the 1999 European Council in Helsinki, the European Drugs Strategy was agreed. Subsequently, the European Commission and the European Parliament adopted the EU Action Plan to Combat Drugs for the years 2000–2004. This action plan includes measures to encourage reduction of supply and demand and international co-operation. EMCDDA was set up to provide information about drug misuse and trafficking in Europe and measures that are in place to combat them.

In summary, it would be mistaken to assume that the extensive list of bodies to promote international co-operation and the measures they have developed have met with universal approval. The number of institutions involved in measures that attempt to control organised crime is high. The sheer volume of reports and recommendations is the product of a bureaucracy of Byzantine proportions. Rivalries between agencies sometimes make effective law enforcement action difficult, although the appointment of international liaison officers is an important step forward. Overall, however, the system of international measures seeking to control, regulate and prevent organised crime is complex. If such a plethora of bureaucracy were to beset organised crime itself, it would be bound to fail! Although many states have signed and ratified the various conventions and instruments, there are continual problems in ensuring that these are converted into action at the grass roots. Despite these negative factors, multilateral co-operation remains the single most important factor in tackling the risks presented by international organised crime.

Conclusion

Organised crime is a complex subject. To respond to the complexity, the study of organised crime set out in this book has reviewed it from a number of different perspectives: a historical perspective through which we could begin to understand its origins and to identify the course of its development; a social perspective to make sense of its basis in social organisation and to assess its impact upon wider society; perspectives drawn from politics and economics in order to grasp its effect upon national and international relations; the framework of international law and treaty obligations because it involves complex legal concepts. To a greater or lesser extent, this book has sought to draw upon all of these perspectives.

Organised crime is also a controversial subject and the modes of explanation that analysts employ are themselves often problematic. For this reason, our debate about the nature of organised crime has reflected as much upon the ways in which we might seek to explain it as upon the object of explanation itself. In this sense, we have reflected both on the *explanans* and on the *explanandum*. In reviewing the literature, the fact that even quite rigorous accounts of the subject sometimes omit this necessary reflection has meant that we have sometimes been critical of the ways in which some writers have sought to explain the phenomenon.

'What is organised crime?' has been the central question upon which we have focused throughout this text. The process of explanation in this context has meant teasing out the variety of meanings that we might appropriately apply to the concept. We have shown that the problem of defining organised crime is both semantic and empirical.

It is semantic in the sense that it is a contested concept, with no possibility of complete agreement about what the term denotes. It is empirical in the sense that there is no absolute consensus about the substantive examples that might fall within its scope.

The question of the extent to which organised crime is 'organised' is at the heart of any attempt to understand the concept. However, some writers who argue that much of it is actually 'disorganised' predicate this claim upon a limited analysis of the notion of organisation. 'Organisation' is itself a term that we need to understand in its historical context and one that we need to revise in the light of contemporary organisational theory. Instead of focusing upon the substance of 'organisation', we should regard the activities of 'organising' groups of criminals as the key that unlocks the meaning of organised crime in late modernity. Van Duyne (1996) rightly suggests that such organising criminals operate through a variety of trading communities in 'a changing landscape of crime in the sense of criminal market opportunities' (Van Duyne 1996: 92). Clearly, the activities of such organising criminals have not remained static. Social change and the globalisation of communications and commerce have brought about a fragmentation of organised crime across the world in the past few decades. This has produced a plurality of forms, ranging from localised gangs to international syndicated crime. Problems of identifying the locus of organised crime also present a number of difficulties. Although there are substantive examples to show that it operates at the local and the international levels, the idea that it may in some sense be transnational in character remains problematic. We also need to understand that its locus is not simply geographic. It operates in a number of logical domains, including the social, political and the economic.

Gangs of all kinds, from youth or street gangs to supposedly more sophisticated forms of organised criminal groups, provide a useful point of departure for the study of organised criminality. In some cases, youth and street gangs may provide a pathway to more highly developed forms of group criminality. This is especially the case in places such as Chicago, where organised crime has a long and interesting history. A review of the literature shows that there is considerable controversy over the nature of gangs, particularly in relation to structures, goals and organisation. Some problems appear to derive from differences in methodology but much of the controversy is about the contested nature of the gang concept. However, we can say that violence and coercion are endemic to gangsterism as a form of life.

Not all organised crime is gang-related crime. Analysis of its range of activities shows that they often revolve around the notion of enterprise crime. We can properly regard enterprise crime as a form of 'dirty business'. It provides goods and services that are on the same continuum as those of legitimate business. However, criminal activities such as protection rackets and drug trafficking are below the legal limits that states permit for security and for the supply of goods. Despite these differences, we can rightly regard both crime groups and legitimate businesses as 'firms' who try to minimise their transaction costs. The ways in which they achieve this will differ, alongside a number of other differences between legitimate and illicit forms of enterprise. Some commentators claim that so-called 'white-collar' and corporate crimes are simply examples of some of the dubious activities that are the reality behind much 'normal' business practice. In some cases, this is true. We cite a number of glaring examples where the officers of large corporations have acted like organised criminals. But, despite these cases, except for those who believe that all capitalist forms of production are themselves illegitimate, there is no evidence that every business is simply a form of organised crime. However, it is certainly true that organised crime groups, businesses and some state enterprises use money laundering to convert the proceeds of their operations into usable assets.

Drug trafficking and trafficking in people are both forms of enterprise crime. In these fields, organised crime groups provide goods and services that are below the legal limits, compared with those within which legitimate pharmaceutical companies and travel agents operate. The extent of drug trafficking is extensive, with centres of illicit opiate production in the Far East and South America. Cannabis is the most extensively produced and most widely traded illicit drug. Supply-chain theory helps to illustrate the structural complexity of the illicit drug industry. We have argued for a typology of traffickers that recognises that they differ according to their antecedents and objectives and to the level of the market that they try to satisfy. We resist the idea of a pyramid of traffickers, controlled by a small number of elites. The smuggling of human beings and the various forms of trafficking in people are also distinct enterprise-crime activities. The former relates mainly to the facilitation of migration by individuals, families, associates and criminal gangs. The latter usually relates to trafficking in women and children for sexual and other purposes, including for domestic labour. In many cases, organised criminal gangs use extortion and coercion to increase their profits. Bearing in mind that even extensive drug trafficking has a relatively short history, these forms of enterprise crime show the extent to which organised crime can flexibly adapt to new conditions and help to 'make' new markets.

So-called 'traditional' forms of organised crime have their origin in the secret societies that developed in Italy, China and Japan to provide protection during periods of bad government. With their origins in Southern Italy and in Naples, the Mafia and the Camorra have developed networks of interlinked (but sometimes opposing) families with an international outreach. Chinese Triad and Tong groups, whose origins were in Hong Kong and mainland China, have spread worldwide, although the influence of the Triads as 'secret societies' may now be taking second place to more venal objectives. The Yakuza, whose origins are in Japan, have developed a range of illicit enterprises. They have also gained considerable political influence in their homeland. All of these groups have developed activities that extend beyond their original aims of providing illicit protection to other forms of organised crime. These include drug trafficking, people smuggling and fraud. In moving into these fields, they have also developed alliances with other criminal groups throughout the world.

Organised crime in the USA provides a fruitful field for study. Much of the literature on the subject emanates from there. From the earliest theories, which suggested that it was the result of an alien conspiracy amongst immigrant populations, to more recent debates about its pluralisation, American organised crime has attracted popular and specialist attention. In the popular literature, the heyday of American organised crime was the period of prohibition, when syndicated crime allied itself with business interests to provide the nation with illicit alcohol. The consolidation of Cosa Nostra style gangsterism thereafter provides a paradigm case of how syndicated crime can thrive in capitalist systems. The more recent development of a plethora of groups, including youth gangs, motorcycle gangs, ethnic crime groups and those whose speciality is corporate crime has extended the field well beyond that occupied by the Italian-American, Irish and Jewish gangs that were dominant until the 1960s. Incursions by so-called 'traditional' organised crime groups, such as the Tongs, Triads and the Yakuza have increased, although they have long had a presence in the USA.

The predominant basis of the response of the authorities to organised crime has been to regard it as a bureaucratic and hierarchical phenomenon, a substantive network which is largely controlled by criminal elites. Much of the criminological debate on the subject in the USA has concerned itself with this assumption, often showing convincingly that it does not reflect the reality of criminal gang activity. The outreach activities of the US authorities in seeking to counter so-called transnational organised crime are a major part of US foreign policy. As we have shown, organised crime in the USA provides an important element of the analysis of organised crime worldwide. The gangster image has been an important one in the development and promulgation of American culture. The celebration of gangster life, as represented in popular entertainment, also shows the extent to which the public in the USA and worldwide has absorbed the gang culture. Although this may entail deeper psychological issues, there is certainly evidence of a long-term public celebration of gangsterism.

The USA has not been alone in experiencing changes to the nature of organised crime in the latter part of the twentieth century. Non-traditional forms of organised crime have also expanded in Europe, through the activities of both indigenous and immigrant gangs. The development of a 'new wave' of organised crime has been particularly evident in the post-Soviet States. It has expanded at a rapid pace in the Russian Federation since the political changes of the late 1980s. Commentators estimate that organised criminal groups controlled around 40 per cent of GNP in Russia by the end of the twentieth century. Privatisation has provided huge opportunities for criminal groups to run protection rackets and to provide illicit goods. Drug trafficking is widespread, alongside corporate crime. An expansion of organised crime is also evident in the newly democratised states of Eastern and Central Europe and in the Baltic Sea region.

Organised crime has also become a global phenomenon. The criminogenic assymetries between the developed and developing world have helped to expand organised crime in territories where it has not been predominant before. Nigeria, for example, is an important generator of international criminal networks, facilitated by hitherto corrupt regimes. Although there is clear evidence of proliferation and of collaboration in some cases, especially in drug trafficking, there is no substantial proof that the Mafia and other major crime groups have merged in a kind of *pax mafiosa*.

Organised crime in Britain has a long history, including criminal groups ranging from highway and town gangs, through illegal thief-takers to bubble companies. Immigrant and indigenous gangs in the late Victorian and Edwardian periods were the precursors to more widespread gangsterdom following the First World War. The heyday of Britain's gangs was the period from the 1920s until the 1960s. Interrupted only by the Second World War, this period generated an identifiable 'underworld' of families and networks of associates whose common origins were in the deprived social conditions of the major cities of Britain. London in particular produced a number of dominant criminal gangs who provided protection at racecourses and other entertainment venues. Although not on the scale of their counterparts in the USA, these gangs ran protection rackets and controlled clubs and fraudulent businesses, often making use of extreme violence for the purpose. The demise of gangs such as the Richardsons and Krays marked the culmination of this era. A more fragmented panorama of indigenous and ethnically-based gangs replaced them. The primary activities of these groups often include large-scale drug trafficking. Many gangs who had specialised in robbery during the 1970s and 1980s switched their activities to this field.

In recent years, as is the case in the rest of Europe, the activities of immigrant criminal groups, many of whom have been predominant in drugs and people smuggling, have supplemented those of indigenous gangs. Armed youth gangs have been extensively active in drug dealing, especially in crack-cocaine. In Northern Ireland, paramilitary terrorist groups have diversified their activities to include drug dealing and robbery. Gangs from Eastern and Central Europe have been active in people trafficking, immigration crime and in the illicit sex trade. Overall, the picture of organised crime in Britain has followed developments elsewhere. A plethora of parallel underworlds has replaced the older, comparatively cohesive, underworld of earlier years.

Since the attack on the World Trade Center in New York in September 2001, terrorism has been the main concern of the international community. This has continued in the light of further attacks in the UK and elsewhere following the wars in Afghanistan and Iraq. Despite this fact, organised crime is likely to remain comparatively high on the political agenda, especially in the longer term if the threat of terrorism recedes. Control measures, however, cannot provide a complete answer to the risks posed by organised crime. Overall, it seems likely that only a well-co-ordinated mixture of law enforcement, regulatory strategies and measures against money laundering will enable states to contain the threats. Anti-money laundering measures that 'follow the money' are increasingly effective in cutting off the flow of funds. Law enforcement activity against organised crime in individual states is necessary to tackle specific cases and to bring offenders to justice, although it cannot provide a long-term solution. Measures such as the UN Convention against Transnational Organised Crime signal the determination of the international community to tackle organised crime by means of co-ordinated action. The G7/8 group also have organised crime clearly on their long-term agenda. The EU has adopted a range of measures intended to have an effect on organised crime. The remit of Europol to tackle it by co-ordinating the work of police in the EU states provides an institution for practical co-operation. As we have already mentioned, the outreach activities of US Federal agencies is an important element of US foreign policy, although sceptics believe that it serves only US interests, not those of the wider community. Whether the sum total of these measures is sufficient to be successful remains an open question.

What is the future of organised crime? We have already remarked on its durability and flexibility. This will continue to enable it to generate new markets and to form new alliances. One particular area of concern may be the increased involvement of terrorist groups. The use of the internet for trading of all kinds is also likely to fuel enterprise crime. Organised crime groups are increasingly likely to make illicit commodities such as drugs available by this means. Counterfeit pharmaceutical drugs are likely to figure in this trade. The use of the internet to facilitate network communications by organised crime groups is likely to increase and there are likely to be more attacks on business targets such as banks using high-tech means.

Although drugs, people smuggling and corporate crime are likely to be the predominant activities of organised crime groups in the short to medium term, new markets will undoubtedly arise. These will continue to have enterprise crime principles as their basis. The extent of the further regression of legitimate business into organised crime is uncertain. More regulation, especially in the fields of banking and financial services, is likely to be necessary if the greed that is endemic in capitalist systems does not increasingly suck legitimate businesses into organised corporate crime. Overall, therefore, we can be certain that organised crime will continue to figure as a major international problem. Only time will tell whether the measures introduced by individual states and by the international community will be effective in containing its worst excesses.

References

Abadinsky, H. (1994) *Organized Crime* (3rd edn). Chicago: Nelson Hall.

Abadinsky, H. (2002) *Organized Crime* (7th edn). Belmont, CA: Wadsworth.

Albanese, J.S. (1996) *Organized Crime in America* (3rd edn). Cincinatti: Anderson.

Albini, J. (1971) *The American Mafia: Genesis of a Legend*. New York: Appleton Century Crofts.

Allum, F. and Siebert, R. (2003) *Organised Crime and the Challenge to Democracy*. London: Routledge.

Anderson, A. (1997) 'Organised Crime, *Mafias* and Government', in G. Fiorentini and S. Peltzman, *The Economics of Organised Crime*. Cambridge: Cambridge University Press.

Arlacchi, P. (1988) *Mafia Business: The Mafia Ethic and the Spirit of Capitalism*. Oxford: Oxford University Press.

Arlacchi. P. (2002) 'Culture, Conflict and Crime: A Global Perspective', in J.D. Freilich, G. Newman, S. Giorna Shoham and M. Addad, *Migration, Culture, Conflict and Crime*. Aldershot: Ashgate.

Arnott, J. (1999) *The Long Firm*. London: Sceptre.

Arnott, J. (2001) *He Kills Coppers*. London: Sceptre.

Arnott, J. (2003) *True Crime*. London: Sceptre.

Asbury, H. (2002 [1927]) *The Gangs of New York*. London: Arrow Books.

Asbury, H. (2003 [1940]) *The Gangs of Chicago*. London: Arrow Books.

Asbury, H. (2004a [1933]) *The Gangs of San Francisco*. London: Arrow Books.

Asbury, H. (2004b [1936]) *The Gangs of New Orleans*. London: Arrow Books.

Association of Chief Police Officers (1986) *Final Report of a Working Party on Drugs Related Crime* (Chairman R.F. Broome). London: Association of Chief Police Officers.

Bannock, G., Baxter, R.E. and Davis, E. (1998) *The Penguin Dictionary of Economics*. London: Penguin Books.

Barnes, M., Elias, R. and Walsh, P. (2000) *Cocky: The Rise and Fall of Curtis Warren: Britain's Biggest Drug Baron*. London: Milo.

Barthes, R. (1983) *The Fashion System*, translated by M. Ward and R. Howard. New York: Hill & Wang.

Bassouni, M.C. and Vetere, E. (eds) (1998) *Organized Crime: A Compilation of UN Documents 1975–1998*. Ardsley, NY: Transnational Publishers.

Bean, J.P. (1981) *The Sheffield Gang Wars*. Sheffield: D. & D. Publications.

Bean, P. (2002) *Drugs and Crime*. Cullompton: Willan Publishing.

Beare, M. (ed.) (1996) *Criminal Conspiracies: Organised Crime in Canada*. Scarborough, Ont: Nelson.

Beare, M. (ed.) (2003) *Critical Reflections on Transnational Organized Crime, Money Laundering and Corruption*. Toronto: University of Toronto Press.

Behan, T. (1996) *The Camorra*. London: Routledge.

Behan, T. (2002) *See Naples and Die: The Camorra and Organized Crime*, London: IB Tauris.

Bell, D. (1960) 'Crime as an American Way of Life', in *The End of Ideology*. Glencoe, IL: Free Press of Glencoe (originally published in *Antioch Review* 1953).

Berdal, M. and Serrano, M. (eds) (2002) *Transnational Organised Crime: New Challenges to International Security*. Boulder, CO: Lynne Rienner.

Berridge, V. (1984) 'Drugs and Social Policy: the Establishment of Drugs Control in Britain 1900–1930', *British Journal of Addiction*, 19: 17–29.

Bigo, D. (2000) 'Liaison Officers in Europe: New Officers in the European Security Field', in J.W.E. Sheptycki (ed.) *Issues in Transnational Policing*. London: Routledge.

Billings, D.E. (1997) 'Chronology of Organised Crime, Money Laundering and Drug Trafficking in Hungary: October 1980–March 1998', *Transnational Organized Crime*, 3/3: 166–90.

Bittner, E. (1970) *The Functions of the Police in Modern Society*. Chevy Chase, MD: National Institute of Mental Health.

Block, A. and Chambliss, W.J. (1981) *Organizing Crime*. New York: Elsevier.

Block, A. (1983) *East Side – West Side: Organizing Crime in New York 1930–1950*. New Brunswick, NJ: Transaction.

Block, A. (1996) 'On the Origins of Fuel Racketeering: The Americans and the "Russians" in New York', in P. Williams (ed.) (1997) *Russian Organised Crime: The New Threat?* London: Frank Cass.

Booth, M. (1999) *The Dragon Syndicates: The Global Phenomenon of the Triads*. London: Doubleday.

Bottom, A.E. (1994) 'Environmental Criminology', in M. Maguire, R. Morgan and R. Reiner (eds) *Oxford Handbook of Criminology*. Oxford: Oxford University Press, pp. 585–656.

Bottoms, A.E. and Wiles, P. (2002) 'Environmental Criminology', in M. Maguire, R. Morgan and R. Reiner (eds) *Oxford Handbook of Criminology*, (3rd edn). Oxford: Oxford University Press, pp. 620–56.

Bowling, B., Phillips, C. and Shah, A. (2003) 'Policing Ethnic Minority Communities', in T. Newburn (ed.) *Handbook of Policing*. Cullompton: Willan Publishing.

Box, S. (1983) *Power, Crime and Mystification*. London: Tavistock.

Boyce, D. (1987) 'Narco Terrorism', *FBI Law Enforcement Bulletin*, 56/11: 24–7.

Brantley, A.C. and Di Rosa, A. (1994) 'Gangs: a National Perspective', *FBI Law Enforcement Bulletin*, May: 1–19.

Bresler, F. (1980) *The Trail of the Triads*. London: Weidenfeld & Nicholson.

Burgess, E.W. (1925) 'The Growth of the City', in R.E. Park and E.W. Burgess, *The City*. Chicago: Chicago University Press.

Burnham, B. (2003) 'Measuring Transnational Organised Crime: An Empirical Study of Existing Data Sets on TOC with Particular Reference to Intergovernmental Organisations', in A. Edwards and P. Gill (eds) *Transnational Organised Crime: Perspectives on Global Security*. London: Routledge.

Cater, F. and Tullett, T. (1990) *The Sharp End: The Fight Against Organised Crime*. London: Grafton.

Chambliss, W.J. (1978) *On the Take: From Petty Crooks to Presidents*. Bloomington: Indiana University Press.

Chibnall, S. and Murphy, R. (eds) (1999) *British Crime Cinema*. London: Routledge.

Chin, K.L. (1996a) 'Gang Violence in Chinatown', in C.R. Huff (ed.) *Gangs in America* (2nd edn). Thousand Oaks, CA: Sage Publications.

Chin, K.L. (1996b) *Chinatown Gangs: Extortion, Enterprise and Ethnicity*. New York: Oxford University Press.

Chin, K.L. (1999) *Smuggled Chinese: Clandestine Immigration to the US*. Philadelphia: Temple University Press.

Chin, K.L., Zhang, S. and Kelly, R.J. (1998) 'Transnational Chinese Organized Crime Activities: Patterns and Emerging Trends', in P. Williams and D. Vlassis (eds) *Combating Transnational Crime: Concepts, Activities and Responses*, Special Issue of *Transnational Organized Crime*, 4/3–4: 127–54.

Chouvy, P.A. (1999) 'Drug Diversity in the Golden Triangle', in *Crime and Justice International*, October, 15(33).

Chouvy, P.A. (2002) 'New Drug Trafficking Routes in Southeast Asia', *Jane's Intelligence Review*, 1 July.

Chu, Y.K. (2000) *The Triads in Business*. London: Routledge.

Clegg, S.W. (1990) *Modern Organizations: Organization Studies in the Postmodern World*. London: Sage.

Cloward, R. and Ohlin, L. (1960) *Delinquency and Opportunity: A Theory of Delinquent Gangs*. New York: Free Press.

Coase, R.H. (1937) 'The Nature of the Firm', *Economica*, N.S. 4: 386–405.

Cohen, A.K. (1955) *Delinquent Boys: The Culture of the Gang*. Glencoe, IL: Free Press.

Cohen, A.K. (1977) 'The Concept of Criminal Organisation', *British Journal of Criminology*, 17(2): 97–111.

Coleman, C. and Norris, C. (2000) *Introducing Criminology*. Cullompton: Willan Publishing.

Council of Europe (2001) *Europe's Fight against Economic and Transnational Organised Crime: Progress or retreat?* Council of Europe Parliamentary Assembly: Recommendation 1507 (2001), 24 April 2001 (11th sitting).

Cox, B., Shirley, J. and Short, M. (1977) *The Fall of Scotland Yard*. Harmondsworth: Penguin Books.

Cressey, D.R. (1967) 'The Functions and Structure of Criminal Syndicates', President's Commission on Law Enforcement and Administration of Justice, *Task Force Report: Organized Crime*. Washington: US Government Printing Office.

Cressey, D.R. (1969) *Theft of the Nation: the Structure and Operations of Organized Crime in America*. New York: Harper & Row.

Cressey, D.R. (1971) *Organized Crime and Criminal Organizations*. Cambridge: Heffer.

Cressey, D.R. (1972) *Criminal Organisation: Its Elementary Forms*. London: Heinemann.

Croall, H. (1992) *Understanding White Collar Crime*. Milton Keynes: Open University Press.

Croall, H. (2001) *Understanding White Collar Crime* (2nd edn). Milton Keynes: Open University Press.

Cyert, R.M. and March, J.G. (1963) *A Behavioural Theory of the Firm*. Englewood Cliffs, NJ: Prentice Hall.

Decker, S.H. (2001) 'The Impact of Organizational Features on Gang Activities and Relationships', in M.W. Klein, H-J. Kerner, C.L. Maxson and E.G.M. Weitekamp (eds) *The Eurogang Paradox: Street Gangs and Youth Groups in the US and Europe*. Dordrecht: Kluwer Academic Publishers.

Decker, S.H. and Van Winkle, B. (1994) 'Slinging Dope: The role of Gangs and Gang Members in Drugs Sales', *Justice Quarterly*, 11(4) (December).

Decker, S.H. and Van Winkle, B. (1996) *Life in the Gang*. Cambridge: Cambridge University Press.

Decker, S.H., Bynum, T. and Weisel, D. (1998) 'A Tale of Two Cities', in J. Miller, C.L. Maxson and M.W. Klein (eds) (2001) *The Modern Gang Reader* (2nd edn). Los Angeles: Roxbury Publishing Company.

Dick, A.R. (1995) 'When does Organized Crime Pay? A Transaction Analysis', *International Review of Law and Economics*, 15(1): 25.

Dorn, N. and South, N. (1990) 'Drug Markets and Law Enforcement', *British Journal of Sociology*, 30/2: 171–88.

Dorn, N., Murji, K. and South, N. (1992) *Traffickers*. London: Routledge.

Downes, D. and Rock, P. (1988) *Understanding Deviance* (2nd edn). Oxford: Oxford University Press.

Drucker, E. (1991) 'US Drugs Policy: Public Health versus Prohibition', in P.A. O'Hare, R. Newcombe, A. Matthews, E.C. Buning and E. Drucker (eds) (1992) *The Reduction of Drug-related Harm*. London: Routledge.

Dunn, G. (1997) 'Major Mafia Gangs in Russia', in P. Williams (ed.) *Russian Organised Crime: The New Threat?* London: Frank Cass.

Dunn, T.J. (2001) 'Border Militarization via Drug and Immigration Enforcement: Human Rights Implications', *Social Justice*, 25(2).

Dunningham, C. and Norris, C. (1999) 'The Detective, the Snout and the Audit Commission: The Real Cost of Using Informants', *Howard Journal*, 38: 67–86.

Ebbe, O.N.I. (1999) 'Political-criminal nexus. The Nigerian Case: Slicing Nigeria's "National Cake"', *Trends in Organized Crime*, 4(3), Spring: 29–59.

Edwards, A. and Gill, P. (eds) (2003) *Transnational Organised Crime: Perspectives on Global Security*. London: Routledge.

Elvins, M. (2003) 'Europe's Response to Transnational Organised Crime', in A. Edwards and P. Gill (eds) *Transnational Organised Crime: Perspectives on Global Security*. London: Routledge.

Emsley, C. (1996) *Crime and Society in England 1750–1900*. London: Longman.

European Commission (2001) 'Joint Report from Commission Services and Europol – Towards a European Strategy to Prevent Organised Crime', Commission Staff Working Paper, SEC (2001) 433 (Brussels, 13 March).

European Commission (2002) *Communication from the Commission to the Council and the European Parliament. Biannual Update of the Scoreboard to Review Progress on the Creation of an Area of 'Freedom Security and Justice' in the European Union* [COM (2002) 261 final]. Brussels: Commission of the European Communities.

European Union (1998) *Article 1 of the Joint Action of the Justice and Home Affairs Council to Create a Criminal Offence to Participate in a Criminal Organisation*. Brussels: European Union, Council of Justice and Home Affairs Ministers.

Fagan, J. (1996) 'Gangs, Drugs and Neighbourhood Change', in C.R. Huff (ed.) *Gangs in America* (2nd edn). Thousand Oaks, CA: Sage Publications.

Falcone, G. (1993) *Men of Honour: The Truth about the Mafia*. London: Warner Books.

Fijnaut, C. (1990), 'Organised Crime: A Comparison between the United States of America and Western Europe', *British Journal of Criminology*, 30(3): 321–40.

Fijnaut, C. (1998) 'Transnational Organized Crime and Institutional Reform in the European Union: The Case of Judicial Co-operation', in P. Williams and D. Vlassis (eds) *Combating Transnational Crime: Concepts, Activities and Responses*, Special Issue of *Transnational Organized Crime*, 4/3–4: 276–302.

Fijnaut, C., Bovenkerk, F., Bruinsma, G. and Van De Bunt, H. (1998) *Organised Crime in the Netherlands*. The Hague: Kluwer Law International.

Finckenauer, J.O. (2001) *Chinese Organised Crime: The Fuk Ching*. Washington: National Institute of Justice.

Finckenauer, J.O. and Voronin, Y.A. (2001) *The Threat of Russian Organized Crime*. Washington: US Department of Justice.

Fox, K. and McDonagh, M. (2003) *Virgin Film Guide* (11th edn). London: Virgin Books.

Fraser, F. (1994) *Mad Frank*. London: Warner Books.

Freilich, J.D., Newman, G., Giorna Shoham, S. and Addad, M. (2002) *Migration, Culture, Conflict and Crime*. Aldershot: Ashgate.

Frost, G. (1948) *Flying Squad*. London: Rockcliff.

Gallie, W.B. (1964) 'Essentially Contested Concepts', in W.B. Gallie *Philosophy and the Historical Understanding*. London: Chatto & Windus.

Gambetta, D. (1996) *The Sicilian Mafia: The Business of Private Protection*. Cambridge, MA and London: Harvard University Press.

Gerth, H.H. and Wright Mills, C. (1948) *From Max Weber: Essays in Sociology*. London: Routledge & Kegan Paul.

Gouldner, A.W. (1954) *Patterns of Industrial Democracy*. New York: Free Press.

Graycar, A. (2002) 'Trafficking in Human Beings', in J.D. Freilich, G. Newman, S. Giorna Shoham and M. Addad, *Migration, Culture, Conflict and Crime*. Aldershot: Ashgate.

Greene, G. (1938) *Brighton Rock*. London: Heinemann.

Gregory, F.E. (2003) 'Classify, Report and Measure: The UK Organised Crime Notification Scheme', in A. Edwards and P. Gill (eds) *Transnational Organised Crime: Perspectives on Global Security*. London: Routledge.

Hall, S., Critcher, C., Jefferson, T., Clarke, J. and Roberts, B. (1978) *Policing the Crisis*. London: Macmillan.

Haller, M. (1990) 'Illegal Enterprise: A Theoretical and Historical Interpretation', *Criminology*, 28(2), May: 207–36.

Hallsworth, S. (2005) *Street Crime*. Cullompton: Willan Publishing.

Hellawell, K. (2002) *The Outsider*. London: HarperCollins.

Heydebrand, W.V. (1989) 'New Organizational Forms', *Contemporary Sociology*, 16(5): 661–4.

High Level Group on Organised Crime (1997) *Action Plan to Combat Organised Crime*, Official Journal of the European Community, C 251, 1–18. Brussels: European Commission.

Hill, B.E.P. (2003) *The Japanese Mafia: Yakuza, Law and the State*. Oxford: Oxford University Press.

Hirschi, T. (1969) *Causes of Delinquency*. Berkeley: University of California Press.

Hobbes, T. (1651) *Leviathan*, edited by M. Oakeshott (1947). Oxford: Blackwell.

Hobbs, D. (1988) *Doing the Business*. Oxford: Clarendon Press.

Hobbs, D. (1994) 'Professional and Organised Crime in Britain', in M. Maguire, R. Morgan and R. Reiner *Oxford Handbook of Criminology*. Oxford: Oxford University Press.

Hobbs, D. (1995) *Bad Business*. Oxford: Oxford University Press.

Hobbs, D. (1998) 'Going down the Glocal: the Local Context of Organised Crime', *Howard Journal*, 37(4): 407–22.

Hobbs, D. (2001) 'The Firm: Organizational Logic and Criminal Culture on a Shifting Terrain', *British Journal of Criminology*, 41: 549–60.

Hobbs, D. and Dunningham, C. (1998), 'Global Organised Crime: Context and Pretext', in V. Ruggiero, N. South and I. Taylor (eds) *The New European Criminology: Crime and Social Order in Europe*. London: Routledge.

Home Office (1985) *Tackling Drugs Misuse: A Summary of the Government's Strategy*. London: The Home Office.

Hopkins Burke, R. (2005) *Introduction to Criminological Theory* (2nd edn). Cullompton: Willan Publishing.

Horowitz, R. (1983) *Honor and the American Dream: Culture and Identity in a Chicago Community*. New Brunswick, NJ: Rutgers University Press.

Huff, C.R. (1996) *Gangs in America*. Thousand Oaks, CA: Sage Publications.

Huspek, M. (2001) 'Production of State, Capital and Citizenry: The Case of Operation Gatekeeper', *Social Justice* 28(2): 51–68.

Ianni, F. and Ianni, E. (1972) *A Family Business: Kinship and Social Control in Organized Crime*. New York: Russell Sage Foundation.

Ianni, F.A.J. (1974) *Black Mafia: Ethnic Succession in Organized Crime*. New York: Simon & Schuster.

Jamieson, A. (1995) 'The Transnational Dimension of Italian Organized Crime', *Transnational Organized Crime,* 1/2: 151–72.

Jamieson, A. (2000) *The Anti-Mafia: Italy's Fight Against Organized Crime*. London: Macmillan.

Kaplan, D.E. and Dubro, A. (1986) *Yakuza: The Explosive Account of Japan's Criminal Underworld*. Reading, MA: Addison Wesley.

Kaplan, D.E. and Dubro, A. (2003) *Yakuza: Japan's Criminal Underworld* (expanded edn). Berkeley: University of California Press.

Kefauver, E. (1951) 'United States Congress, Senate Special Committee to Investigate Organized Crime in Interstate Commerce', *Third Interim Report*. Washington: US Government Printing Office.

Kelly, L. and Regan, L. (2000) *Stopping Traffic: Exploring the Extent of, and Response to, Trafficking in Women for Sexual Exploitation in the UK*. London: Home Office (Police Research Series Paper 125).

Kelly, R.J. (2000) *Encyclopedia of Organized Crime in the United States: From Capone's Chicago to the New Urban Underworld*. Westport, CT: Greenwood.

Klein, M. (1971) *Street Gangs and Street Workers*. Englewood Cliffs, NJ: Prentice Hall.

Klein, M. (1995) 'Street Gang Cycles', in J.Q. Wilson and J. Petersilia (eds) *Crime*. San Francisco: Institute for Contemporary Studies.

Klein, M. (1996) 'Gangs in the United States and Europe', in J. Miller, C.L. Maxson and M.W. Klein (eds) (2001) *The Modern Gang Reader* (2nd edn). Los Angeles: Roxbury Publishing Company.

Klein, M. and Maxson, C. (1994) 'Gangs and Cocaine Trafficking', in D.L. McKenzie and C.D. Uchida (eds) *Drugs and Crime: Evaluating Public Policy Initiatives*. Thousand Oaks, CA: Sage Publications.

Klein, M., Maxson, C. and Cunningham, L. (1991) '"Crack", Street Gangs and Violence', *Criminology*, 31: 623–50.

Klein, M.W., Kerner, H-J, Maxson, C.L and Weitekamp, E.G.M. (eds) (2001) *The Eurogang Paradox: Street Gangs and Youth Groups in the US and Europe*. Dordrecht: Kluwer Academic Publishers.

Klockars, C.B. (1974) *The Professional Fence*. London: Tavistock.

Koslowski, R. (2001) 'Economic Globalization, Human Smuggling and Global Governance', in D. Kyle and R. Koslowski (eds) *Global Human Smuggling: Comparative Perspectives*. Baltimore: Johns Hopkins University Press.

Kray, R. and Kray, R. (1988) *Our Story*. London: Pan Books.

Kyle, D. and Koslowski, R. (eds) (2001) *Global Human Smuggling: Comparative Perspectives*. Baltimore: Johns Hopkins University Press.

Lawrence, P.R. and Lorsch, J.W. (1967) *Organization and Environment: Managing Differentiation and Integration*. Boston: Graduate School of Business Administration, Harvard University.

Levi, M. (1997) 'Money Laundering and Regulatory Policies', in E. Savona (ed.) *Responding to Money Laundering: International Perspectives*. Amsterdam: Harwood Academic.

Levi, M. (ed.) (1998) *Reflections on Organised Crime: Patterns and Control*. Oxford: Blackwell (for The Howard League).

Levi, M. (2002) 'The Organization of Serious Crimes' in M. Maguire, R. Morgan and R. Reiner (eds) *Oxford Handbook of Criminology* (3rd edn). Oxford: Oxford University Press.

Levi, M. (2003) 'Organised and Financial Crime', in T. Newburn (ed.) *Handbook of Policing*. Cullompton: Willan Publishing.

Levi, M. and Maguire, M. (2004) 'Reducing and Preventing Organised Crime: An Evidence-based Critique', *Crime, Law and Social Change*, 41: 397–469.

Levi, M. and Osofsky, L. (1995) *Investigating, Seizing and Confiscating the Proceeds of Crime* (Crime Detection and Prevention Series Paper No. 61). London: The Home Office.

Liddick, D. (1999) *An Empirical, Theoretical and Historical Overview of Organised Crime* (Criminology Studies V, 6). New York: Edwin Mellen Press.

Lippens, R. (2001) 'Rethinking Organizational Crime and Organizational Criminology', *Crime, Law and Social Change*, 35: 319–31.

Locker, J.P. (2004) '"This Most Pernicious Species of Crime": Embezzlement in its Public and Private Dimensions, *c.* 1850–1930'. Keele University, unpublished Ph.D. thesis.

Loftin, C. (1984) 'Assaultive Violence as a Contagious Process', Bulletin of the New York Academy of Medicine, 62: 550–5.

Lupsha, P.A. (1996) 'Transnational Organized Crime versus the State', *Transnational Organized Crime*, 2/1: 21–48.

Lyman, M.D. and Potter, G.W. (1997) *Organized Crime*. Upper Saddle River, NJ: Prentice Hall.

Lyman, M.D. and Potter, G.W. (1999) *Organized Crime* (2nd edn). Upper Saddle River, NJ: Prentice Hall.

Lyman, M.D. and Potter, G.W. (2004) *Organized Crime* (3nd edn). Upper Saddle River, NJ: Prentice Hall.

Maas, P. (1968) *The Valachi Papers*. New York: Putnam.

Maguire, M. and John, T. (1995) *Intelligence, Surveillance and Informants: Integrated Approaches* (Crime Detection and Prevention Series Paper No. 64). London: The Home Office.

Maltz, M. (1976) 'On Defining Organized Crime: The Development of a Definition and a Typology', *Crime and Delinquency*, 22(3): 338–46.

Mars, G. (1999) 'Criminal Social Organisation, Cultures and Vulnerability: An Approach from Cultural Theory', in D. Canter and L. Alison, *The Social Psychology of Crime: Groups, Teams and Networks*. Aldershot: Ashgate.

Mawby, R.C. (2003) 'Completing the "half-formed picture"? Media images of Policing', in P. Mason (ed.) *Criminal Visions: Media Representations of Crime and Justice*. Cullompton: Willan Publishing,

Miller, J., Maxson, C.L. and Klein, M.W. (eds) (2001) *The Modern Gang Reader* (2nd edn). Los Angeles: Roxbury Publishing Company.

Miller, S., Blackler, J. and Alexandra, A. (1997) *Police Ethics*. St Leonards, NSW: Allen Unwin.

Moore, J.W. (1978) *Homeboys: Gangs, Drugs and Prison in the Barrios of Los Angeles*. Philadelphia: Temple University Press.

Moore, J.W. (1991) *Going down to the Barrio: Homeboys and Homegirls in Change*. Philadelphia: Temple University Press.

Morton, J. (1992) *Gangland, Volume 1*. London: Little Brown.

Morton, J. (1993) *Bent Coppers*. London: Little Brown.

Morton, J. (1994) *Gangland, Volume 2*. London: Little Brown.

Morton, J. (2002) *Gangland Today*. London: Time Warner.

Morton, J. and Parker, J. (2004) *Gangland Bosses*. London: Time Warner.

Mueller, G.O.W. (1998) 'Transnational Crime: Definitions and Concepts', in P. Williams and D. Vlassis (eds) *Combating Transnational Crime: Concepts, Activities and Responses*, Special Issue of *Transnational Organized Crime* 4/3–4: 13–21.

Muir, J. (1999) 'Middle East Drugs Haul from Iranian Camel Caravan', *BBC News*, Thursday 24 June 1999.

Munn, M. (1993) *The Hollywood Connection: The Mafia and the Movie Business*. London: Robson Books.

Nash, J.R. (1993) *World Encyclopedia of Organized Crime*. Cambridge, MA: Da Capo Press.

National Criminal Intelligence Service (n.d.) *Definition of Organised Crime*. London: National Criminal Intelligence Service (NCIS).

Naylor, R. (1997) 'Mafias, Myths, and Markets: On the Theory and Practice of Enterprise Crime', *Transnational Organized Crime*, 3/3: 1–45.

Naylor, R. (2002) *Wages of Crime: Black Markets, Illegal Finance and the Underworld Economy*. Ithaca, NY: Cornell University Press.

Naylor, R. (2003) 'Follow-the-Money Methods in Crime Control Policy', in M. Beare (ed.) *Critical Reflections on Transnational Organized Crime, Money Laundering and Corruption*. Toronto: University of Toronto Press.

Nelken, D. (2002) 'White Collar Crime', in M. Maguire, R. Morgan and R. Reiner (eds) *Oxford Handbook of Criminology* (3rd edn). Oxford: Oxford University Press.

Nevins, J. (2001) *Operation Gatekeeper: The Rise of the "Illegal Alien" and the Making of the US-Mexico Boundary*. New York: Routledge.

Oakeshott, M. (1947) (ed.) *Hobbes' Leviathan* (1651). Oxford: Blackwell.

Observatoire Géopolitique des Drougues (2000) *The World Geo-Politics of Drugs: Annual Report for 1998/1999*. Paris: OGD.

Oyster Bay Conference (1965) *Combating Organized Crime: Report of the 1965 Oyster Bay, New York, Conferences on Combating Organized Crime*. Albany, NY: Office of the Counsel to the Governor.

Padilla, F.M. (1992) *The Gang as an American Enterprise*. New Brunswick, NJ: Rutgers University Press.

Parker, H. (1974) *The View from the Boys*. Newton Abbot: David & Charles.

Passas, N. (1995) *Organized Crime*. Aldershot: Dartmouth.

Passas, N. (1996) 'The Genesis of the BCCI Scandal', in M. Levi and D. Nelken (eds) *The Corruption of Politics and the Politics of Corruption*. Oxford: Blackwell.

Passas, N. (1998) 'Globalization and Transnational Organized Crime: Effects of Criminogenic Assymetries', in P. Williams and D. Vlassis (eds) *Combating Transnational Crime: Concepts, Activities and Responses*, Special Issue of *Transnational Organized Crime*, 4/3–4: 22–56.

Pearce, F. (1976) *Crimes of the Powerful: Marxism, Crime and Deviance*. London: Pluto.

Pearson, G. (1994) 'Youth, Crime and Society', in M. Maguire, R. Morgan and R. Reiner (eds) *Oxford Handbook of Criminology*. Oxford: Oxford University Press.

Pearson, J. (1973) *The Profession of Violence: The Rise and Fall of the Kray Twins' Vicious Criminal Empire*. London: Panther Books.

Porter, M.E. (1985) *Competitive Advantage: Creating and Sustaining Superior Performance*. New York: Free Press.

Punch, M. (1996) *Dirty Business: Exploring Corporate Misconduct*. London: Sage.

Puzo, M. (1969) *The Godfather*. New York: Putnam.

Quinn, E. (2005) *Nuthin' but a "g" thang: The Culture and Commerce of Gangsta Rap*. New York: Columbia University Press.

Rahn, R.W. (2002) 'Nightmare on FATF Street', *Washington Times*, 9 June.

Rawlinson, P. (1997) 'Russian Organised Crime: A Brief History', in P. Williams (ed.) *Russian Organised Crime: The New Threat?* London: Frank Cass.

Rawlinson, P. (1998) 'Mafia, Media and Myth: Representations of Russian Organised Crime', in M. Levi (ed.) *Reflections on Organised Crime: Patterns and Control*. Oxford: Blackwell (for the Howard League).

Read, L. and Morton, J. (1992) *Nipper*, London: Warner Books.

Reuter, P. (1983) *Disorganised Crime: Illegal Markets and the Mafia – The Economics of the Visible Hand*. Cambridge, MA: MIT Press.

Richardson, C. (1992) *My Manor*. London: Pan Books.

Riis, J. (1902) *The Battle with the Slum*. Montclair, NJ: Patterson Smith.

Robinson, J. (1996) *The Laundrymen: Inside Money Laundering, the World's Largest Business*. New York: Arcade.

Robinson, J. (2002) *The Merger: The Conglomeration of International Organized Crime*. Woodstock and New York: The Overlook Press.

Ruggiero, V. (1996) *Organised and Corporate Crime in Europe: Offers that Can't be Refused*. Aldershot: Dartmouth.

Ryan, P.J. and Rush. G.E. (1998) *Understanding Organised Crime in Global Perspective*. London: Sage.

Sanchez-Jankowski, M. (1991) *Islands in the Street: Gangs and American Urban Society*. Berkeley: University of California Press.

Santiago, M. (2000) *Europol and Police Co-operation in Europe* (Criminology Studies V, 11). New York: Edwin Mellen Press.

Savona, E. (1997) 'Introduction', in E. Savona (ed.) *Responding to Money Laundering: International Perspectives*. Amsterdam: Harwood Academic Publishers.

Savona, E. (1999) *European Money Trails*. Philadelphia: Harwood Academic Publishers.

Savona, E. (ed.) (2000) *The World Report on Money Laundering*. Amsterdam: Harwood Academic Publishers.

Savona, E. and De Feo, M.A. (1997) 'International Money Laundering Trends and Prevention/Control Policies' in E. Savona (ed.) *Responding to Money*

Laundering: International Perspectives. Amsterdam: Harwood Academic Publishers.

Savona, E., Lewis, C. and Vettori, B. (eds) (2005) *EUSTOC – Developing an EU Statistical Apparatus for Measuring Organised Crime, Assessing its Risk and Evaluating Organised Crime Policies* (2003 AGIS programme). Brussels: European Commission.

Scherer, F. (1970) *Industrial Market Structure and Market Performance.* Chicago: Rand McNally.

Schelling, T. (1967) 'Economic Analysis of Organized Crime', in *Task Force Report: Organized Crime.* Washington: US Government Printing Office.

Schelling, T. (1984) *Choice and Consequence.* Cambridge, MA: Harvard University Press.

Scholenhardt, A. (1999) 'The Business of Migration: Organised Crime and Illegal Migration in Australia and the Asia-Pacific Region'. Paper Presented to the University of Adelaide Law School, May (unpublished).

Scott, W.R. (1992) *Organizations: Rational, Natural and Open Systems.* Englewood Cliffs, NJ: Prentice Hall.

Sharpe, J. (2004) *Dick Turpin: The Myth of the English Highwayman.* London: Profile Books.

Shaw, C.R. and McKay, H.D. (1942) *Juvenile Delinquency and Urban Areas.* Chicago: University of Chicago Press.

Sheldon, H.D. (1898) 'The Institutional Activities of American Children', *American Journal of Psychology*, 9/4: 425–48.

Shelley, L. (1995) 'Transnational Organized Crime: An Imminent Threat to the Nation State', *Journal of International Affairs*, 48/2: 463–89.

Shelley, L. (1997) 'Post-Soviet Organised Crime: A New Form of Authoritarianism', in P. Williams (ed.) *Russian Organised Crime: The New Threat?* London: Frank Cass.

Sheptycki, J. (2003a) 'Against Transnational Organized Crime', in M. Beare, *Critical Reflections on Transnational Organized Crime, Money Laundering and Corruption.* Toronto: University of Toronto Press.

Sheptycki, J. (2003b) 'Global Law Enforcement as a Protection Racket: Some Sceptical Notes on Transnational Organised Crime as an Object of Global Governance', in A. Edwards and P. Gill (eds) *Transnational Organised Crime: Perspectives on Global Security.* London: Routledge.

Short, J.F. and Strodtbeck F.L. (1974) *Group Process and Gang Delinquency.* Chicago: University of Chicago Press.

Siegel, L. (1991) 'The Criminalization of Pregnant and Child-rearing Drugs Users: An Example of the American Harm Maximization Program', in P.A. O'Hare, R. Newcombe, A. Matthews, E.C. Buning and E. Drucker (eds) (1992) *The Reduction of Drug-related Harm.* London: Routledge.

Sillitoe, P. (1955) *Cloak without Dagger.* London: Pan Books.

Skolnick, J. (1966) *Justice without Trial.* New York: John Wiley.

Skolnick, J., Correl, T., Navarro, T. and Rabb, R. (1990) 'The Social Structure of Street Drug Dealing', *American Journal of Police*, 9/1: 1–41.

Slapper, G. and Tombs, S. (1999) *Corporate Crime*. Harlow: Pearson.

Smith, D.C. (1975) *The Mafia Mystique*. New York: Basic Books.

Spergel, I. (1966) *Street Gang Work: Theory and Practice*. Reading, MA: Addison-Wesley.

Steinberg, J. (1995) 'The Golden Crescent Heroin Connection', *Executive Intelligence Review*, 13 October.

Stelfox, P. (2003) 'Transnational Organised Crime: A Police Perspective', in A. Edwards and P. Gill (eds) *Transnational Organised Crime: Perspectives on Global Security*. London: Routledge.

Sterling, C. (1994) *Crime without Frontiers: The Worldwide Expansion of Organised Crime and the Pax Mafiosa*. London: Warner Books.

Sutherland, E. (1983) *White Collar Crime: The Uncut Version*. New Haven: Yale University Press.

Tappan, P. (1947) 'Who is the Criminal', *American Sociological Review*, 12: 96–102.

Thompson, M., Ellis, R. and Wildavsky, A. (1990) *Cultural Theory*. Boulder, CO: Westview Press.

Thrasher, F. (1927) *The Gang: A Study of 1313 Gangs in Chicago*. Chicago: University of Chicago Press.

Troubnikoff, A.M. (2003) *Trafficking in Women and Children: Current Issues and Developments*. New York: Nova Science Publishers.

United Nations (1976) *Fifth UN Congress on the Prevention of Crime and the Treatment of Offenders: Report* (A/CONF.169/15/Add.1). New York: UN Department of Economic and Social Affairs.

United Nations (1995), *Naples Political Declaration and Global Action Plan Against Organized Transnational Crime*, reprinted in *Transnational Organized Crime*, 1995, 1:1, 118–27.

United Nations (1997) *World Drugs Report*. Vienna: UN Office for Drugs and Crime.

United Nations (2000a) *Convention against Transnational Organized Crime*. Palermo, Sicily: United Nations.

United Nations (2000b) *Protocol Against the Smuggling of Migrants by Land, Air and Sea, Supplementing the United Nations Convention Against Transnational Organized Crime*. New York: United Nations.

United Nations Office for Drugs and Crime (2002) *Global Programme against Money Laundering*, Vienna: UN Office for Drugs and Crime.

United Nations (2004) *World Drugs Report*, Vienna: UN Office for Drugs and Crime.

US Bureau of Justice (1992) *Data Report*, Washington: Department of Justice.

US Drug Enforcement Administration (2001) 'The Drug Trade in Colombia: A Threat Assessment', in *DEA Intelligence Reports*. Washington: US Department of Justice.

US Drug Enforcement Administration (2002) 'Drugs and Terrorism: A New Perspective' in *DEA Drug Intelligence Brief* (September). Washington: US Department of Justice.

US Federal Bureau of Investigation (2003) *Statement to the US Congress on Eurasian Organized Crime by Grant D. Ashley, Assistant Director, Criminal Investigation Division*, October. Washington: US Federal Bureau of Investigation.

US President's Commission on Law Enforcement and Administration of Justice (1967) *The Challenge of Crime in a Free Society*. Washington: US Government Printing Office.

US President's Commission on Organized Crime (1984) *Report on Organized Crime of Asian Origin* (Record of Hearing 23–25 October 1984). Washington: US Government Printing Office.

Van der Heijden, T. (1996) 'Measuring Organized Crime in Western Europe' in M. Pagon (ed.) *Policing in Central and Eastern Europe: Comparing Firsthand Knowledge with Experience in the West*. Ljubljana: College of Police and Security Studies.

Van der Heijden, T. (1998) *Assessing the Nature and Extent of Organised Crime in the European Union*. Paper Presented to UN ad hoc Meeting on National Capacities for Collection of Criminal Justice Information and Statistics, 17–18 March, Veldhoven, NL (Cited HEUNI Newsletter July 1998: 24).

Van Duyne, P.C. (1996) *Organized Crime in Europe*. New York: Nova Science Publishers Inc.

Varese, F. (2001) *The Russian Mafia: Private Protection in a New Market Economy*. Oxford: Oxford University Press.

Viano, E. (1999) *Global Organised Crime and International Society*. Aldershot: Ashgate.

Vlassis, D. (1998) 'Drafting the United Nations Convention against Transnational Crime', in P. Williams and D. Vlassis (eds) *Combating Transnational Crime: Concepts, Activities and Responses*, Special Issue of *Transnational Organized Crime*, 4/3–4: 356–62.

Weick, K.E. (1974) 'Middle Range Theories of Social Systems', *Behavioral Science*, 19: 357–67.

Wensley, F.P. (1931) *Forty Years of Scotland Yard*. New York: Garden City Publishing Company.

Williams, P. (ed.) (1997) *Russian Organised Crime: The New Threat?* London: Frank Cass.

Williams, P. and Savona, E. (eds) (1996) *The United Nations and Transnational Organised Crime*. London: Frank Cass.

Williamson, O.E. (1981) 'The Economics of Organization: The Transaction Cost Approach', *American Journal of Sociology*, 87: 548–77.

Wolf, D. (1991) *Rebels: A Brotherhood of Outlaw Bikers*. Toronto: University of Toronto Press.

Woodiwiss, M. (2001) *Organized Crime and American Power*. Toronto: University of Toronto Press.

Woodiwiss, M. (2003a) 'Transnational Organized Crime: The Strange Career of an American Concept', in M. Beare (ed.) *Critical Reflections on Transnational Organized Crime, Money Laundering and Corruption*. Toronto: University of Toronto Press.

Woodiwiss, M. (2003b) 'Transnational Organised Crime: The Global Reach of an American Concept in Edwards', in A. Edwards and P. Gill (eds) *Transnational Organised Crime: Perspectives on Global Security*. London: Routledge.

Wrench, P. (1997) 'The G8 and Transnational Organised Crime', in P.J. Cullen and W.C. Gilmore (eds) (1998), *Crime Sans Frontiers: International and European Legal Approaches*, Hume Papers in Public Policy, 6:1&2. Edinburgh: Edinburgh University Press, 39–43.

Wright, A. (1997) 'Organized Crime in Hungary: The Transition from State to Civil Society', *Transnational Organized Crime*, 3: 1, 68–86.

Wright, A. (1998) 'The Illicit Drug Industry', *Lectures on Drug Trafficking*. Bramshill: National Police College (unpublished).

Wright, A. (2002) *Policing: An Introduction to Concepts and Practice*. Cullompton: Willan Publishing.

Wright, A. and Waymont, A. (1989) *Police Drugs Enforcement Strategies and Intelligence Needs in England and Wales*. Report to ACPO. Southampton: Southampton University Centre for International Policy Studies.

Wright, A., Waymont, A. and Gregory, F.E. (1993) *Drugs Squads: Law Enforcement Strategies and Intelligence in England and Wales*. London: The Police Foundation.

Yablonsky, L. (1962) *The Violent Gang*. New York: Penguin Books.

Young, J. (1999) *The Exclusive Society*. London: Sage Publications.

Zhang, S. and Chin, K-L. (2003) 'The Declining Significance of Triad Societies in Transnational Illegal Activities: A Structural Deficiency Perspective', *British Journal of Criminology*, 43: 469–88.

Zorbaugh, H.W. (1929) *The Gold Coast and the Slum: A Sociological Study of Chicago's Near North Side*. Chicago: University of Chicago Press.

Index